INTENTIONAL INTEGRITY

INTENTIONAL INTEGRITY

How Smart Companies
Can Lead an Ethical Revolution

Robert Chesnut
Chief Ethics Officer of Airbnb
with **Joan O'C. Hamilton**

St. Martin's Press
New York

Disclaimer: Prior to taking on this project, I spoke with leaders at Airbnb, who have been terrific champions of the company's ethics program and the importance of integrity inside Airbnb. I am grateful to Airbnb founders Brian, Nate, Joe, and to so many members of Airbnb's leadership, including Belinda Johnson, Beth Axelrod, Chris Lehane, Greg Greeley, Ari Balogh, Rich Baer, and others, for contributing their thoughts about ethics to me over the years. While I was employed by Airbnb during the writing of *Intentional Integrity*, though, this is not an "Airbnb" book. Airbnb did not exercise editorial control over the book and has not endorsed or approved any of the material herein. All opinions expressed in these pages (including views about the law or any legal related matters) are my personal views except where specifically stated otherwise, and are not necessarily the views of Airbnb Inc., its officers, or employees. Finally, this book does not contain privileged material from any company where I have served either in a legal or advisory capacity.

First published in the United States by St. Martin's Press, an imprint of St. Martin's Publishing Group

www.stmartins.com

Design by Meryl Sussman Levavi

Library of Congress Cataloging-in-Publication Data

Names: Chesnut, Robert, author.
Title: Intentional integrity : how smart companies can lead an ethical revolution /
    Robert Chesnut, Chief Ethics Officer, Airbnb ; with Joan O'C. Hamilton.
Description: First Edition. | New York : St. Martin's Press, 2020. |
    Includes bibliographical references and index.
Identifiers: LCCN 2019059170 | ISBN 9781250239709 (hardcover) |
    ISBN 9781250272478 (international, sold outside the U.S., subject to rights availability) |
    ISBN 9781250270818 (ebook)
Subjects: LCSH: Corporate culture. | Management. | Organizational behavior.
Classification: LCC HD58.7 .C484514 2020 | DDC 658.4/08—dc23
LC record available at https://lccn.loc.gov/2019059170

Our books may be purchased in bulk for promotional, educational, or business use. Please contact your local bookseller or the Macmillan Corporate and Premium Sales Department at 1-800-221-7945, extension 5442, or by email at MacmillanSpecialMarkets@macmillan.com.

First U.S. Edition: 2020
First International Edition: 2020

10 9 8 7 6 5 4 3 2 1

To my family:
my wife, Jillian,
my children, Bianca and Cliff,
my parents, Kitty and Bob,
my extended family Justin, Amanda, Blake, Nick, and Brock,
and of course Uncle Brother

Contents

INTENTIONAL INTEGRITY

Introduction

Show of hands?
A new approach to integrity

I look out over a room filled with about 50 new hires and throw out the question that always provokes uneasy laughter and side-eye glances.

"Show of hands—who in this group has integrity?"

I wait.

Some hands go right up. Others go halfway, the hires swiveling their heads to scan the room, wondering: Is it cool to raise my hand?

"A few," I observe, smiling.

Laughter breaks the tension, resolving into silence; hands start to go down. People shift in their seats.

This is how it begins—a direct, open, mostly enjoyable but sometimes uncomfortable conversation with new employees about what it means to have Intentional Integrity in the workplace.

✦

In 2016, I joined Airbnb as the company's general counsel. Founded in 2008 by three twentysomethings who rented out airbeds on their small San Francisco apartment floor, the company now helps tens of millions of travelers connect with unique accommodations. Airbnb's founders were pioneers in the "sharing economy," in which Internet platforms like eBay,

Uber, Lyft, Turo, Upwork, Poshmark, and many others leverage existing capacity in everything from shelter and artwork to clothing and vehicles.

So many of these companies, initially praised and celebrated as innovators, now find themselves at the center of important debates about the impact of technology on society. Politicians and the press are asking tough questions about their most significant impacts: Are platforms like Upwork, for example, enabling new flexible ways of working that unlock human potential, or are they just enabling large companies to exploit "gig" workers? Are ride-sharing companies offering new income sources and making the roads safer, or are they a collection of unregulated operators with too much information about where customers come and go? Is Airbnb helping thousands of people leverage unused space to augment their incomes, or is it reducing the quality of life in neighborhoods? Should we nurture these platforms? Regulate them? Tax them? Or break them up?

For over three years I managed a global legal team that confronted these questions daily, and worked with legal issues impacting our business model in over 190 countries and more than 100,000 cities. At times it was head-spinning. One minute we were concerned with regional conflict overseas, the next with a small-town ordinance governing short-term rentals. We had to figure out how to deal with white supremacists in the United States who had advised their supporters to stay in Airbnbs while traveling for rallies. And then there were the typical duties of any legal team, such as preparing contracts and managing disputes.

Ideally, platform companies like ours would partner with all levels of government leaders and focus on solving at least some of these challenges with well-reasoned policy solutions. However, that has become very hard to do. Our politics have become so fractured and our world's problems so complex. And even though we've largely avoided the kind of scandals that have plagued so many other companies, I nonetheless understand why politicians, and more importantly the public, are sometimes wary of corporate motives. Data privacy abuses, sexual misconduct, greedy self-dealing, and various other instances of arrogant and entitled behavior have contributed to an erosion of the public's trust in institutions in general.

This might sound grim. But I'm an optimist by nature, and I'm more convinced than ever that all businesses have a great opportunity right now to step into the leadership void and chart a proactive, ethical course that is good for their full slate of stakeholders. A company's stakeholders are commonly defined to include customers, employees, business partners, communities in which it operates, and, yes, investor shareholders. But to me, especially coming from a global platform company, "stakeholders" means everybody. Literally. I believe tech companies can make the world better, not just more digital. And if businesses of every size in every industry commit to principles like promoting ethical supply chains, lowering a company's carbon footprint, and declaring a commitment to fight discrimination of all kinds, then these organizations are poised to play a leadership role and make a meaningful and positive difference.

But here's the catch: to be taken seriously, to have the impact I am convinced they can have, business leaders must embrace what I call Intentional Integrity.

✦

Intentional Integrity is not just a vow to be virtuous. It means making a serious and thorough effort to, first, identify an organization's purpose and the values it stands for; then develop specific rules that reflect those values; and finally, drive the importance of following the rules into every corner—and level—of a company. It's often not a straight-line journey, and you need to be prepared for setbacks. But in my experience, the effort can deliver both business success and positive social value. In fact, there is growing evidence that failing to establish trust and ignoring issues important to an organization's entire slate of stakeholders will hurt companies' bottom-line performance.

Drilling down

Just as I was finishing this book in the fall of 2019, I transitioned from my role as Airbnb general counsel to run the company's ethics office. I made the move because the Integrity Belongs Here program we started at Airbnb had such an impact on our organization and on individuals that I wanted a chance to focus even more on ethics and push our ideas out into the larger business community. (I could never have imagined the turmoil that would erupt just a few months later as the COVID-19 virus spread around the world. In the postscript, I've addressed the topic of integrity during a crisis, material that was added after this book was finished and ready for publication.)

As you read, you'll notice that I've always had a fascination with ethics and how to motivate positive behavior. It's been an important aspect of every job I've ever held, beginning with my years as a federal prosecutor. But in the corporate setting, to achieve the change I want to see, I've come to think about integrity in a specific way.

✦

What put these ideas in motion for me at Airbnb was that soon after I arrived, there was an explosion of news accounts involving scandals at tech companies. Some of the worst offenses happened literally down the street from our San Francisco offices. Accusations ranged from sexual harassment to illegally selling customer data to foreign actors and even out-and-out fraud (in the case of Theranos). The who's who of tech high-flyers—Facebook, Uber, Google—were being summoned right and left to testify before Congress, and the media were treating them as poster children for arrogance and unethical leadership.

Bad acting isn't confined to tech of course. Across many industries, unethical behavior in recent years has meant the tarnishing of once proud and respected brands, like Volkswagen and, more recently, Boeing. Then there is the #MeToo movement, prompted by a long list of prominent business executives and media figures who engaged in years of inappropriate behavior with junior employees, resulting in scandal, resignations, and in some cases lawsuits and even criminal charges. A number of top universities have been in the spotlight for allowing students to essentially bribe their way in through fraudulent athletic credentials. Even organizations like the Boy Scouts and the Catholic Church have been exposed for covering up thousands of sexual assaults. Talk about a depressing list.

I became preoccupied with the sheer number of these scandals. I thought, *These situations are outrageous and wrong. And the failure of leadership in these organizations is doing terrible harm to individuals and destroying trust in these brands. As Airbnb's general counsel, I cannot just sit here with my fingers crossed. I need to do something proactive to make sure that every single Airbnb employee*—and by this time we had thousands—*realizes this behavior is not OK. I need to try to prevent our company from becoming a fixture in these kinds of headlines.*

I came to Airbnb in the first place because I was impressed with the leadership of CEO Brian Chesky and his team. I had heard from others and observed myself that they had a mature and thoughtful style not always found among young tech entrepreneurs. They project a sincere sense of mission—to create a feeling of belonging in the world. Brian talks about it a lot, and you hear employees all over the world refer to the mission constantly.

However, the brutal reality is that you can have great leaders and the right intentions, but it's not enough. A very small number of rogue employees can have an outsized negative impact on your reputation. And so you need a deliberate, intentional commitment to promote and enforce specific rules that are tuned to your company's unique business and culture. There needs to be an environment where those rules are owned broadly within the company, discussed openly in a positive way so that they feel woven into the culture. There need to be fair, appropriate consequences for breaking those rules.

This challenge is one that many good leaders admit they struggle with. I attended the University of Virginia, which has a long-standing emphasis on its honor code, but even President James E. Ryan and I have discussed how creating an ethical culture is something you're never finished with. While Ryan reinforces messages of integrity and honor constantly, he admits that at the end of the day "the institution's reputation is still at risk if even one person fails to heed that message."

◆

At Airbnb I decided two things. First, we needed to write a code of ethics specific to Airbnb's unique mission and business model. Second, we would not outsource communication of that code by just making employees watch some boring video created by a third party. The stakes were just too high, and the threats were just too big.

So we developed the written code (which I'll talk more about soon), and I began traveling and personally addressing employee groups all over the world on the topic of Integrity Belongs Here. And I will be honest: almost everybody admits to me that they dread coming to a talk on corporate ethics. But the good news is, the majority end up enjoying it and even want to learn more.

◆

As I indicated above, I always start sessions by asking, "Who here has integrity?" Then, either during these sessions or in conversations afterward, employees ask me more questions about the question itself:

Are you asking if I'm honest?
Does it mean abiding by the letter of the law?
Does it have anything to do with the law?
Is integrity the same thing as loyalty?
Do you mean something very specific, or is integrity a subjective thing?

My impression is that most people think the following: I'm a good person, so of course I have integrity. But these questions show me how vital it is that employees understand exactly what an organization expects of them. If they don't, they are vulnerable to what I call the integrity trap. The integrity trap is circular reasoning that goes like this: Because I feel confident that I have integrity, my integrity will point me toward the right thing to do when I encounter a dilemma. I will choose the solution that represents integrity. Even if I break a rule, it's OK, because, obviously, I have a good reason.

In fact, it's not OK.

We need more cherry-tree moments

The word "integrity," of course, suggests a fundamental sense of honesty and ability to behave with civility and fairness. There was a time when every schoolkid in America learned the story of how George Washington's integrity was on display at a very young age. He supposedly (although likely not, but it's how the story was told) cut down a cherry tree as a boy, and when he was asked about it, he admitted his guilt, adding, "I cannot tell a lie." The story may be quaint, but our society seems to have evolved to a point where teaching a child the importance of telling the truth and taking responsibility for mistakes is not a priority for some parents. The recent cheating and bribery scandals at some of America's top universities reinforce that.

So yes, integrity in the workplace *is* about "doing the right thing." I also like the comment widely (but alas erroneously) attributed to C. S. Lewis that integrity is about doing the right thing "even when no one else is watching." But I will concede that workplaces today are diverse, and it's not always clear what the right thing to do is. At Airbnb, our workplace, like most, is steadily becoming more diverse, more global, which means there's no common set of values, no one religion, no agreed-upon set of ethics or morals that we bring to this new highly connected workplace. We each have our own unique background, our own sense of right and wrong, and our own beliefs about what's appropriate. We are grappling with how to promote collegiality and trust; at the same time, we're realizing that what one person considers a friendly hug may make the person to whom the hug is offered uncomfortable. The world is changing quickly, forcing us to consider new topics—like who owns our data in the virtual world—for which there are not always established norms.

Although codes of ethics have many common themes, there is in fact no one list of rules that works for every company. Rather, the point is that companies must intentionally determine what their values are and state them, and then each and every employee at every level, including the board, must agree to behave in a manner *consistent with the values everyone has pledged to adhere to*—even when it's hard to do so, even when another course may also have value to the individual or others. This is not just a top-down exercise. At the highest level of the company, it means that leaders agree to adhere to the same rules that apply to everyone else and to manage by those rules. For example, a manager ignoring the rules until someone she or he doesn't like breaks one should be held accountable for violating the spirit of the code.

Over the years, I have led legal teams and served as an advisor at more than a dozen companies and nonprofits. I have heard many versions of integrity-trap logic from employees at all levels. "C'mon, we don't get paid enough as it is, and you're going to nickel and dime me on my expense report?" Or, "I didn't mention that my brother owns the company I hired to do our printing because I knew I could negotiate a better deal out of him than we'd get from anybody else. Trust me!" I once had to terminate a leader who assaulted another employee at a Christmas party. "I would never do something like that, but I was hammered," he argued. We fired both him and his alter ego.

Keeping leaders, employees, and companies out of integrity traps is one reason why I'm writing this book. Ambiguity is the enemy of integrity.

Silence and poorly conceived incentives set integrity traps. Intentional Integrity requires a deliberate process, not just a policy announcement.

The good news is that creating a workplace with a strong sense of integrity is a more welcome notion than many realize.

Trust is critical

In early 2019, the global public relations firm Edelman released its 19th Annual Edelman Trust Barometer,[1] which tracks trends in public opinion involving trust in institutions like the media and government, as well as in the workplace. According to the firm's CEO, Richard Edelman, "People have low confidence that societal institutions will help them navigate a turbulent world, so they are turning to a critical relationship: their employer."

I was already working on this book when this data dropped on my desk. These findings inspire me, because they reflect what I see every day when I talk to our employees and read headlines concerning companies facing public scrutiny and vocal and contentious pushback from their workforce. Despite the frustration and the mistakes many companies have made, employees want to be proud of where they work; they yearn to be what Edelman calls "partners in change" with their employers. Says Edelman, "This significant shift in employee expectations opens up an enormous opportunity for employers to help rebuild societal trust, as the general population sees business as being able to make money and improve society (73 percent)."[2]

The Edelman trust study reinforced that employees are looking for leadership to speak up and clarify the boundaries and set out clear expectations for how employees should treat each other, interact with partners, and represent the company's values to customers. And, most importantly, model the right behavior themselves.

It just makes sense. The path to integrity requires commitment, focus, and attention *from everybody*. What makes Intentional Integrity such a powerful concept is that it means asking "What is the right thing to do?" so often that it becomes a reflex, not a distraction. The return on this investment in reinforcing the importance of doing the right thing is measured not just by the problems you avoid but in the trust that is created within an organization and among stakeholders.

✦

For example, at Airbnb, my ethics advisor team and I have been debating a question that is not in any way a scandalous emergency. One of our in-house recruiters managed the successful hiring of a highly skilled employee. After accepting our offer, the new employee sent the recruiter a thank-you letter and a $200 gift card as a token of his appreciation. Pretty generous token, right? The recruiter, noting that a simple note would have been sufficient, immediately reported this to our ethics team, unclear whether this represented a prohibited form of a gift.

Airbnb has a specific set of rules governing gifts, including one that prohibits employees from accepting gifts from vendors valued in excess of $200. We are also firm that customer service folks who interact with our guests and hosts may not accept free stays or any other kind of gift. However, we do not have a policy about employees giving gifts to one another. It has never surfaced as an issue for us before.

All of our 30 ethics advisors are copied on every inquiry submitted to our ethics inbox. The gift card email prompted spirited reactions from many of them. Some said the gift card didn't seem like a problem—since the new employee was now effectively done with the recruiter and there was no reporting relationship, where was the conflict of interest? A few others found it inappropriate and suggested that the recruiter should return the card, worrying that the employee might send friends seeking employment to the recruiter. It was fascinating to me to see the group devote so much energy to sorting out a fairly minor, isolated event.

Personally, I am inclined to think this gift is unusual, but not unethical. Recruiters don't hire; they present slates of candidates who are hired or not by a manager based on their merits. But the reason I bring this up is that I believe it shows that our people trust our approach to ethics. That the recruiter's first instinct was to check to see if this was OK tells me that employees are hearing the messages we're sending: Integrity matters. Think before you act. Ask if you're not sure if you're about to do the right thing. People only ask questions like this when they trust you and feel that you'll treat them with respect. This is why I have hope that companies can overcome what Duke University researcher Dan Ariely has explained to me is a basic tendency of most people to act in a self-interested way and rationalize situations where they stand to gain something if they believe they will not be called out or punished. Our recruiter didn't have to tell us about the gift card, but she determined that asking about it was the right thing to do.

✦

I believe that open, respectful dialogue in any organization builds trust. In 2018, a report by the worldwide consulting firm Accenture suggested that companies put considerable revenue at risk if they do not invest in measuring, managing, and exhibiting trust as an organizational value. Accenture's report, *The Bottom Line on Trust*, noted, "In the not-too-distant past, trust was considered a 'soft' corporate issue." In other words, it was something a company's leaders focused on after the hard work of delivering profits was done. No more. Today, "companies need to execute a balanced strategy that prioritizes trust at the same level as growth and profitability. Those who do benefit from greater resiliency from trust incidents, making them more competitive. Those who don't are putting billions in future revenue at risk."[3]

According to Accenture, trust is vital for companies to survive the changing dynamics of globalization and increased transparency. Accenture developed what it called the Competitive Agility Index, which predicts the financial impact of negative "trust incidents" like scandals or revelations of hypocritical behavior. They concluded that customers today punish companies for bad behavior by withholding their business. According to Accenture's calculus, for example, "a $30 billion retail company experiencing a material drop in trust stands to lose $4 billion in future revenue."

Let's talk. Seriously.

Where does this journey to regain and nurture trust begin? By having some honest and straightforward conversations. The trouble is, most companies don't talk much about integrity. Many seem to fear that it might attract unwanted attention, scrutiny, or accusations of hypocrisy. Others worry that attempts to actively enforce integrity or other workplace interaction concepts like "radical candor" or "civility" will be seen as tools to further advance the agendas of the powerful. Legal officers who deal firsthand with the consequences of companies' and employees' problematic acts may feel like they are professionally constrained from addressing the larger issues and speaking about unreported facts, motives, and dilemmas. Meanwhile, some leaders say that they just don't want to seem "holier than thou," or appear to "virtue signal" just for public relations purposes.

As a result, many companies have their human resources department download a code of ethics template, put their logo on it, and send it out in an email for their employees to read and agree to. They hang a laminated poster created by a compliance company in the breakroom, with legally mandated information about how to file complaints with various state agencies. They ask their employees to watch a video about sexual harassment. But then they never mention ethics again, and the lawyers can only hope that if something goes wrong, the thin document in the breakroom will be their legal and brand shield.

There is no shield against the damage a lack of integrity can inflict. And the problem is, silence about integrity creates ambiguities about right and wrong that make everyone in an organization a little uncertain, a little nervous. Regrettably, a minority of people will exploit that uncomfortable silence to rationalize selfish behavior. And so the lack of specificity about the values an organization expects its employees and managers to model is one reason why we have so many ethical crises erupting.

✦

It's clear to me that pressure on companies to act ethically is bubbling up from inside their own ranks. Many employees are no longer content to just cash their paychecks—they want to understand the lines their employers will and will not cross. Some employees, and particularly millennials, see their employer as inseparable from their own identity. When their company makes a mistake or a controversial decision, it becomes public, shared on social media, and visible for their friends to question them about. If evidence emerges that the company is spewing huge amounts of carbon into the air or exploiting child labor overseas, employees will demand answers, and they may hold a walkout or even quit if they don't like what they hear. And their actions may inspire or amplify consumer boycotts or prompt customers to take their business elsewhere.

In 2018, more than 600 employees of Salesforce signed a petition asking the company to end its contract with the U.S. Customs and Border Protection in protest over the Trump administration and the CBP's policy of separating migrant children from their parents at the border.[4] By June 2019, employees of the online marketplace Wayfair staged a walkout to protest the company's sale of beds and home goods to a contractor who was sending them to a facility in Texas designed to house detained migrant children.[5] Google employees, meanwhile, have organized several public demonstrations to protest executives receiving large severance packages after being accused of sexual harassment. They've also spoken out against Google's use of confidential, mandatory arbitration.[6] The press has uncovered a "private" Facebook group where 18,000-strong Amazon employees unhappy with their pay and workload routinely air their complaints.[7]

Broadening support

Smart leaders in many fields, including tech, are seeing these public protests by employees and realizing it's important for company leaders to think more deeply about ethics and integrity and what their companies stand for. For example, LinkedIn cofounder and now venture capitalist Reid Hoffman and I met when I was working at eBay and he was COO at PayPal. You won't find a more vocal tech advocate than Reid, but he and I spoke recently about narcissistic CEOs fueling the techlash with their "I'll worry about ethics later" attitude. Instead, he says, "Integrity is a mantle that companies need to take up. People are yearning for companies to take on a broader purpose than just short-term profit."

In April 2019, the *Wall Street Journal* wrote a story about how the outdoor products company Patagonia had disallowed customization of its vests with the logos of corporate customers who are not "mission-driven companies that prioritize the planet."[8] The popular fleece vests had become a Wall Street fashion staple in recent years. The tone of the story was wry, but the idea of a company literally "disqualifying" customers anxious to purchase their products or service over a fundamental values and integrity issue once would have seemed radical, but we're seeing more and more companies do just that. It's grounded in a desire to project to customers and employees that a brand is aligned with its most aspirational values even at the expense of revenues and profits. As you'll read, we've made some decisions like this at Airbnb as well.

Recently, 181 members of Business Roundtable, all CEOs of the nation's largest companies, took a courageous step in asserting that companies must embrace a more stakeholder-oriented corporate governance posture rather than simply making shareholder return their sole focus. The BRT drew fire from some investor groups, but a wide variety of other organizations, including the U.S. Chamber of Commerce, endorsed its position. The fact that 181 of the top CEOs in the country could agree on such a dramatic departure from the historic purpose of corporations is a sign of how ready the world is for companies to step up to the challenge.[9]

I do want to be clear on one point, however. I am not suggesting that most people or companies used to have integrity at one point and now they don't. Both heroes and hypocrites have always walked among us. I am also not suggesting that most companies have not cared about integrity in the past or don't care about it today. I would argue instead that we are at a moment when we clearly need companies to lead the way on integrity, because it's the right thing to do and it makes sense from a business standpoint for them to do so. That said, I perceive a real nervousness among companies and other institutions in talking about the importance of integrity and grappling with what it means. That's what I want to change.

Integrity is a superpower

At Airbnb, the founders of the company realized from the beginning that integrity had to be the foundation of a business based on hosting complete strangers in your home. For one thing, we have data about some of our customers' most personal activities—where and how they live and where they travel. Beyond that, our Airbnb hosts welcome strangers into their homes; our business model relies on our customers' basic trust that this will be a safe, pleasant, as-advertised experience where both parties benefit. The damage to our reputation can be swift and severe if any of us—the hosts, the guests, or Airbnb as the facilitator—do not act with integrity. As you'll read, in some instances we've learned that lesson the hard way.

We've also evolved to advocate that companies adopting an attitude of Intentional Integrity can lead a broader embrace of it across society, even around the world. We will always need governments to manage defense, infrastructure, social services, law enforcement, and other basic functions of a society. But the private sector has opportunities to take on a much more active role as an engine for social good. Think about it. Companies must use sensitivity and flexibility, not bluster and military threats, to succeed in the myriad cultures and political complexity of global markets. Unencumbered by national boundaries, fractious party polarization, and deadlocked legislative branches, company employees can be united by a common belief that their company's work has purpose, and they can react more quickly and creatively to customer needs and concerns. And if something doesn't work, companies are better able to shift and try something else.

More and more companies accept that a commitment to diversity and inclusion, a preference for less environmental impact, and a promise to avoid suppliers with offensive labor practices and even customers who exhibit behavior inconsistent with their values are positions they should embrace publicly. These companies are well positioned to lead broader progress in each of these areas—if they act with integrity.

It's also true, by the way, that forging a better relationship with stakeholders will give them insights that support every facet of their business. For example, you will later meet an Airbnb employee named Srin Madipalli, who helped open our eyes to a very important set of stakeholders in our guest community: individuals with physical disabilities. Put simply, these guests need more information about listings than we used to provide. Srin has a medical condition that requires him to use a powered wheelchair, which he has done for his entire life. He also loves to travel, but travel becomes challenging when accommodations are not as described, or when listings lack the details he needs to determine if they will work for him.

After Srin came to work at Airbnb, he not only helped improve how we help hosts be specific about access issues—in fact we've added 27 different measures to our host profile forms—but he also helped us make sure our own activities and facilities don't unintentionally exclude employees with physical challenges. Seeing the world through the eyes of a single stakeholder acting on authentic concerns and issues can help a company create a more inclusive corporate culture, and in this case it literally made the world easier to navigate for millions of other people with physical challenges. To me, that's a bold endorsement of Intentional Integrity.

Myths of millennialism

Occasionally when I talk about our commitment to integrity with friends or folks outside work, I hear: Doesn't this take a lot of time? Do employees actually care? There is a lingering myth that the hottest companies are propelled by young hipster employees' hard-partying, sexually free-wheeling, self-indulgent energy.

Well, a few companies have tried that bro culture thing. And we've seen where that leads. And more importantly, myths like these sell talented, principled young workers short.

Intentional Integrity is compatible with an intense, high-pressure workplace. And specifying what a company stands for is not a preachy, smug exercise. It's about providing guidance to encourage lawful, respectful behavior and to prevent and fix, not cover up, mistakes. It's an approach that's as relevant to a start-up catering to vegans as it is to a 75-year-old processed-meat company. It's as relevant to a tech company as it is to a bank or a grocery chain. It's agnostic toward religious beliefs and conservative or liberal politics.

Intentional Integrity means stating clearly and with specificity: here are *our* values. While not every employee may agree philosophically with every rule, the rules are a reflection of the company's mission and culture, and every employee agrees to abide by every rule in the workplace during their employment.

Intentional Integrity does not have to be a cultural buzzkill. At Airbnb, our employees can bring their dogs to work and enjoy a draft beer in the company breakroom. Even the legal department has happy hours. We have not declared war on fun. What we have done is make clear that the workplace, like every other aspect of life, must have boundaries. As long as those boundaries are set mindfully, based on the given company's own circumstances, and not arbitrarily, and as long as they're followed by everyone from the CEO on down, they create a workplace where people can feel respected, do rewarding work, and, yes, have some fun in the process. And the feedback I get from employees of every age is that they appreciate, even enjoy, engaging with fellow workers about integrity, about where and how to set these boundaries. They're proud to have their personal brand associated with a company that makes a conscious effort to do the right thing. So Intentional Integrity, done right, can play a big part in attracting and retaining talent.

Who's watching?

On a global basis, transparency is a powerful behavior modifier that supports Intentional Integrity. To be clear, integrity is about your personal choices, not about whether anyone is watching or knows what you did. But we all have to accept that something has changed: in the twenty-first century, *somebody is always watching.*

Even in theoretically private corporate spaces, it doesn't matter if you're the CEO or if you work in building maintenance, your badge system and your company's parking lot security video can record exactly when you come and go. And your head of IT can monitor exactly what websites you visit. A friend who works for a global IT consulting firm tells me it's become a running joke for members of her project team to say out loud, "There he goes again," referring to an executive at their client company who makes multiple visits to a porn site each day—easily visible to team members monitoring the network as part of their job.

This level of monitoring makes everyone, me included, uneasy. It feels like an intrusion, and I'm not advocating for more of it. But it is the new normal. Today, any lapse in judgment can become public at the speed of Wi-Fi. An executive who has too much to drink at the Christmas party may find his karaoke rendition of "Hiccup Sanna Claus" has gone viral by midnight. If you're in retail or the hospitality industry, good luck if you insult a customer or fail to return a call: Yelp and Facebook offer real-time megaphones for your customers' anger and frustration. In the twenty-first century, George Washington might not have had the chance to confess to chopping down the famous cherry tree . . . he would have been caught, ax in hand, on a security camera and outed on YouTube before he could utter his famous line.

What used to be personal is now public. The person you're competing with for a promotion may have a copy of a text you sent that ridiculed a board member—or the hiring manager. The sheer number of watching eyes ratchets up the need for our deeds to match our words and our commitments. If they don't, we're going to hear about it.

There is no going backward on this. NBA commissioner Adam Silver told me that he constantly advocates for the importance of transparency when ethical dilemmas arise, and he believes leaders must model the highest possible ethical standards. "In part, the Internet is driving this. There is always a camera, always a microphone holding you accountable. In the past, training [about ethical conduct] has focused on liability and the law, but going forward it needs to be about doing what's right, and as leaders we need to be specific about core values and speak openly about, and engage on, these subjects."

✦

Without question, Airbnb has had its own challenging ethical issues: our business model is changing the face of travel, and of course this means that there are economic winners and losers. Neighbors are concerned about impacts on housing prices and neighborhoods. Tensions arise among our guests and hosts. The same folks who love to stay in our variety of accommodations, ranging from remote yurts to urban apartments, do not love dealing with loud parties in an Airbnb rental next door to their home.

Employees expect us to address those issues head on and creatively, and we have. For example, we have launched a $25 million initiative in different regions of the country where affordable housing is scarce. We have a division that is looking to create small pop-up cottages that can be assembled in the backyards of suburban homes, which can support the Airbnb model of leveraging existing properties to rent to guests without taking longer-term rental properties off the market. And we're exploring ways that we can help reduce friction points between hosts, guests, and communities.

✦

One irony is that in tech companies, which are drawing so much fire, employees can actually risk making their concerns over ethical matters public. This is because, in part, highly coveted technical talent cannot be easily replaced. If company leaders don't listen and respond to concerns in a respectful way, they risk alienating employees who will take their talent elsewhere. They may even take customers, who also want to work with partners who are aligned in their values, with them. I suspect that valued and influential employees in any industry will notice this and feel empowered to become more vocal with their concerns.

After analyzing the results of his company's trust survey, Richard Edelman concluded that employers have a unique opportunity to attract and keep employees, and capitalizing on it requires four things: establishing an audacious goal consistent with the company's business (for example, increasing revenues while reducing carbon output); supplementing mainstream and social media with presentations about current events presented on company channels; supporting local communities and encouraging employees to give back through volunteering; and requiring the CEO to take a prominent role in speaking up in support of values such as diversity, inclusion, and social issues like immigration or homelessness.

All good ideas. But I would add that each of these steps is doomed unless it occurs as part of a larger commitment to integrity. If the CEO is seen as cynical or opportunistic about initiatives with a social-good component, it will be worse than doing nothing.

◆

Even when they find the "why" of Intentional Integrity pretty clear—attracting and retaining top talent; forging trust with customers; and, of course, avoiding scandals—many leaders today find it a daunting subject to take on. My goal is to convince every business leader, using the stories and experiences that have shaped my views, that it's worth it to get practical and tactical. It's not difficult to make ethics part of a company's cultural DNA, and I will discuss the most important risks companies must address in a code of ethics. But also, very critically, I will cover how leaders can engage and empower employees to recognize and tackle integrity dilemmas as they would other business challenges, by considering both short- and long-term consequences. I think you'll find it more interesting, and fun, than you might have imagined.

1

Spies, jarts, and racism:
The roots of corporate culture shocks

There is nothing new about bad behavior, but technology has created new integrity dilemmas. As a lawyer who's worked in public service and in corporations, the evidence is clear to me that proactively addressing integrity dilemmas is far better than cleaning up the damage they can cause.

Anyone considering advice about integrity should ask an obvious question: Who are you to tell me how to behave? Maybe Rob Chesnut knows what is legal since he's a lawyer, but how does he know "what is right"?

People are naturally wary of anyone who is trying to influence how they think or behave. So here's my background. I'm a middle-aged white guy from the South. I was an only child with a Marine Corps father who left when I was thirteen. Thanks to my mom's hard work and my uncle's generosity, I graduated from both the University of Virginia and Harvard Law School. I then worked as a federal prosecutor before joining eBay in 1999, and I have worked in high tech ever since as both a legal officer and advisor.

Like most people, I have faced integrity dilemmas where I wished in hindsight that I or the organization I worked for had made different choices. I don't pretend to be a superior judge of personal decisions or what's right or wrong in the abstract. Nor do I have a foolproof system to inoculate your workplace from amoral actors or criminals. But I do have unique experience sorting out ethical dilemmas for disruptive business platforms.

✦

I distinctly remember my very first e-commerce experience. It was 1998, and I had an unusual hobby: I created art prints by manipulating the surface of "instant" camera photos. To make it work, I needed a specific camera—the Polaroid SX-70. The problem was, Polaroid no longer made the camera, so I looked for used ones at flea markets and swap meets. Somebody told me that a new auction "dot com" called eBay included vintage cameras among its listings. I went to eBay's homepage and typed "SX-70" in the search box, hoping I'd find one or two.

The search returned dozens. I was amazed—dumbfounded actually. At the time, I had no idea that that moment would change the course of my career.

People are basically good

After law school, a clerkship with a federal judge, and a short stint as a civil constitutional law attorney with the U.S. Justice Department, I joined the U.S. Attorney's Office in Alexandria, Virginia. Coincidentally, an integrity issue involving a colleague led to my first significant promotion. A federal judge found that a prosecutor at my office had knowingly withheld exculpatory evidence from a defendant charged with kidnapping. After the prosecutor was moved out of his leadership role in the criminal section of the office, I took over his position running the major crimes unit, and within weeks, the FBI came to my office and presented me with the prosecution of Aldrich Ames, a former CIA officer who spent years spying for what was then the Soviet Union.

The consequences of Ames's spying were horrific—literally deadly. Because of the intelligence Ames shared with the Soviets, a number of U.S. operatives were arrested, and some were executed.[1] At least 100 operations were undermined, and U.S. national security was directly compromised for nearly a decade. Ames is still serving a life sentence today.

Espionage cases are fascinating, but I never saw myself as a career prosecutor. By the late 1990s, I was looking for new challenges, right at the time my search for old SX-70s led me to eBay. I sent my resume to their general "jobs@ebay.com" email address. Someone called me the next day, and within two weeks, I was on a plane to California to meet with CEO Meg Whitman. In March 1999, I became eBay's third lawyer.

The founder of eBay, Pierre Omidyar, had a motto about the eBay community: people are basically good. In those days eBay had no access to PayPal or online credit card processing. The buyer wrote a check or bought a money order, put a stamp on an envelope, and waited for days while it made its way to the seller's mailbox. The seller waited for the check to clear before packaging the item to ship it. When I first mailed a $50 money order for a Polaroid SX-70, I remember thinking, *Well, I'll be lucky if I ever see the camera.* But in this exchange, and in virtually all of my 1,000-plus transactions since, everyone did exactly what they were supposed to do.

The magic of eBay was that it created a way for people with shared passions to connect. Many transactions were just business, but others were a marriage of desire and object, making both parties happy and sometimes leading them to crave even more interaction.

Most of the time, eBay users experienced a positive interaction with a stranger, reinforcing that most people, in fact, do value and demonstrate integrity. I see that same energy in our Airbnb community today. Hosts and guests tend to enjoy their shared experiences; they like learning about each other's worlds. Whether it's following rules about noise or taking pains to return an item left behind, they mostly try to do the right thing. Some even become friends.

Unfortunately, there is also the small number of people in any community who exploit others, who bend and break rules. I quickly learned that if you don't create policies that protect the good folks from those with bad intentions, your entire platform can dissolve. If you don't listen and respond to frustrations that surface from other members of your community about your policies and behaviors, you won't succeed.

I was employee number 170 at eBay, and I can assure you its eventual success was far from guaranteed when I joined. We grew so fast that our computer architecture could not handle the exploding transaction traffic, and we had frequent system outages. We had lots of competition too: at one point, there were a couple hundred online auction platforms, including short-lived efforts from Yahoo! and Amazon. And behind the scenes we were encountering significant legal and business dilemmas for which there were few precedents and no guides to best practices. That's one reason Meg Whitman took a chance on a federal prosecutor with no experience in corporate law.

Barely used brain

In the early days of eBay, the media loved to do stories about our bizarre and hilarious listings: The jar that supposedly contained a ghost. "Civil War era" dirt. A "barely used" brain. A grilled cheese sandwich with an image of the Virgin Mary seared into one side. But some listings were not so funny—they were illegal, or dangerous, or they perpetrated some kind of fraud. In some cases, they deeply offended segments of our community—such as instances of people auctioning locks of hair or other items connected to serial killers. Sorting through the complexity of human desires, imagination, and dark urges became part of a typical workday for the eBay Trust and Safety team.

Sometimes the listing was fine but the seller was unreliable—slow to ship, unresponsive to questions, sloppy in packaging fragile merchandise. Finally, online commerce began to raise unique legal issues; for example, was eBay a neutral platform, or was it liable for allowing listings of stolen or unsafe merchandise? That attracted the attention of law enforcement, legislators, and government regulators. Our competitors were happy to try to use the law to put us out of business.

My team was charged with sorting a lot of this out, and I soon realized that eBay listings offered a peek into an astonishing variety of human passions. Some were fun and harmless: at the point when Pierre was first developing eBay, his girlfriend Pam collected Pez dispensers, and they would become part of eBay lore.

However, the platform surfaced other complicated human desires as well. We became aware of listings for used, unwashed underwear from models. There were listings for body fluids that ranged from excess breast milk (desired both by mothers who could not produce enough and some sex fetishists) to urine (desired by people who needed "clean" samples at hand for random drug tests).

Weapons of many kinds, from automatic rifles to antique spears, were listed. Sellers listed T-shirts and other items with racist, profane, and violent imagery. We learned people were also listing narcotics, bomb-making ingredients and plans, and live animals like parrots and snakes.

In the beginning, Pierre's attitude about what could be listed on eBay was simple: if it's legal to sell "on land," it's legal on eBay. If something was illegal on land and eBay learned about it, we would take the listing down.

But Pierre feared that prohibiting items that were legal but offensive would demand endless value judgments, a worry companies like Facebook and Twitter wrestle with to this day. Who would . . . should . . . could make those calls?

Also, U.S. law (the Communications Decency Act of 1996) provides Internet companies that qualify as "online service providers" with limited immunity. It treats them as "common carriers" as long as they do not act as editors on content that users post on their sites. A common carrier is an entity that provides a lawful service indiscriminately and is not held responsible for its content or any consequences that could result from it. For example, if someone posts a libelous review about a seller on eBay, a court does not hold eBay legally responsible for the false review. But if eBay were to start monitoring and editing reviews, then much like a newspaper it could be sued for false statements on its site.

We at eBay were concerned that proactively intervening in ANY listings might change the scope of our liability as it pertained to ALL listings, not to mention that the cost of employing enough people to do this would be astronomical. At the same time, we cared about our community; we did not want to take an approach that encouraged crimes or made our marketplace feel unsafe or unreliable.

How clean is your marketplace?

Meg Whitman and the board weighed many different opportunities in creating a brand image. There was no lack of "adult" products being listed on the site, or firearms or fetish gear. We made money from all those transactions. But our leaders came to the conclusion that we needed to intentionally shape our brand; we needed to reject the swap-meet ethos and become a welcoming, safe, "clean, well-lit marketplace," as Meg began describing it. We didn't want a family checking their bid for Sam the white bear Beanie Baby to mistype and be presented with a list of S&M paraphernalia. Meg decided we would emphasize our commitment to ethical transactions and a safe, family-friendly space and directed me to create and run the Trust and Safety group to make rules to govern the marketplace.

Issue by issue, category by category, my team, which originally was two people and eventually grew to 2,000, researched specific dilemmas and submitted rule recommendations to the executive team. We had to think not just about legally defensible situations but also about practical policies that were "right" for our community and our brand. Meg's "clean, well-lit marketplace" was an important metaphor to intentionally guide our thought process. However I must admit that we often felt more like traffic cops in a sprawling new city without stoplights whose population was doubling every week than ethical strategists. We were awash in issues—fraud, stolen accounts, and controversial items like breast milk and blessed sacrament wafers—and had to triage the most important ones, make recommendations, and move on. We existed to protect our platform from fraud and bad behavior, all in support of the eBay community and brand,

These challenges created some unforgettable moments for me, one of which showed me just how deep an emotional connection people can forge with a company they like and respect. Meg once sent me to Chicago to appear on *The Oprah Winfrey Show* with a woman who won an auction for a wedding dress on eBay, sent a $3,500 check, but never received the dress. Oprah's producers invited us to participate in a show about her experience.

Talk about nerve-racking. Oprah's team gave us no details on who would be on the show besides the bride and me. Would there also be consumer watchdogs? Would there be a politician about to introduce legislation cracking down on e-commerce? Or might there be 200 angry people in the audience who'd also experienced fraud or had bad eBay experiences? What was I walking into?

Meg pulled me aside and said, "You've got a half million dollars in your pocket if you need it. Talk with people, and if they had a bad experience, fix it on the spot." She encouraged me to offer to buy this fraud victim a replacement wedding dress. She reinforced our message: eBay cares about its community and doing the right thing.

Hey, no pressure!

Somewhat to my shock, the show could not have been a better experience for me or for eBay's reputation. Long before the taping, when the designer of the wedding dress heard from Oprah's team about the fraud, she stepped up and gave the bride a brand-new dress. There were no angry victims in the audience; in fact, they cheered when I assured them that eBay was as angry and frustrated about the bride's experience as she was. I said that we take fraud very seriously and we are pouring a lot of resources into finding and prosecuting criminals and shutting them down. Oprah was sympathetic and gracious. When the show was over, she came to me in the front row and held my hand up as if I'd won a prizefight, and the crowd went crazy, clapping as we walked off the stage together.

This incident offered important lessons. First, "let the buyer beware" could not be a guiding philosophy for our marketplace—it was up to us to proactively make it as safe as possible—or suffer the consequences. Second, and equally important, customers *love* companies that demonstrate an effort to do the right thing. And I didn't even have to spend that pocket money to learn the lesson.

House rules

Soon eBay realized that it did not want to hide behind the "platform" shield or use the letter of the law as its minimum standard. There is a lesson here that I think is essential for all companies today: to have any credibility with employees, customers, investors, or other stakeholders, a company must commit to obeying laws and regulations, both their details and the spirit in which they were created. That seems so obvious, and yet, over the years at multiple companies, I have occasionally been surprised when executives pay more attention to what they can get away with than to how they can achieve their goals and objectives honestly and legally. It's appropriate and ethical to work to change laws or regulations that a company considers unfair or ill-advised. That's what democracy is all about. But how can you ask employees to obey your rules if you don't respect the laws that apply to the company?

So, the first priority of eBay's Trust and Safety group was to ban listings for products that were illegal for the average person to sell. Among them: child pornography, narcotics, human organs (somebody tried to auction their kidney), human tissues or fluids (blood, breast milk, semen, eggs), stolen merchandise, and explosive devices and regulated chemical components like dynamite or C4.

That seems like a simple list. But those illegal goods were only the beginning of my introduction to a universe of laws I had never encountered in law school or as a federal prosecutor. For example, counterfeit goods were a headache. People have every right to list a Chanel handbag they no longer want for sale on eBay. However, it is illegal to sell a counterfeit Chanel handbag, even if the description in a listing plainly represents it as a counterfeit. And without that disclaimer, how would a buyer or eBay know the difference? Luxury goods makers constantly accused us of not doing enough to stop counterfeit trading, even though we had every incentive to stop it: in our view, counterfeit goods cheapened our marketplace by undermining our most treasured asset—trust.

Then, we had to address items that were not illegal per se but that violated contracts between other parties. For example, none of us initially realized that, by contract, schools aren't supposed to sell or give away teacher's-edition textbooks. Of course, they do. Homeschoolers love to get their hands on them. This type of trading happened under the radar until eBay made it public. Then, we received angry letters from publishers threatening to drag us into who knows how many lawsuits, so we had to ban teacher textbook listings. Which made homeschoolers furious at us.

Then, there were controversial items that were legal but were fraught with social or safety implications. Initially eBay did allow listings for alcohol, tobacco, and firearms. If you think about how heavily regulated all of these items are on land, you can imagine why they became problematic on eBay. Liquor, tobacco, and gun laws and taxes vary from state to state (and sometimes by county or even city). With guns, some states require background checks and other security precautions. All three were banned from listings shortly before I arrived.

When we banned gun listings, some accused us of trying to be the morality police or said that we were anti–Second Amendment. I fielded an angry call from an agent of the U.S. Bureau of Alcohol, Tobacco, and Firearms; he traded firearms on eBay and vehemently opposed our decision. We discussed it and agreed to disagree.

The Columbine High School massacre occurred just two months after eBay banned firearm sales. One of the early rumors was that the underage killers had bought some of their weapons on eBay. The rumor turned out to be false, but it reinforced why we did not want to be in the business of facilitating gun transactions when they could so easily end up in the wrong hands.

The gun experience also made clear the double-edged sword of why companies try to avoid making policies of this kind and why it was absolutely necessary to have them. Sometimes integrity means having the courage to prioritize risks and make hard choices, such as between freedom and safety. It means acting consistently with a set of values the organization has committed to, even when you know some customers or community members won't like it. And when something terrible does happen, it's important to show that your organization doesn't operate in denial or with its head in the sand: it tries to anticipate problems and prevent them.

What happens when users break the rules?

A different but also critical element of my job in Trust and Safety was determining consequences for people who broke *our* rules. It was easy enough to make a list of prohibited items and then write software to flag listings that mentioned key words like "autopsy" or "urine." If someone complained that a listing violated our policy, or if we found it ourselves, we would send an email and then remove it. If the person kept posting banned items, we had the option to cancel their account. If we identified true criminals who would take buyers' money and run off with it without shipping the purchased items, we would turn the case over to the police.

However, we also tried to be consistent with Pierre's foundational belief that people are basically good. Not all cases of banned items or fraudulent listings were equivalent, and some were not intentional. Some sellers had themselves been duped when they acquired the item they were now selling. In the beginning, if there was an accusation of fraud, our team or I would sometimes just call a seller and try to figure out what was going on.

For example, there was once a listing for a baseball ostensibly signed by New York Yankees catcher Thurman Munson. An eBay shopper reported the listing to us as a counterfeit. I called the seller of the ball, who angrily and adamantly defended the authenticity of the autograph until I pointed out to him that Munson died in a plane crash in 1979; the ball had the official symbol of the president of the American League, Bobby Brown, who didn't become president until 1984. I was prepared to remove the item and chalk this instance up to a misunderstanding, but that was before we checked into his account. He had been personally bidding on the item to drive the price up, which also violated our rules, so instead we kicked him off the platform.

Almost more difficult to deal with were sellers who just pushed the limits of legality or were lazy or sloppy. Some sellers consistently described items as being in better condition than they really were, or they were slow to ship items after receiving payment. Dealing with these shabby sellers gave me insight into a fact of corporate life I think any executive who wants to promote integrity in their workplace has to consider: you must think long and hard about the performance target numbers you post on the wall because they can have unintended and damaging consequences.

Obviously, there can be tension between profits and the larger ideals of your brand. If you reward your sales or marketing teams on the basis of certain raw numbers—I'll use eBay as an example and say the number of listings posted, or the dollar volume of transactions in a category—you may unconsciously be incentivizing employees to overlook unethical behavior. At eBay, I became frustrated at times with our marketing category managers who defended sellers we would internally rate a C- or D, whom I thought we should kick off the platform. The pushback was that they still were driving business to us. An eBay employee who was evaluated on the basis of growing the number of listings or the dollars made by eBay actually had no incentive to crack down on C- sellers. The manager personally achieved the same benefit from the C- transaction as from an A+++ transaction.

The trade-off I would pose was: How much are we losing when a buyer has a bad experience and goes away and doesn't come back? Still, I angered some colleagues whose compensation was based in part on transaction traffic. Since these managers never suffered performance deductions based on the quality of the transactions, they became an internal obstacle in protecting the brand reputation. Eventually, our team collected hard data that buyers who had a bad experience curtailed future purchases. Over time, we added more factors to our performance incentives, some of which addressed the quality of sellers as judged by complaints and other feedback about how smoothly their transactions resolved, not just total number of items listed in a category.

There are some parallels to certain issues that come up with our Airbnb hosts and guests today. The vast majority of these people are ethical, responsible partners. But some have dubious definitions of what constitutes "clean" or "quiet," or they may describe a home's location as within "walking distance" of an event venue when it would be better described as "hiking distance." On the other hand, it's also true that a few Airbnb guests have done significant damage to a host's property or have hosted loud or prohibited parties in defiance of clearly stated terms for the listing.

All of these points of friction require our attention, and they can be complicated to unravel. We create insurance policies for our hosts to cover damage by guests, and we give hosts feedback when we get complaints about descriptions of properties not matching up with guests' expectations. We make clear that these descriptions are part of a contract. If they misrepresent their properties, we can't allow them on our platform. In late 2019, we banned party houses on Airbnb altogether.

Looking back, I wish I had been more aggressive earlier in eBay's life in arguing for even more crackdowns on unethical and problematic sellers. Our failure to aggressively deal with mediocre sellers and focus on providing an outstanding buyer experience was, I believe, at the heart of eBay's gradual slide from its position as the e-commerce leader. Meg Whitman was never stingy in giving me resources, but we had so many issues to worry about, and it was a different time; many elements of e-commerce that we take for granted today were still evolving.

For example, in the late 1990s, our feedback system was considered revolutionary—eBay allowed buyers and sellers the opportunity to research and evaluate each other, which you couldn't do for newspaper want ads or people at a swap meet. But over time it was clear that our feedback system had flaws that undermined its integrity. Scams like phishing and stealing account data might allow scammers to operate under a legitimate eBay user's profile for multiple transactions before the fraud was discovered. Also, buyers and sellers posted their reviews independently, and so each feared retribution by the other for being the first to post a negative review. A buyer and seller might exchange vicious and accusatory private emails, but there was no incentive to give anything but a positive public review for fear of your own rating being hurt. Thus, over time, the review system lost some integrity.

Airbnb figured out a good solution to this issue years before I arrived. Hosts and guests have two weeks to submit a review after an Airbnb stay. Airbnb won't post either side's review until both weigh in or two weeks pass. If the guest writes a review but the host does not, or vice versa, the single review is posted after two weeks, and the other party cannot respond (or retaliate). This helps to increase the odds of a more honest review from both parties. Other companies like Amazon and Yelp are evolving online reputation even further, using algorithms and AI to identify and reduce the impact of unreliable reviews.

It's not just about the letter of the law

I could list 200 more examples of tricky decisions we had to make at eBay as we tried to build a high-integrity business. In those days, the focus of our work was not so much on rules for our employees but on the rules of the marketplace. Still, it was my introduction to many points of friction I continue to see playing out at Internet companies involving conflicts around fraud, free speech, data privacy, and a platform's liability for content. It also gave me insight to how broad the term "stakeholder" could be. One minute I'd find myself talking with a homeschooling mother just trying to obtain resources to educate her child, the next I'd be on the phone with a law enforcement official who wanted help with a criminal investigation, and the next I'd be mollifying an angry stamp collector about what constituted "mint" condition. But I want to end this chapter with two stories that I think speak to the external benefits of establishing a reputation for ethical and honest behavior.

"You're all going to jail"

One of my most memorable days at eBay came early on when I received an email from a user that said: "You're all going to jail for selling jarts."

Perhaps like you, I asked: What are jarts? A "jart" is a combination javelin and lawn dart. It has a long, sharp spike and is designed to be thrown toward a target on grass. I don't know how many backyard birthday party guests were maimed by these things before the U.S. Consumer Products Safety Commission (CPSC) wisely banned them for sale in all 50 states in 1988.

Consumers don't have to return or stop using a recalled or banned product. Therefore, it's not surprising that many ended up in attics or in garage sales. And once eBay appeared, some ended up listed on eBay.[2] However, it's against the law to sell a banned product.

As a lawyer, this presented a real dilemma. We could have tried to make the common carrier argument. But it was true that we were *profiting* from the sale of a dangerous, banned product that could physically harm our customers. More broadly, jarts made us realize that there were likely many other recalled or illegal products that were being sold on eBay, from makeup to tires to fireworks. What should we do about this?

I did something that shocked many of my legal colleagues: I called the CPSC and asked for an appointment with their general counsel. I flew to Washington alone to meet with him.

There had been no official complaint, and the CPSC's office was unaware of the jart issue on eBay. But I sat down and laid it out: the Internet is coming at all of us, and we need government to partner with business to protect consumers. Let's put aside the issue of "who's liable" and start with the basic premise that as a responsible company, we don't want to sell defective or dangerous goods. We don't have all the answers yet, but we want to work together to figure it out.

That meeting set the tone, and within months we announced a partnership to work together to protect consumers from dangerous goods being sold on eBay. We prohibited listings for banned products, put warnings in categories like children's toys and power tools where recalled items were common, gave the CPSC a free page on our site to educate consumers and link to their database of recalled items, and even hired a team to learn about recalled items and search the site to remove the most common ones.

Maybe it was because I had worked in government, but I had a high confidence that if we demonstrated integrity, if we were transparent and reasonable, regulators would be reasonable too. Meg Whitman backed me. It was a risk, but it paid off. On an ongoing basis, we worked together with the government to identify dangerous and banned products, sharing information and resources. To my knowledge, eBay has never had any kind of legal action filed against it by the government over this issue.[3]

No room for racism

In the same way that jarts were a wake-up call, the media began running stories within weeks of my 2016 arrival at Airbnb about complaints by African American guests who reported that they had been discriminated against by some Airbnb hosts. Some hosts were refusing to book guests after viewing profile photos. In some cases, we learned that guests had been turned away at the door when hosts saw their faces. Some guests filed lawsuits in addition to complaints, and the California Department of Fair Employment and Housing (DFEH) filed a class action alleging that Airbnb was legally responsible for the discrimination.

We could have fought the cases one by one, arguing that Airbnb had not committed or abetted the discriminatory act (in fact, such discrimination violates our user policies). Led by our CEO, Brian Chesky, we took a different course. It's not a legal issue, Brian said publicly, it's bigger than that. "Discrimination is the opposite of belonging, and its existence on our platform jeopardizes this core mission," he wrote in a letter to the Airbnb community. "Every time you make someone else feel like they belong, that person feels accepted and safe to be themselves. While this may sound like a small act of kindness, we are a community of millions of people strong. Imagine what we can do together."[4]

In the years since the problem became public, Airbnb has taken concrete steps to reduce discrimination on the platform. For example, we've required all customers globally to take a pledge when joining Airbnb that they will accept everyone without regard to race, religion, nationality, sexual orientation, or other protected factor. We've moved guest photo displays to post-booking confirmations. And most importantly, we've created a special team to investigate allegations of discrimination.

◆

An exciting business model and solid value proposition are huge advantages for a start-up. At the same time, new technologies raise new challenges. In each case, I'm proud that the companies I've worked for have made real changes to their business processes to get to the root of a serious issue, and, as time has gone on, they have monitored the impact and tweaked the processes.

It's critical to have leadership that commits to a set of values even when it's not easy.

2

Six Cs:
Critical steps to fostering integrity
in the workplace

Choosing Intentional Integrity is an opportunity. It is not just about outlawing certain acts. It's about shaping a positive attitude toward ethical, value-based behavior. Intentional Integrity also promotes an empowered and energetic culture. It's a way to drive ethical choices about common dilemmas and challenges to every level of the company.

Entrepreneurs often joke that running a start-up is like building an airplane while flying it. Teams work night and day to ready a product for launch and capture market and mindshare. It's intense and exciting. Focus is critical. But processes and structures you ignored in favor of launch inevitably start to create problems. You may be an innovator, but you also have to do some traditional things companies do: hire and train people, buy equipment, rent facilities, understand applicable laws. The absence of clear policies and structure in a fast-growing company can create a crisis that sends the company plunging to earth faster than a blown engine.

When I arrived at Airbnb in 2016, I saw an innovative and fast-growing platform with high-integrity leaders, but no written code of ethics or specific guidelines for our employees' interactions with the community or with one another. Before I could go out and talk to employees about integrity and appropriate behavior, I realized that we had to have our own code of ethics to make sure we were all operating off the same playbook.

The code I helped to institute at Airbnb builds on the basic principles I came to value and embrace while working at several companies throughout my career. These principles are not exotic: we committed to follow the law . . . to not discriminate . . . to reject conflicts of interest and unethical and illegal practices like bribery . . . to protect customer privacy . . . to safeguard the company's intellectual property . . . to prohibit sexual harassment or any other behavior that made employees feel unsafe. There also are some elements of the code that are unique to Airbnb's mission, such as that we foster belonging among strangers.

And then we created a community standards document about behavior on our platform. It reflected in part my years at eBay observing the interaction between buyers and sellers; this time, I had to recalibrate my perspective to the related but also unique context of interaction between hosts and guests. The golden rule is a good basic guide: if you treat others the way you'd like to be treated, you can generally sort through most issues. But just as the list of eBay's rules governing prohibited and banned items eventually grew very, very long, the guidance we've had to give to our platform users has become increasingly explicit, as a universe of local laws and issues impact Airbnb hosts, not to mention the very personal nature of staying in another person's home.

I had the full support of CEO Brian Chesky, the board, and the executive management team, and we created a code we are all proud of. Then, we developed processes and techniques to reinforce the code and make sure its messages remain top of mind inside the company. And, over time, we also created processes aimed at reporting violations, investigating reports, and assigning consequences. As I contemplated what I wanted to emphasize in this book, I evaluated the processes that we used to create the code and that we still use to drive its spirit into the company. I now call the overall effort, for simplicity's sake, the Six Cs.

The first C stands for Chief. Make no mistake: If your CEO does not embrace the importance of integrity and commit to both live by the company's code of ethics and enforce it, forget about the other five Cs. You're done. You will not build a high-integrity culture. Hypocrisy and ambiguity are the enemies of integrity, and if the CEO (and this also goes for the entire executive team and board members) bends or breaks the rules or only enforces them selectively, employees will never take your program seriously.

The second C stands for Customized Code of Ethics. You must have a specific, published code of ethics that reflects your company's core values as well as the norms of its particular industry, geographic location, and culture. This is so important that I will talk about it in the next two chapters. First, we'll discuss your brand, what you stand for, and the practical activities and nuances of your business. As you address specific issues and rules, you'll do so within that larger brand context.

In chapter 5, I will tell you about the 10 most common integrity violations every company needs to think about and address. This will include the stories behind the rules, where the code meets real life. The reason I emphasize some parts of a code or advocate certain kinds of processes will become clearer. I'll explain the rationale for some specific policies that any company operating in today's more transparent, networked, and digital world, as well as one with changing social mores, should consider. Some of the examples I discuss will help explain one of our code's fundamental principles: "You're always at work when you're with someone from work."

The third C stands for Communicating the Code. As general counsel and as head of the ethics team, I give in-person small-group presentations on integrity to all new employees in offices around the world. Using senior leaders to communicate and reinforce the code is crucial. If all you do is paste an ethics code on a web page or print it out and bundle it with documents about the health plan and parking procedures, you will send the wrong message to the company about the importance of the code. If you try to teach the code with a canned online program or video, you will make very little impact. Think about your own experiences in this regard. If you delegate the training to a mid-level HR manager, you are suggesting that it just isn't very important.

Lilian Tham, head of executive recruiting at Airbnb, has worked for a number of global companies. After I gave the integrity talk during her orientation week, she sought me out to say how much she appreciated it. Later, she shared a few more thoughts about the

"Check-in" talk with me: "I do think that the cultural norms that are shared with new employees during Check-in sets the stage for how they engage with the company and their colleagues moving forward. While I've worked for companies like Disney, American Express, and Google, I've never been in a company where the message on ethics or harassment has been led by the GC or a senior executive at Rob's level. It's often led by a junior HR person who pushes a button on a video that feels outdated and out of touch. Having Rob lead these discussions with the new employees, integrating real-life examples and with him sharing his vulnerabilities and his own imperfect interactions, underscored how important integrity and ethics are to our mission and our culture. It lays down the foundation for how we should think about interacting with our colleagues and how we should conduct ourselves well after Check-in."

The fourth C stands for Clear Reporting System. Make it easy for employees to report ethical lapses, corruption, and fraud. This is far superior to learning about problems from media inquiries, lawsuits, government regulators, or social media. Former Applied Materials CEO and chairman James Morgan, a highly respected technology executive who ran Applied for nearly three decades, had a good motto that was well known to his managers: "Bad news is good news—if you do something about it." In other words, he wanted to hear about problems as early as possible, because then the company could fix them before they became crises. It can go against human nature to be a "fink" or a naysayer, but at Applied, people who found problems early were celebrated. That's a great habit to reinforce.

Companies that want a culture of integrity must make the process of reporting all problems, especially violations of the code, easy, straightforward, and clear. You cannot just say, "It's your job, employees, to tell us what's going on," then ignore the barriers that restrict them from doing just that.

We'll talk about anonymous tips, investigating violations, and the due process all accused parties should receive. Ideally, there should be multiple reporting avenues. There are organizations that are actually developing interesting online reporting platforms for companies to try to solve some of the fear and retaliation issues that can surround reporting.

The fifth C stands for Consequences. A code must be enforced. Violations at any and every level bring consequences, which might be a warning for a first offense but can ramp up to termination. A high-integrity culture depends on fair and reasonable responses to violations. A code without consequences risks two things: First, if employees never hear about the code being referenced or enforced, they will forget about it. Your culture will develop in spite of your code rather than being shaped by it. Second, a code that exists but is not consistently enforced can become weaponized. A Silicon Valley CEO once told me, "Nobody ever reads the corporate handbook unless they're trying to stick it to someone." Executives and employees trying to sabotage a colleague have been known to scour old emails or expense reports for ethical "dirt" or even to try to trap someone into violating a rule. This happens more often than many folks realize. For example, the #MeToo movement has unearthed situations where senior executives received complaints about a CEO's inappropriate behavior, and in response they told the complainers' managers to scour their records for reasons to fire the employee who complained. That is toxic behavior that destroys a culture of trust.

Human beings (and valuable employees) make mistakes for many reasons, and everyone deserves a fair hearing and consequences that reflect the specifics and magnitude of an offense. That said, we'll talk about the complexity of consequences.

The sixth C stands for Constant. Integrity presentations, videos, and internal electronic and paper posters are all designed to create repetition, or what I call a "constant drumbeat." We want employees to think about the company's values constantly when they make decisions or take initiatives that have an integrity component. Researchers have studied what motivates people to behave in more or less honest ways, and constantly reinforcing the expectation and direction to be honest and ethical makes a difference. We also want employees to remember what their employer stands for when they are making comments on social media or anonymous workplace discussion sites.

Another element of being constant is that you want to monitor integrity issues, violations, and actions taken. In the legal department you need a dashboard that indicates the number and nature of code violation inquiries, reports, and disciplinary actions, and which way they are trending. Be alert to specific divisions that might need more training or support. Identify geographic regions where certain messages are not getting through or where special circumstances are creating issues.

Finally, you want to constantly revisit, refresh, and update your Intentional Integrity process to reflect new legal, business, or technology realities. As the company grows and adds business lines or activities, it must incorporate the new cultural implications of that growth and other unique issues into the code. Communication about integrity must not become background noise—it needs to be imaginative and memorable. You have to look for opportunities to provide teaching moments when a controversy at another company arises so you can prevent the same scenario happening in your company. In my integrity talks, I have a slide with headlines of other companies' mistakes and scandals. It's sobering. I see grimaces in the audience. But even when it's not your own crisis, it can be an opportunity to focus everyone's attention on specific behaviors, both good and bad. You must constantly refresh and reinforce your values.

Code moments

I may be a lawyer, but dry handbook language makes even my eyes glaze over. I find that complicated and nuanced subjects are best explained by storytelling, by connecting rules to the spirit and intention of what you're trying to achieve. For the most part, I will use real-life examples for each of the "Cs" I'm going to explain in subsequent chapters. I find that almost each and every day brings new examples of companies facing, and sometimes failing, integrity dilemmas.

However, I want to address one sensitive issue directly. I cannot reveal the details of discussions I have had with the management of Airbnb about specific cases or situations where I provided legal counsel. Those conversations fall under the category of attorney-client privilege. I cannot go beyond whatever the company has publicly stated. Figuring out how I could bring real-life dilemmas to life proved to be problematic. How could I follow my ethical obligations and still provide meaningful insight?

What I've settled on is presenting what I call "Code Moments." These are composite scenarios that reflect details from real but unidentified situations, integrity dilemmas, and ethics issues that I have investigated, made recommendations on, talked with legal colleagues about, or otherwise seen in my career. Several also reflect my writing collaborator's involvement with specific stories when she worked as a national business magazine reporter.

I want to be clear: these Code Moments are based on real-life situations, but they are written as composites. Nonessential identifying details have been changed. There is no one case study based entirely on the facts of one case. I have chosen this format so that I can be completely candid in sharing my analysis of the concerns and legal issues these situations raise without violating any of my own professional duties and ethics as a legal officer.

But I also want to stress, these are NOT wild hypotheticals—they are common challenges. I often tell our Airbnb employees, "I have no doubt that in the next year every one of you will have at least one significant Code Moment." But I believe they have lower-level dilemmas far more frequently, much more often, in fact, than executives realize or would like to admit.

Each Code Moment will include, first, a summary of the facts. I've plucked the topics from the most common categories we're going to explore in more detail in chapter 4. They include:

Romantic entanglements
Alcohol and drug issues
Misuse of company resources or property and expense account issues
Conflicts of interest
Abuse of access to customer data
Sexual harassment or assault
Bribes and improper gifts
Trade secret and confidential information disclosure
Fraud
Social media issues

Then in the appendix I'll lay out action options, ways to think about these dilemmas, and my take on the larger issues. You'll notice in these Code Moments that they frequently contain multiple code violations, and often by multiple parties, around the same triggering incident. This reflects real life: many people who make a bad decision are ashamed of their behavior. They sometimes go into denial and resort to lies and cover-ups that can make code violations spread faster than mold on an abandoned sandwich in the breakroom fridge.

My hope is that you will read the examples and, first, ponder the possible responses a leader might have. Then, turn to the back of the book where I'll discuss the scenario and options in more detail. Do they remind you of conflicts or quandaries that worked out well . . . or not so well?

I have always believed that each of us goes through life peering through lenses that are colored by our personal experiences and histories. Some experiences have given us wisdom; some have warped our perceptions of others' actions and motives. They can be fogged by desire or cracked by disappointments.

When we encounter people whose lenses are different from ours, sometimes we hit impasses. It's useful from time to time to remove our personal lenses and imagine situations from another person's point of view. As a parent I have often told my children to do this when they find themselves angry at authority figures or in conflict with friends.

Empathizing with others can be helpful at work as well. We don't always make time to consider other points of view or issues beyond those that impact our career, our deliverables, our ambitions. After all, every day we have to hit targets, get the job done. Time is precious, competition is fierce, resources are scarce. As so many organizations have demonstrated, it can be tempting to cut corners, fudge the truth, and ignore the bad behavior of top performers. But I think we've also seen that such a myopic approach often ends badly.

Solving integrity dilemmas can mean removing the lenses of our own biases and preoccupations and putting on a set of "ethics goggles." These goggles focus our attention on shared and common values and principles, and they can help us see and choose the right path.

My goal is to help you polish your ethics goggles so you'll reach for them instinctively and broaden your context for making decisions. Using a solid and tested process to create the culture is critical—but you must be prepared for dilemmas that will challenge the rules and processes in one way or another.

If you're a leader, I hope Code Moments reinforce the need for you to lay out in fairly specific detail what you expect from your employees. But whether you are a leader or an individual contributor, I hope they demonstrate the slippery slope of rationalizing behavior. These examples may raise questions you want to explore further or talk about with friends or colleagues. These are the conversations I want to start.

3

C is for Chief:
Integrity begins at the top

The tone at the top of your organization is critical to building a high-integrity culture.

I haven't slept or eaten properly in days, and I'm exhausted. My strength is gone, and as I pick through the wreckage, clean up this mess and try to piece my life back together, I realize the only thing that sounds appealing now is to go spend a few months near a beach, somewhere calm and sunny. Somewhere like Mexico, or Bali.

But ideas like this, adventurous and enticing travel ideas that I've had so many times before, are now plagued with a question I've never before had to worry too much about: How would I find a place to stay?[1]

In June 2011, an Airbnb host identified only as "EJ" posted a horror story in a lengthy blog about returning from a business trip to discover that a guest had trashed her apartment. Understandably, she felt violated and frightened at the intensity of the vandalism. From Airbnb's point of view, meanwhile, her post was a scary counter to our brand and values, our belief that people are basically good and can share great experiences and travel adventures in a community built on trust. It also formed the basis for what Airbnb CEO Brian Chesky today recalls as the most intense "integrity moment" he had faced at the then three-year-old company.

EJ, a corporate event planner in her thirties, explained that she had rented her apartment in San Francisco to a guest who went by "DJ Pattrson."

EJ's previous experiences renting out her New York apartment on Airbnb had gone well, and she figured that while on business trips she might as well make some money from her empty space. She wasn't able to meet DJ before she left for a few days, but she was reassured by the several texts she received from the guest, complimenting her on her beautiful apartment and thanking EJ for being such a good host.

After a week on the road, EJ returned home to find almost psychopathic destruction: someone (witnesses said more than one person was in and out of her place) had pulled her clothes off their hangers and out of drawers and left them in a wet pile under bathroom towels; sprinkled cleanser powder all over her kitchen; dumped a mystery crud all over her bathroom; punched through a wall to her locked closet and stolen her grandmother's jewelry, as well as a laptop, camera, and backup drives. It was summer, but the guest had burned several logs—and a set of sheets—in the fireplace with the flue closed, so there was a film of ash throughout the unit. She discovered that DJ also took discount coupons from her apartment and used them while ordering merchandise with EJ's credit card. Horrifying.

At the time, it was Airbnb's explicit policy that it was not liable for any damage done by a guest. Airbnb would assist the host in getting a resolution, but the host had to seek and obtain restitution from the guest. While she mentioned in her blog post that the company was sympathetic and helpful, EJ also raised the point that Airbnb promoted how transparent its process was, but the system process meant that Airbnb did not provide any ability for a host or guests to research the other in a meaningful way in advance of a booking. She argued in her blog that this created an impression that Airbnb had already vetted the other party.

Once the blog post aired, it went viral. It prompted some other hosts to say they had experienced bad guests as well. Brian Chesky watched the media coverage go from bad to worse. He recalls: "We did not handle it well initially. We bungled the customer service response. We tried to optimize the PR outcome frankly, and the more we tried to optimize the PR outcome, the worse it got. We kept doing it, and nothing worked." There was disagreement among company leaders about how to stem the criticism. Some thought it best to be quiet and wait it out. Others thought the company should take more responsibility. Someone from Airbnb reached out to ask EJ to take her blog post down, offending her and prompting another post. The situation dragged on for several weeks as reporters looked for other stories of damage or problems from Airbnb guests.

Brian says he finally hit a wall. "At one point, and out of desperation, frankly, I thought, screw the outcome. I am going to think about how I want to be remembered. I decided to make a business decision to do the right thing. The principled decision." He realized many situations are just too complex to try to solve for a desired outcome. "If you don't know how a situation that's complicated is going to play out, figure out how you want to be remembered. That is different from making a decision because you believe it's going to play out a certain way."

Step one, he decided, was to issue a frank and clear apology. Step two, the company needed to offer some kind of protection to hosts from this kind of rare but devastating event. He called a board member to discuss his plan to offer $5,000 worth of insurance to hosts, incurring a charge that was going to lower Airbnb's profit. He figured the director would be concerned about the cost, but Brian felt it was the right thing to do. Instead, the board member said, "Yes, and add a zero to it." Soon after, Brian issued a statement that said, among other things, "We have felt paralyzed, and over the last four weeks, we have really screwed things up." He announced going forward the $50,000 guarantee for all hosts to make things right in the event of damage.

Airbnb worked with law enforcement to try to identify "DJ Pattrson," and a suspect was later arrested and charged with possession of stolen items.[2] The company withstood the controversy, and Brian's decision to take a principled path became a source of pride for employees.

I was not at Airbnb when this situation took place, but I can tell you that people still talk about Brian's apology and how he made things right. It became part of the Airbnb culture, a show of integrity I subsequently have heard a number of employees and executives and investors point to with pride. "That's when I really saw what Brian was made of," Joe Zadeh, then head of product management, later told *Fortune* magazine.[3]

When a CEO acts with integrity, it sends a message throughout an entire organization that is not soon forgotten. Employees do not expect their leaders to be perfect, but too many leaders assume that admitting a mistake is a sign of weakness. In fact, it's the opposite. If a CEO cannot admit a mistake, how can you expect anyone in an organization to instinctively take responsibility and fix a problem rather than try to avoid blame or even cover it up? If a CEO instead acts with integrity and expects it from others, it's more likely to be the default option throughout the organization.

◆

I believe this is true in any company in any industry. Recently, I was in a hotel lounge watching a basketball game, and I struck up a conversation with a gentleman who was alone at the adjoining table. He was low-key and said very little about his background, and it took me over an hour to realize that I was talking with the cofounder of the giant retailer Costco, Jim Sinegal. For about two hours we talked about the state of the country, integrity as a concept, ethical sourcing of goods, treating employees with respect, and the idea of managing companies on a long time horizon instead of quarter to quarter.

Later, I did some research and learned that Costco has one of the lowest turnover rates in retailing, and that around 90 percent of its employees have access to health insurance versus an industry average of about 6 percent.[4] I am sure the company is a fierce competitor, but I did not find any stories about Costco scandals or questionable ethics. During our conversation, I told him about my belief in the concept of Intentional Integrity, and he quietly said, "Only one thing matters. It all starts at the top."

In late 2018, the *New York Times* technology columnist Kara Swisher wrote a column about tech company executives in which she listed one troubling behavior after another. Swisher observed that "slowly, then all at once, it feels like too many digital leaders have lost their minds."[5]

The larger point of Swisher's column was a question: since Silicon Valley CEOs have been failing at demonstrating integrity by deed and word, is it time to create a "chief ethics officer" position? "As one ethical quandary after another has hit its profoundly ill-prepared executives, their once-pristine reputations have fallen like palm trees in a hurricane," she noted.

◆

A chief ethics officer role may become an important one for platform companies that must grapple with complex, global issues. But it might surprise you that I say this with some caveats. On one hand, establishing a position like chief ethics officer is a strong statement that a company prioritizes ethics and doing the right thing. And for companies who've experienced scandals or who need to reboot their brand and culture, hiring or appointing a chief ethics officer can offer valuable outside perspective and wisdom.

But I don't want to give the impression that only a sizable company can adequately address integrity issues. The leader of any company, for that matter any sole proprietorship, must shoulder responsibility for thinking through its purpose, its values, and the basic rules of its interactions with stakeholders and then commit to act on those values. A CEO or business owner cannot "outsource" responsibility for an organization's integrity to a chief ethics officer or anyone else. A chief ethics officer can be a valuable partner to a CEO, focusing on details of difficult and complex dilemmas and ways to shape the company's policies and training. But as Jim Sinegal and other seasoned leaders know so well, Intentional Integrity must begin at the top—the very top. When a leader forgets that, it can spell disaster.

The agony of defeat

When I was a kid, the Volkswagen Beetle sold for less than $2,000. It was cute, fun, and, along with the iconic VW van, it and its brand stood for the "hippie" values of peace and love and living simply. Over the years, the company also acquired and produced more performance-oriented cars. I always liked Volkswagens; the first family car I bought when my daughter Bianca was born was a Passat.

A decade ago, Volkswagen's CEO tasked the company with the goal of turbocharging sales of diesel engines in the United States. Company leaders put intense pressure on its engineers to deliver the power consumers wanted despite also having to pass strict U.S. fuel emission standards that reduced engine performance. They appeared to have done the nearly impossible, and sales soared.

But in 2015, outside engineers curious as to why VW's U.S. cars seemed to have lower emissions than its European models discovered that, in fact, they didn't. Volkswagen cars in the United States were being sold with "defeat" software code that gave false readings during emissions tests. Put simply: responding to corporate directives to become the world's largest automaker, multiple VW employees came up with a plan involving deliberate fraud.[6] The company eventually paid $25 billion in fines and restitutions and retrofits for more than half a million cars sold. One U.S. employee was sentenced to seven years in prison. The CEO resigned and was later criminally charged by German prosecutors,[7] and the company is still trying to rebuild its reputation.

Reading about VW's fall from grace was another motivator for me to write this book. What that company did infuriated me as a customer. I owned one of those so-called low-emission Volkswagens. The company will never regain my trust.

How could this possibly have happened? How could a company think it could get away with a fraud this big? A number of management experts have researched this question and have written about how even though VW had a code of ethics that explicitly prohibited fraud, leaders minimized its importance, rationalized that the end goal of success justified interim unethical behavior, and figured that the consequences would be minimal even if they were exposed. Bottom line: the company's leaders so elevated hitting performance targets above all others that they created catastrophic consequences for the brand.[8]

This is a staggering indictment of what happens when a CEO fails to lead with Intentional Integrity. Pursuit of short-term goals and competitive glory destroyed the reputation of a once-storied brand.

Model what you mean

For any CEO, job one is to realize that developing the code you want is within your scope, but it is an abdication of duty to ignore it. If a company's top leaders are not willing to embrace each and every provision in the code, then the rejected provisions should not be in the code at all. It has to be all or nothing, because that is what secures buy-in from everyone else.

When I talk to our employees, I stress that no one at Airbnb operates above our code. And it's true—everyone from the CEO to our board to our management team explicitly buys in and supports the Intentional Integrity program. I can tell from employees' reactions, and from one-on-one conversations, that the fact that what applies to them also applies to the CEO is *very* important.

Obviously, for a CEO to insist on a code of conduct he or she doesn't feel compelled to follow is the height of hypocrisy. People rightly resent the existence of two sets of rules. Applied Materials' former CEO James Morgan has also emphasized that idea: "As a leader, the character of your organization will never exceed your own. Make sure you exhibit every trait and quality you want your people to exhibit."[9]

Of course, this can be complicated. In day-to-day life in the corner office, CEOs may set integrity traps for themselves. They may not necessarily make an explicit decision to break the law or ignore the company's own rules, but they may rationalize false trade-offs. For example, a chemical manufacturing leader might think, "There are environmental regulations that require us to spend money on waste treatment, but if I ignore them now and invest the money in R&D instead, we can prevent the waste problem entirely within a few years. Violating the law in this narrow situation is a decision that supports the greater good, right?!"

Another example is that a business owner might consider rules prohibiting gifts to be relevant only to lower-level employees. After all, their lack of sophistication and judgment might make them vulnerable to small bribes, while the owner of course will always put the company's needs first—so doesn't it follow that there is no need to be rude and reject a vendor's or partner's gift? Isn't getting gifts just an accepted perk of the job?

That kind of rationalizing rubs off on others, which is why it's so important for the CEO to not only follow the rules but also actively advocate for behaving with integrity among direct reports.

A colleague who previously worked at Amazon told me about a practice that founder and CEO Jeff Bezos repeats each quarter to model integrity in Amazon's financial reporting. Now, there is no question that Bezos is a complicated leader. Plenty of critics have condemned his intense focus on growth and perceived insensitivity to stakeholders, including his own employees and merchants on his platform.

But my colleague says that when it comes to financial reporting, Bezos is unrelenting in that the numbers Amazon reports must have integrity. He and his general counsel sit down every quarter and go over the draft of the numbers the chief financial officer of each group is reporting. Bezos looks each CFO in the eye and asks, "Is there any entry here that makes you uncomfortable?" That is powerful, specific, and direct CEO engagement that validates integrity as a value. It communicates that Bezos wants to hear bad news before it comes back to haunt the company.

He does not want to have to defend overly optimistic forecasts. That is a practice other CEOs should model.

Venture capitalist and entrepreneur Ben Horowitz told me that he used to do something similar when he was the CEO of Opsware. Every quarter, he would sit with his accounting team and drill down into any suspiciously positive numbers. He told them clearly and consistently not to manipulate the numbers or violate any accounting or disclosure obligations. He recalls saying once, "'Look, we're going to lose deals, we might go bankrupt. But we're not going to jail.' It's not just 'do the right thing'—you have to be really explicit."

I thought about the critical nature of leadership when I read *Bad Blood*, the book by John Carreyrou about the rise and fall of the blood-testing company Theranos. The CEO's concern for, and emphasis on, accurate reporting appeared to be the opposite of what we've seen from Bezos and Horowitz. *Bad Blood* describes Elizabeth Holmes as a CEO who repeatedly overpromised, underdelivered, and lied to cover up problems. Holmes packed her board with famous people who were not experts in the company's domain—her second in command was also her boyfriend—and she told investors and partners whatever she thought would keep the company's valuation high in the short term. The result: the company failed, and the name Theranos is now synonymous with fraud and frothy promotion. Holmes is facing both criminal charges and civil liability for her role in its demise.

Paul Sallaberry is a venture capitalist who previously held senior executive positions at Oracle and Veritas. Paul tells me he believes integrity must be woven early into a company's DNA, a theme he repeats to the CEOs he coaches. "There is a myth that there are two kinds of companies, old blue-blood tortoises who care about integrity and ethics, and then fast, nimble, modern companies. That's wrong—you can do both. The only way to build a great culture is to have a value system people want to be part of. When you ask people to do the right thing, you get trust. People realize you'll do the right thing by them. Otherwise you get a bunch of mercenaries who leave the minute times get tough."

This brings up another important element of integrity a company's top leadership should model: not throwing junior people under the bus when there's a setback. In that vein I respect how Starbucks acted in the wake of a 2018 incident in which the manager of a Philadelphia location told two African American men they could not use the restroom because they had not purchased anything. The manager eventually called the police when the men refused to leave. They complained to authorities and Starbucks received strong criticism in the local community and negative national press.[10]

In response, Starbucks did not issue knee-jerk denials. Its founder and executive chairman, Howard Schultz, spoke at some length about the incident, and he did not dismiss it as one store manager's mistake. He repeatedly said that the company had created the problem because its policy about individuals in stores who had not purchased food or drinks had been vague. The company took the time to be thoughtful, eventually creating a policy that allows individuals to be inside a Starbucks or to use the restroom regardless of whether or not they are a paying customer, as long as they are not disruptive or discourteous. Starbucks also closed its doors for half a day to give employees "racial-bias education," and CEO Kevin Johnson spoke publicly of the importance of listening to customers, communities, and store partners in shaping this new policy.

In this situation, Starbucks directly acknowledged that ambiguity is the enemy of integrity. Vague guidelines and case-by-case responses to challenges result in biased or expedient decisions that can chew at the character of a company. They can drive away customers and hurt morale. Inconsistent, impulsive decision-making is something employees also notice. They stop trusting management. They stop believing their issues will be treated fairly and on their merits.

No exceptions

At Airbnb, of course, we have had to respond to unanticipated issues. But I believe our CEO and executive team have gone to great lengths to identify dilemmas before they occur as well as the best path forward—a much better idea than resolving a mess after the fact.

For example, since 2018, we have had a rule that no one on the executive team is allowed to pursue a romantic relationship with an Airbnb employee. Period. No exceptions. Every one of us, single or not, including Brian, specifically and personally agreed to abide by this rule. I'll admit that when I first raised this with the executive team, someone laughed and said, "We're all in serious relationships or married anyway.

No big deal." I pointed out that many of the #MeToo cases involved married executives. Nobody laughed at that, and after a short silence, we all signed up.

Some executives and friends I've told about that policy are shocked. Isn't that extreme—even harsh—to forbid a relationship between consenting adults? Look, we have watched too many executives and companies mess this up. We at Airbnb have decided that the potential for difficult and distracting issues in the workplace stemming from romantic relationships is too great to risk, so we insist on this rule.

The "no relationship" rule is limited to the executive team, as the power dynamic is such that a senior leader could make a junior employee feel pressured in certain situations. At Airbnb, other romantic relationships involving employees are OK, as long as one person doesn't fall under the other's span of management control. If you work in sales and develop a relationship with someone in logistics, there is no reporting relationship and no issue. If you are a manager in customer service and find yourself attracted to someone who reports to you, you may not pursue that relationship. Should a relationship blossom in spite of this rule, the senior employee is held accountable for violating the code of ethics.

Our rule extends to anyone who has a control relationship over another employee. For example, suppose a particular human resources professional is responsible for supporting a sales team. While there is no formal reporting relationship, that HR professional has a control relationship with the team they support—he or she is aware of any investigations and performance issues on the team. The HR person has access to confidential salary and bonus information for each team member. That HR professional could not have a romantic relationship with someone on the team without undermining their impartiality and ability to perform their duties.

The general counsel might be called upon to investigate a complaint about literally any employee, so I would have been unable to pursue any romantic office relationships while I was in this role—or in my current role running our ethics office. Sure, a GC might recuse him- or herself from an investigation, but there would be speculation and gossip that would distract everyone involved and raise questions about what was going on behind the scenes. Common sense says the solution is that senior leaders should not get romantically involved with any employee.

There are leaders I consider ethical who handle this issue differently. Some rely on timely disclosures and a commitment to move employees to avoid a relationship in a chain of command. I don't think that's ideal. By the time that disclosure happens, there is already a relationship, and there has already been some distracting secrecy or activity. People don't just see each other across a crowded room and run to report an attraction.

Even if a relationship is open and disclosed, it doesn't solve the problem. There will be situations where the junior employee will have a broad awareness of things going on across the company due to their relationship with the C-level or other senior executive. There will be a perception, right or not, that the junior employee has an inside track on the best work and promotion opportunities. And how can a manager effectively discipline a junior employee if that person has a sympathetic ear at the top of the company?

Instead, we have agreed as an executive team: I am not going to seek an exception or put off a decision about this on someone else. If I feel the need to pursue a romantic relationship with an employee, I will seek another position at another company.

Customer privacy

Customer data privacy is another area where companies should have specific rules to discourage employee overreach. Airbnb has firm rules about employees not accessing customer data for any reason other than to perform official duties.

Uber learned how important it is to follow that kind of rule in 2016 after reports surfaced in the media about Uber's "God View" tool. In essence, Uber employees created a tool that enabled its employees to track any user in real time through their system. They became so cavalier about it that a New York Uber executive once met a journalist at the curb where she stepped out of an Uber. They were scheduled for an interview, and he greeted her adding, "I've been tracking you." A former security chief quit and then sued the company, claiming employees commonly accessed data for politicians and celebrities.[11]

According to published reports, employees also used the tool to spy on the trips of ex-partners, friends and family members, current crushes, and others. When the abuse was reported, users were outraged, and the company later paid fines and agreed to privacy audits by the Federal Trade Commission for the next 20 years. The message to companies was clear—customer data is a trust that employers must respect by preventing such widespread employee abuse.

Different lenses, different filters

So those are two specific elements of Airbnb's code, and I've explained how the code in some ways demands more of senior executives than of the rank and file. Now, there is no question some CEOs at other companies are put off by the idea of specific rules like this. There is a tradition of business lore that celebrates and even lionizes rebels. I'm thinking of entrepreneurs like Steve Jobs, for example, or Richard Branson or Ted Turner. When Jobs was starting out as an engineer at Atari, he was famous for going everywhere barefoot, and later he turned the act of rejecting the establishment and the rules into a rallying cry for Apple.

Cultivating a company culture where employees resemble a merry band of pirates who spit in the competition's eye can create a unique brand. Sometimes it can be a recruiting advantage as well. And of course it can be done ethically. But there is a point where "ask forgiveness, not permission" can backfire. High-spirited people can lose control and egg each other on to the detriment of others, and eventually the company, if there aren't guidelines about what the line is and what it means to cross it.

Let's go back to the relationship issue. Some CEOs clearly believe that they have earned the right to judge when and if a relationship with another consenting adult employee or partner is a problem. They see their role as driving the stock price, period. If their bottom-line performance is strong, they feel they don't deserve to be hemmed in by any rules.

There may have been a time when that argument reflected popular norms. But times have changed. I can name a few CEOs who probably agreed with the thinking that they are accountable only to the bottom line—Harvey Weinstein, Les Moonves, and Steve Wynn come to mind. All were powerful, self-assured CEOs who lost their jobs after many accusations surfaced of inappropriate relationships spanning many years. They have all defended their actions in the context of "consensual" relationships, even when their accusers have claimed that intimidation—or worse—was involved. It's also worth noting that in each case, reporters—and in the case of Wynn, government regulators—have uncovered evidence that other employees and executives knew about their behaviors or even arranged for assignations or helped cover up what the CEO was doing. *The consequences of inappropriate romantic relationships at work almost never remain confined to the "consenting adults."*

Setting the right tone at the top also involves the difficult dilemma of how CEOs treat highly valued or "favorite" employees when those individuals abuse their power or break rules. Most of us have seen at one time or another the "golden boy" or "golden girl" phenomenon, often a charismatic top sales performer or dealmaker or coder who may be seen throughout the company as one who can "do no wrong" in the CEO's eyes.

It's bad enough when the CEO's pet annoys colleagues in myriad small ways—acts imperious with support staff, parks in others' spots, is always too busy to attend "mandatory" meetings. But when they turn in record sales numbers the same month that they're accused of sexual harassment or abusing customer data, then what? We've seen too many examples where the official response was a cover-up and a quiet settlement. I think those days are fast coming to an end, thanks to #MeToo and activist employees who are demanding more accountability. A culture that uses cover-ups to respond to ethics violations has a serious, company-wide problem that goes beyond any individual incident.

Imagine that your best performer and most valuable employee just harassed someone in the office. What are you willing to assign as a consequence to that person? Treating the offender less harshly than someone else who did the same thing after you've created a supposedly ironclad rule is not the path of integrity and risks a quiet—or not-so-quiet—revolt.

Most CEOs like being the ultimate deciders. They like their freedom. Narcissistic CEOs take it to an extreme. But mature people understand that, ultimately, many jobs come with sacrifices to one's personal life, friendships, and freedoms, whether it's working long hours or not being able to trade stocks when you're an insider. Everyone must follow the law, but nobody is forced to work for a company with a detailed ethics policy. Over time, in an ethical company, policy will evolve to keep pace with social norms, recruiting issues, and other variables.

6,000 chief ethics officers

In one sense, I'd like every person in our company to think of themselves as an ethics officer, a guardian of our brand. We are not perfect, we all know we are not perfect, and we treat integrity as a journey where we may stumble, not as an action item to cross off our to-do list. We actively encourage ethics questions and reports, and any effort to intimidate any-one into not reporting a violation they have experienced or observed is also forbidden. Also, personal loyalty is not a defense or a work value that rises above others.

There are three specific roles and entities I want to emphasize that also represent the idea of ethics leadership by a "chief."

Board leadership

If the media coverage of the various scandals and revelations over the last couple of years has carried an underlying theme, it is this: Where was the board? Ultimately, directors have a fiduciary duty to a company's share-holders to protect their assets. While the CEO has operational authority, the board can fire a CEO. One excuse boards tend to give when a com-pany has run amok or an executive has acted inappropriately is that the CEO hid what was really going on from them.

Boards are getting less and less sympathy for that posture. An article in *Corporate Counsel* made an important and timely point: "#MeToo has been a catalyst for change across business and society. It has forced a spotlight on culture as a critical corporate asset. Forward-thinking boards should seize the moment to enhance corporate governance practices and reimagine a workplace that has a safe, inclusive, fair and healthy culture aimed at long-term value creation."[12]

In some cases, gung-ho investors dominate a board to such a de-gree that they become part of the problem. In the fall of 2019, the New York–based shared office space company WeWork suddenly occupied the scandal spotlight when it delayed and then withdrew its much-anticipated public offering. It had already lost $1.3 billion on revenues of just $1.5 billion in the first half of the year, but the bigger story was corporate governance. WeWork was exposed as an ethical train wreck. Its cofounder Adam Neumann soon left the company amid accusations of self-dealing, hiring family members for key positions, traveling on the company's lavish $60 million corporate jet, and encouraging excessive drinking and raucous work parties.

Where was the board? Well, one board seat belongs to SoftBank, whose Vision Fund has put over $10 billion into the company. SoftBank chairman Masayoshi Son scoffed as recently as 2018 at how conservative he felt many tech investors were being, according to the *Los Angeles Times*. "Why don't we go big bang?" he told Bloomberg. "The other shareholders, they try to create clean, polished little companies. And I say: 'Let's go rough. We don't need to polish. We don't need efficiency right now. Let's make a big fight.'"[13] Meanwhile, in 2017, Neumann told *Forbes* about a conversation he had with Son: "Masa turns to me and asks, 'In a fight, who wins—the smart guy or the crazy guy?' I say, 'Crazy guy,' and he looks at me and says, 'You are correct, but you and [Neumann's cofounder] are not crazy enough.'"[14]

Should we be surprised if an already hard-charging entrepreneur like Neumann, showered with billions in cash and exhorted to "go big bang" by an iconic investor, went . . . well, big bang?

The principles I advocate in the rest of this book will mean nothing unless CEOs embrace them and boards monitor the CEO's implementation of them—and demand the information they need to do that.

The general counsel

The second specific and relevant ethics leadership role in a fairly large company would be the company's general counsel. General counsel have a broad scope of responsibility. They must monitor the operational concerns of compliance with regulations, both U.S. and foreign laws, and ongoing lawsuits. They must weigh in on contracts, business deals, litigation, and personnel-related challenges. And on a higher level, they must partner with the leadership team to figure out how to say yes to innovation and creative ideas that may carry certain risks or hard-to-predict elements.

The GC role is unquestionably secondary to that of the CEO in terms of setting the tone and reinforcing ethics as a priority, but when the GC role exists, it is critical to the implementation of Intentional Integrity. The GC position is one of the few operational checks on senior leaders, including the CEO, when they've gone off track, and the legal team is vital to making sure relevant laws and regulations are interpreted correctly and consistently by company managers. This oversight can sometimes draw flak from managers who prefer looser interpretations, and that's to be expected. But the legal team has a professional duty to uphold the law and give sound advice. A GC who displays questionable ethical behavior is, in my opinion, a serious liability.

I was dismayed, as I know other general counsel were, when I read about the controversy involving Alphabet's chief legal officer, David Drummond. As first reported in the *New York Times* in 2018 and more recently in an August 27, 2019, article for *Medium*, a Google contracts attorney named Jennifer Blakely said she and Drummond began an affair in 2004.[15] Drummond was then Google's general counsel, and Blakely was a member of his team. In 2007, he fathered a child with her. "After our son was born I received a call from HR notifying me that one of us would have to leave the legal department where David was now Chief Legal Officer, so I transferred to the sales department despite having zero experience in sales," she wrote in *Medium*.[16]

Unhappy with her new role, Blakely left Google a year later. Blakely claimed that Drummond never told anyone at Google about their relationship before the child was born, despite realizing Google had a policy banning direct-report relationships. Drummond subsequently released a statement admitting they shared a son, but he claimed that there were "two sides" to the story and disputed some of her facts. Drummond also said he "discussed the details of our relationship with our employer at the time" but would not be discussing the situation further.[17]

The situation got even more complicated, but let's first focus on the events to this point. I appreciate that human relationships are complex and that individuals can have very different views about a breakup. But there were two fundamental ethical mistakes here. The first was when one of Google's top leaders engaged in a romantic relationship with a member of his own team apparently in direct contradiction of the company's policy. And this fundamental mistake was compounded by the second error—the company failing to hold that leader accountable for the first mistake, and instead implementing a "solution" that moved the brunt of the consequences onto the junior employee. Being moved out of one role—here a role for which Jennifer Blakely was trained and experienced—and into another less enjoyable or satisfying one is an all too familiar story in corporate America. The person without power bears the consequences. An article posted on Law.com quoted human resources expert Jaime Klein noting the commonality that companies frequently protect people viewed as too important to lose: "It's these high talents, these subject matter experts we can't lose. I constantly see companies making exceptions for them. Until we stop making exceptions and create rules that apply to everyone, these things will continue to happen."[18]

Clearly, many Google employees want better leadership on this issue. On November 1, 2018, over 20,000 Google employees worldwide walked off their jobs after two other "high talents" (as Klein called them) left the company with large severance payouts despite having been accused of sexual misconduct. *Business Insider* reported that a social media account for Google walkout organizers tweeted that Blakely's 2019 blog post reflected "the systemic culture of treating people like objects at the highest levels of Google. This hurts all of us—of all genders and at all levels of the company."[19] I have to agree that Google's failure to hold Drummond to its supposed standard makes it hard to imagine how its general counsel and HR team could ever lead a discussion about ethics and be taken seriously.

Subsequent news did not change my thinking on that: multiple media outlets reported that shortly after he issued the "two sides" statement about Blakely in 2019, Drummond married a Google employee from the legal department.[20] In 2019, a group of shareholders filed suit against Alphabet alleging it covered up sexual misconduct allegations, and the company announced it had launched an internal investigation (as of this writing it had not released any findings). The first week of January 2020, in an upbeat email, Drummond announced he was retiring. Turns out, he had spent the preceding months selling more than $200 million in stock. Alphabet confirmed that Drummond was not getting an exit package.[21] And we wonder why there's a techlash?

Head of human resources

The final specific, critical role that represents the idea of ethics leadership by a "chief" is the head of human resources. I've been lucky to work with one of the best, Beth Axelrod, at both eBay and Airbnb. Again, sometimes HR duties in a small company are shared by founders who wear many hats. But in a larger organization, the head of human resources generally is tasked with building and maintaining the company's human capital. That means recruiting and training employees, overseeing benefits, implementing specific workplace policies, and maintaining a safe facility. Situations with ethical components can crop up among all of these duties.

Writing and following through on employment contracts is also an HR function. It's worth noting that corporate contracts have come under more intense scrutiny because some companies have made payouts to individuals accused of sexual harassment and other behaviors. They have claimed that the contract details gave them no choice but to pay out significant sums. Going forward, HR chiefs need to think deeply about how contracts should address violations of the company's code of ethics before they agree to provisions without consequences for bad behavior.

Stand up for intentionality

Whatever your role in a company, whether it's the CEO, the owner, an executive team member, a mid-level manager, or even an individual contributor, it behooves you to think about the environment you want to live in and work to make it happen. In fact, think of yourself as the CEO of your own reputation and that of a team you manage, and then make sure your own actions match up to that challenge.

Know your current ethics policy if your company has one, and think about whether it goes far enough based on what you see going on around you. Don't shrug off ethical violations because they don't seem to involve you. As an employee, your company's brand and reputation extend to you. You may end up answering for a problem you could have helped prevent.

As you read the examples and Code Moment studies I will offer, think about what the parallels might be in your workplace. Would you know how to sort through these integrity dilemmas? Are there rules or policies that would improve the integrity of your workplace?

If you don't have a code of business ethics, perhaps you can lobby human resources to develop one. Too intimidating? Send a note to the CEO or general counsel about any ethical or integrity dilemmas that you encounter for which you feel the company would benefit from more specific guidance.

I don't love anonymous memos, but I realize that other employees sometimes treat those who raise these issues like the kid who asks the teacher five minutes before the bell rings if any homework is going to be assigned. And yet those same cynics will go to websites like Glassdoor or Blind and anonymously post negative things about their boss or company. They are quick to complain; they often seem fueled by personal resentments and jealousy; but do they want to *resolve* these issues?

It's a rare GC who would not take seriously a memo from an anonymous employee concerned about their company's reputation, ability to recruit good people, relationship with partners or customers, or increased liability because of a certain situation. If you do find yourself concerned and want to alert your company's GC, provide evidence and facts to support your contentions if you can.

Alternatively, you may not want to invest this energy in the company you currently work for if you suspect your concerns about integrity will not be taken seriously. But when you decide to make a career move, probing a potential new employer about how the company's leadership prioritizes and nurtures integrity might help you find a job in a company more aligned with your values. Paul Sallaberry adds, "I see that employees really associate themselves with their companies today. When they're deciding where they want to work, they're asking 'Who am I?' As a company, when you display honesty and integrity, you'll attract people who want that. When you make bad habits standard operating procedure, it will come back and kill you."

CODE MOMENT 1: REGINA AND THE TELLTALE TEXT

For 11 years, Regina has worked as an executive assistant to Mike, who was made CEO two years ago. She's been to Mike's home for staff holiday parties, and she's friendly with his wife, Sally.

One day, Sally calls and tells Regina, "Mike left his iPad home; I just read a flirty text from a number in Illinois. Regina, is Mike having an affair?"

Regina's heart sinks. Mike has been distant lately, and he has asked Regina several times to coordinate his schedule with that of a vendor's female executive who lives in Chicago.

"Sally, I don't know anything about that," Regina tells her. "Might it be a wrong number text?" Sally just hangs up.

Minutes later, Mike calls Regina and yells: "What the hell is wrong with you? Why didn't you cover for me with Sally?"

"Mike, I didn't know what to say."

"MIGHT be a wrong number," he again yells. "That's all she heard. Why didn't you tell her you were SURE it was a mistake? Regina, you're supposed to have my back. I need an assistant I can trust." He hangs up.

The ball's in Regina's court. What should she do next?

For discussion, see appendix, page 232.

CODE MOMENT 2: WHO'S YOUR CUSTOMER, CHARLIE?

Charlie is the CEO of ISP-Co, a Midwestern telecom provider that has experienced a number of regulatory setbacks. His government affairs chief, Larry, calls to tell Charlie that one of the telecom commission members told Larry she is having a problem with her email account, hosted by ISP-Co. Her password is no longer working. But here's the thing: her estranged husband is the account holder, and customer service has told her they can only talk to or investigate issues for account owners. She's worried he is reading her email. Larry told her he might be able to help.

Larry tells Charlie this is a chance to help her and the company and improve their relationship. He wants Charlie to relax the rules.

Although it's not one of his own making, this is a Code Moment for Charlie. What's the right thing to do?

For discussion, see appendix, page 235.

4

Who are we?
Defining what integrity means to
your organization

You can't download integrity by finding a "universal" template and adding your name and logo to it. You must do the work of figuring out your values and crafting rules that reflect your specific business model, industry standards, stakeholder concerns, and external challenges.

There are companies whose brand names have long stood for appealing and aspirational ideas. Think Levi's—"Quality never goes out of style." Nike—"Just Do It." Visit Disney's "Magic Kingdom." A "Kodak moment" is still a euphemism for something fleeting and precious that a photo can help you capture forever (even in these days of cell phone cameras).

But then there is a company whose name, even nearly 20 years after it went bankrupt, is shorthand for complete ethical collapse. That company is Enron.

Enron became a Wall Street and business press darling in the 1990s by selling energy contracts after natural gas markets were deregulated. After a decade of skyrocketing stock increases, *Fortune* called Enron the most innovative large company in America in 2000. Its market capitalization was $60 billion. *Chief Executive* magazine listed its board of directors as among the top five in the nation.[1] And the executives' arrogance was legend: on a conference call attended by dozens of investors and analysts, CEO Jeffrey Skilling once famously said to a fund manager who questioned Enron's confusing balance sheets, "We appreciate that . . . Asshole."[2]

Oops.

By November 2001, Enron's stock price plummeted from $90 to less than $1. A month later, Enron filed for bankruptcy, the largest in U.S. history. Turns out the cheeky fund manager had the last laugh: Enron's tangled mess of accounting tricks and unethical financial reporting doomed it, also leading to the demise of its auditor, Arthur Andersen. Several Enron executives were indicted and went to federal prison—Skilling was released in February 2019 after serving 12 years. The board was soundly criticized for issuing "waivers" to the company's own code of ethics that specifically enriched individual executives involved with some transactions.

Enron's demise in large part motivated Congress to pass the Sarbanes–Oxley Act in 2002. That law remains in force today. It mandates a specific and written code of ethics for every publicly traded U.S. corporation. Among other rules, it calls on the leadership of public companies to disclose the "fundamental business values by which the senior management of companies operate"; the SEC went further, later demanding that public companies produce a full code of ethics governing their directors, officers, and employees and disclose any waivers granted to that code.

These rules apply only to publicly traded companies, but many private companies adopt a code of ethics and business practices consistent with these standards. Such guidelines serve several important purposes—not just regulating what conduct is and is not allowed but also defining the culture of the company and framing the brand so that customers, potential employees, and partners can choose to buy from, work for, and do business with brands that have similar values.

Enron's demise hurt a lot of people. Employees lost their jobs, smaller investors suffered heavy losses, and some saw their retirement funds wiped out. The fraud and deception perpetuated by Enron was an egregious abuse of the public's trust. However, there is a silver lining to the Enron story. Laws such as Sarbanes–Oxley mandating public companies to create a specific code of ethics and business practices support the notion of intentionally planting and nurturing cherry trees—a much more satisfying and high-return activity than having to admit you chopped one down.

What needs to be in the code?

Over the years, companies' codes of ethics and business practices have taken on a standard structure, which can typically be divided into five basic parts[3]:

1. An **introduction** signed by the CEO that lays out a company's basic mission or purpose. It makes clear that the code applies to everyone in the company.
2. A specific **statement of core values and principles**. Not a generic and all-encompassing "Don't be evil" (sorry, Google) but rather a deliberate, affirmative commitment to values like honesty, fairness, and respect for the law, as well as values related to the business mission, which might include excellent customer service, low prices, maximizing shareholder value, respecting and empowering employees, or a commitment to ethically sourced ingredients or materials.
3. A specific set of **rules and practices tuned for a specific workplace**, accompanied by **examples** designed to bring to life the values and principles in an accessible context. The use of examples is critical and sometimes overlooked. The idea is to show your employees how to handle themselves when they encounter a Code Moment, not just tell them.
4. Detailed **consequences**—a listing of actions specifying how the code will be enforced, as well as the **resources available to employees** with questions, those who want to report an infraction, etc.
5. Last but certainly not least, language clarifying that **employees who want to work at the company will be expected to read, understand, and sign a pledge to follow the code.** It's a code violation to discourage anyone from reporting a code violation or to retaliate because of a report. And in some companies, for certain positions such as the financial reporting structure, a failure to report a code violation is a code violation.

A code with these five basic elements will work for the majority of companies who sell goods and services—and even for nonprofits. The format is straightforward and scalable, as relevant to a 150-person cowboy boot manufacturer as it is to a global Internet platform company or a restaurant chain. In addition, I believe companies with significant Internet platforms also need to consider formulating a set of standards that I'll discuss in chapter 11 about community standards and integrity.

Step 1: What do we stand for?

The CEO and the board need to go all in supporting the creation or revision of the code of ethics. Obviously, the CEO is not going to manage the tactical assembly of the code, but the executive team must kick off this effort to make sure everyone is aligned with the company's values. They must determine:

- What does the company stand for?
- What are the basic moral or human aspirations that the company commits to, such as honesty, respect for law, respect for individuals, rejection of discrimination on the basis of race, religion, ethnicity, national origin, gender, sexual orientation?
- What are the key operational and or/business values the company believes in? These could include quality, workplace safety, excellence in service, transparent financial reporting, ethically sourced ingredients or materials, empowered employees, or deep concern for customer satisfaction.
- What are the values specific to the company's brand?
- Does the company have a unique workplace culture or position in a community or point of view that is integral to its brand?

This is not an exercise in determining objectively right and wrong values. It's about who you are and how you intend to demonstrate who you are. Eventually you're going to want to be able to draw a straight line from every core value to every rule in the code of ethics.

In early 2018, Brian Chesky released an open letter to the Airbnb community in which he talked in detail about his feeling that companies need to change their operating values and even their time horizons if they're going to survive and prosper. He wrote:

> It's clear that our responsibility isn't just to our employees, our shareholders, or even to our community—it's also to the next generation. Companies have a responsibility to improve society,

and the problems Airbnb can have a role in solving are so vast that we need to operate on a longer time horizon.

Technology has changed a lot in my lifetime, but how companies run has not. Companies face pressures based on legacies from the 20th-century, and the convention is to focus on increasingly short-term financial interests, often at the expense of a company's vision, long-term value, and its impact on society. You could say that these are 20th-century companies living in a 21st-century world.

Brian rejects the antiquated way of thinking about corporations, one that goes back to the 1970s when economist Milton Friedman famously argued that corporate leaders should "conduct the business in accordance with [shareholders'] desires, which generally will be to make as much money as possible while conforming to the basic rules of the society."[4] Many experts credit that line of thinking with pushing publicly held corporations toward a fixation on quarterly results, sometimes at the expense of quality, customer service, employee safety, and other investments that can undercut profits.

We'll talk more about that later, but Brian is not the only business leader calling for a mind-set change. In early 2019, Blackrock, Inc. CEO Larry Fink wrote a letter to the heads of companies that Blackrock had invested in. He referred to the current ethical and social challenges swirling around companies, and he focused on the power of knowing a company's purpose.

Purpose is not the sole pursuit of profits but the animating force for achieving them. Profits are in no way inconsistent with purpose—in fact, profits and purpose are inextricably linked. Profits are essential if a company is to effectively serve all of its stakeholders over time—not only shareholders, but also employees, customers, and communities. Similarly, when a company truly understands and expresses its purpose, it functions with the focus and strategic discipline that drive long-term profitability. Purpose unifies management, employees, and communities. It drives ethical behavior and creates an essential check on actions that go against the best interests of stakeholders. Purpose guides culture, provides a framework for consistent decision-making, and, ultimately, helps sustain long-term financial returns for the shareholders of your company.[5]

What Larry Fink calls the "framework for consistent decision-making" is the payoff for intentionally discussing and stating your company's core values. And his broadening of a company's purpose to embrace and serve all stakeholders, not just shareholders, is refreshing to hear from a significant investor and thought leader for entrepreneurial companies.

So how does all this play out in the pages of a code? Let's look at examples of core values expressed by three companies, and then at how those values inform very specific policies.

At the giant retailer Walmart, the company's statement of global ethics begins: "Our unique culture drives our purpose of saving people money so they can live better, and the foundation of our culture is a commitment to operating with integrity."[6]

At the premium outdoor products company Patagonia, the mission statement is:

> At Patagonia, we appreciate that all life on earth is under threat of extinction. We aim to use the resources we have—our business, our investments, our voice and our imaginations—to do something about it.
>
> Patagonia grew out of a small company that made tools for climbers. Alpinism remains at the heart of a worldwide business that still makes clothes for climbing—as well as for skiing, snowboarding, surfing, fly fishing, mountain biking and trail running. These are silent sports. None require an engine; rarely do they deliver the cheers of a crowd. In each, reward comes in the form of hard-won grace and moments of connection with nature.[7]

At Airbnb, we say, "Our culture is built around four Core Values: Champion the Mission, Be a Host, Embrace the Adventure, and Be a Cereal Entrepreneur.[8] Our Code of Ethics articulates the principles we must practice to live up to our values. It clarifies expectations around our behavior and reinforces our shared responsibility for this incredible Airbnb community."

Each of the three companies' statements is aspirational, but they are not interchangeable. Patagonia does not say a word about low-cost products, because Patagonia is not about low-cost products. There is nothing in Walmart's statement about the environment because that is not Walmart's core concern. Airbnb's code is designed for an Internet platform that does not produce or sell products; Airbnb is committed to pursuing policies and activities that speak to nurturing businesses organized around hospitality, adventure, connections, and belonging. And all three companies demonstrate Intentional Integrity by stating unique value propositions and creating policies that reflect those values.

Reflecting core values in specific rules

A common ethics dilemma companies wrestle with is whether or not they should allow employees to accept gifts, which is a good example to show how core values inform specific rules in different ways. Gifts can range from benign "business courtesies," like a coffee mug with the logo of a new product a partner is introducing or an invitation to a comedy club for all attendees of a partner meeting, to gifts that are designed to influence if not outright buy a specific business outcome.

Walmart's code of ethics maintains that employees may not accept gifts of any kind or size. Not lunch, not a T-shirt, not a pair of concert tickets, not a ticket to a luxury box at a ballgame organized to entertain a supplier's customers. In fact, employees are expected to alert partners and suppliers that they cannot accept gifts in advance of any situation where a gift might be involved. I've heard stories of some Walmart employees pulling a dollar out of their pocket to pay for water when visiting a vendor's office.

Walmart's code states, "Our policy on gifts and entertainment services stems from our values of complete transparency and objectivity and our principle of maintaining Everyday Low Costs. Since such gifts and entertainment services increase the cost of doing business, we try and help our suppliers to give us lower costs on products by not expecting the gifts and entertainment services they may have to spend on other customers." To me, this explanation is clear and consistent and flows straight from Walmart's core value—low prices. It doesn't rely on a vague sense of morals or ethics. Walmart employees may not love turning down gifts, but it's a model of a well-articulated purposeful policy.

As a general rule at Airbnb, as I mentioned earlier, we allow employees to accept gifts and occasional entertainment experiences from our vendors and business partners as long as they don't exceed a value of $200. So, you're wondering, if I like Walmart's policy so much, why don't I also support banning all gifts?

The issue is not whether you "like" or "dislike" a policy in the abstract. The question is, does the policy reflect the specific organization's mission and purpose, as well as its business realities? Airbnb is in the hospitality industry, and our business is about providing and facilitating meaningful, memorable experiences. Core to hospitality is being gracious and making others feel welcome and appreciated. The industry's marketing practices often involve gifts and events. Also, our headquarters and many of our offices are in urban areas where we compete for buzz and mindshare among potential employees as well as customers. Potential employee groups pay attention to "collateral" like T-shirts, ball caps, imprinted tote bags, and other branded items. If we're going to give those away, it would be weird for us not to accept them. Unlike Walmart, we are an enabling platform and don't set prices, so the logic Walmart applies to prohibiting gifts is not generally relevant to us.

OK then, why $200? Why any limit? Because ambiguity sets integrity traps. Of course we recognize that our employees are in a position to influence business decisions by choosing among partners or vendors, and we don't want to create conditions that would tempt our partners to offer (or our employees to accept) valuable or coercive gifts or experiences. And we have more detailed rules about gifts than just a dollar limit. For example, we might approve a gift above the $200 limit for something like an entertainment event—but only if the organizer attends it (in other words, a "business courtesy" gift is not a voucher for dinner for an employee and their spouse). We have other specific rules about gifts, including one stating that we don't *offer* gifts valued above $200 or those designed to influence business decisions. Giving or accepting certain higher-value gifts—like a unique guided excursion to an exotic location opening up to tourism or an exclusive relationship-building event—may be OK even if they are over the $200 limit, but these would require consultation with an ethics advisor and approval by a manager. There must be a specific business purpose or educational experience involved.

When I was a federal prosecutor at the Department of Justice in the 1990s, we had a rule that forbade us from accepting gifts or meals over $25. This meant that someone from another agency or a lawyer from a team you were working with could save you time by talking with you over a simple meal or coffee, and you didn't have to report it. A low threshold like that made sense—there can't even be a whiff that a prosecutor is being influenced by gifts. Each of these different approaches represents a perfectly good option if it's well considered, applies equally to everyone, and fits with your values and the nature of your business and culture.

Step 2: Driving the code process

OK, so you're a CEO who has decided to develop an Intentional Integrity code, or you've convinced your own CEO to put you in charge. How do you get started?

I'll start here with two essential points: (1) Nobody wants another committee, and (2) sorry, you *need* a committee representing as many different roles and parts of the company as possible if you want to create a code that represents your organization's values *and* have everyone buy in.

If you don't get input from all parts of the company, you risk creating what I call the "Moses syndrome." This happens when the GC or the leader of the ethics code project is perceived to have gone off on a spiritual retreat and returned with a long list of ethics rules everyone else is supposed to follow. The Moses syndrome presents the opposite message you want to give employees. Intentional Integrity needs to be inclusive and reflect diverse points of view and the experiences of employees across the company. That means you need to listen, challenge employees to think deeply about some of these issues, and write policies that reflect not only the law and the practices of other companies but also employee concerns, questions, and points of confusion.

I won't lie to you: in my experience, people invited to craft these codes of ethics initially dread it. It sounds tedious, right? I clearly recall the response of the Airbnb employee I asked to lead the project: "Oh gawwwwd," she moaned. And yes, there is a certain element of unglamorous sausage-making in arguing over the wording of rules. But before long, those involved often admit that it's interesting, thought-provoking, and even fun.

If you think about it, the success of advice columns like Dear Abby has been writers' willingness to take on ethical quandaries. Examples may involve dilemmas like: "I love my mother-in-law but can't stand my father-in-law—can I just invite her over for the holidays?" or "I'm worried my neighbor might be abusing his dog—should I talk to him first, or just report him?" The way human beings prosecute and resolve conflicts and dilemmas with an ethical component is inherently fascinating.

Dear Abby cleverly built humor into her responses to keep readers coming back for more, and that's relevant to the spirit of writing an ethics code as well.[9] Human foibles and weird curveballs are often on the table when talk turns to ethics; as a result, members of a committee drafting a code will likely find themselves laughing much more than they expected. For example, when we were discussing if we should allow dogs in our offices, a team member told the story of their experience at a prior company where a dog there used to sneak into conference rooms and leave "input." There was a suspicion that he was an agent of a competitor, since he invariably did this right before important meetings with investors, who got to smell the consequences. This story led to another about an executive at a dog-friendly company who was meeting with a potential partner from another country. The executive arrived in the lobby to discover his guest had mistaken a dog treat in a glass jar for a cookie and was munching on it, and then offered him one. He gamely put it in his mouth so as not to embarrass the guest.

Not only is coming up with reasonable solutions to everyday dilemmas often fun, it's also satisfying. Participants realize that the whole subject of ethics means recognizing that you have complex and sometimes conflicting obligations within your company. When you tackle them head on, there is a genuine feeling of empowerment.

In terms of the makeup of the committee, the key again is diversity. You want to represent all crucial divisions of the company (e.g., sales, marketing, legal, HR, building maintenance). While it's not possible to tick every box, the ideal committee will also capture people of different ages and racial and ethnic backgrounds. If you're a nonprofit, you might want donors or advocacy partners or clients that your group is serving to be represented. If you're a start-up, the only practical approach may be for one person to take a stab at writing a code and circulate it to everyone for input. But don't make it one person's turf; the code needs to belong to everyone to have credibility.

Step 3: Well-mapped ground

So the CEO has bought in, the executive team has created a statement of values to guide the process, and a committee has been formed. I've discussed some of the material you'll cover and why diverse voices and thinking are useful, but let me back up. What is the actual process for writing a comprehensive code?

I've seen this done two ways. At eBay, we wrote an entire Internet body of law from scratch for the Trust and Safety group, while at Airbnb we looked first at other codes of conduct from respected companies. The fastest and most efficient way to jump-start the process is to review existing codes of ethics for several categories of public companies, which, thanks to Sarbanes–Oxley, are published on their websites. I recommend reviewing the following:

Codes from companies that tend to be respected in general for their commitment to ethics and good business practices. You can easily search online for lists that identify transparent, responsive, and ethical companies.

Codes from at least two public companies in your business space. These could be competitors or companies that are likely to face the same business dynamics as you face.

Codes from local companies that may have specifically addressed regional or state laws that you also must consider. You may make custom sports gear for fans, but you may also have something to learn from a manufacturer of lighting systems who has incorporated state and local personnel or environmental laws into their code of ethics.

Companies whose codes of ethics were written or revised to address issues that have initiated lawsuits or controversies. For example, if you run a chain of smoothie shops, you might think about Starbucks' experience in Philadelphia when coming up with policies for managers to guide them in dealing with people who come in but don't buy anything. What is the brand image you want to represent? Are you like Starbucks, wanting to create a welcoming environment that people come back to for meetings, to visit friends, or to sip a drink and relax and read? Or are you like Dunkin' (formerly Dunkin' Donuts), whose focus is on online ordering and getting people in and out quickly?

At your first meeting, we'll assume that everyone has read sample codes, so you can begin by addressing the company's mission statement. You may already have one, you may want to improve on the one you have, or you may need to write one from scratch. One of the most important principles in the process is that every rule you write must somehow reach back to reflect your sense of mission and purpose.

Don't use general platitudes. Think hard about the history of your company, why it was founded, and what it wants to be. Consider these statements of purpose from three established companies:

At Coca-Cola, the code begins in a warm, conversational fashion and is headlined "Integrity—The Essential Ingredient": "What makes Coca-Cola one of the most admired brands in the world? It is not just our products. It is also how we do our work and the integrity of our actions. Ingrained in our culture, integrity inspires our work and strengthens our reputation as a Company that does extraordinary things and always does what is right. Integrity is the essential ingredient to our success."[10]

At Amazon, the code of ethics and business practices begins, "In performing their job duties, Amazon.com employees should always act lawfully, ethically, and in the best interests of Amazon.com."[11] It's businesslike, no-nonsense.

Hewlett Packard Enterprise: "At Hewlett Packard Enterprise (HPE), how we do things is as important as what we do. The HPE Standards of Business Conduct (SBC) sets the standards that guide our business practices and govern our behavior. Every decision we make matters in our effort to deliver meaningful contributions to people, organizations, our communities, and the world. We are accountable for our actions, responsible for their consequences, and proud of our efforts. Together, let's build trust by emphasizing ethics in everything we do."[12]

For me, these codes leave distinct impressions of the companies, just from the statements. When I read Coca-Cola's, I feel like the company values what its customers think of it. It seeks admiration and respect. When I read Amazon's, I feel less warmth—I feel the heartbeat of an aggressive competitor, but one committed to acting within the law. The HPE code values having a global, outward-facing awareness, reminding employees that they have impact beyond their immediate environment.

This is a subjective exercise, and these are my personal impressions. For your code, think about what impression, however subtle, its tone and mission statement will leave on a reader. Companies that have faced scandals or accusations or lawsuits sometimes find that the press or their accusers unearth these statements and judge their behavior accordingly. Road test statements a bit and see how people respond. Early in Google's life, the statements "Don't be evil" or "Be googly" probably sounded like a sort of hip, "We use common sense" message. For many Google employees, these were inspiring principles. But in stories where Google employees have been accused of inappropriate behavior, sometimes the taglines are referred to as evidence of a culture of arrogance or high-handedness. As you get into the body of these codes, I am sure some rules will resonate with you and others will put you off.

Another exercise I recommend is challenging every person on the committee to write down five issues related to ethics or business practices that they see as points of friction in their domain. Different industries and diverse functions within a company may encounter unique challenges that make some sample code elements irrelevant but demand much more detail in other spots. Codes of companies that operate globally need to address federal statutes about bribery and foreign laws, for example, while a regional auto-repair chain will have none of those concerns but may need to spell out specific policies related to installing used parts, standing behind their work, or calculating time for purposes of labor charges.

Here's an interesting point of debate inside many companies: policies related to conference attendance. Employees who love to travel and network argue that conferences are essential to their work, helping them raise brand awareness and make valuable connections. Others worry that conferences too often become boondoggles of one kind or another and even potential conflicts of interest if the conference expenses are covered by a customer or potential vendor.

So the committee gathers input. In the case of travel, sales will argue that they need the flexibility to attend any conference their customer leads are planning to attend. CEOs and CFOs want to attend "thought leader" conferences with their peers. Another manager may point out the negative effect on their team's productivity when employees are away. Accounting may point to the cost of traveling to meetings and announce it has to come down by 30 percent. A code that states that "employees should only go to conferences that reasonably support their work mission" does not seem to offer enough guidance for real dilemmas.

In this classic situation, employees working on a code of ethics come to realize that the exercise is not just about allowing or banning things, it's about reflecting the company's priorities and motivating good behavior. For example, let's say the CEO agrees with accounting: we need to reduce our conference costs. The ethics code committee might debate: How do we motivate productive conference attendance while discouraging costly boondoggles?

One code option is to allow employees to go to conferences where a partner or vendor pays the expenses. That cuts costs. But another option is the opposite choice: you will pay your way to any conference worth attending. Now, you have business line managers devoting chunks of their budgets to sending employees to conferences; they are more likely to demand that employees make a strong business case to attend. The first scenario might benefit a company that is low on cash and in a very sales-oriented phase; the second may go a long way to cutting out employees wasting time at nonproductive conferences.

There is no hard and fast way to create this kind of policy. In the wording of a rule, be as specific as possible. Specificity promotes integrity. As the leader of an ethics initiative, you may allot a certain amount of time for discussion and then hold a vote, or you may take the discussion under advisement and write the rule yourself according to what seems to be the reasonable approach.

In my experience, having all departments represented in your committee will surface hidden issues, such as those surrounding dogs in the office. At Airbnb we allow dogs—having them around reinforces a sense of home and belonging, our core values. But dogs have needs—water, elimination breaks, exercise. People may have allergies. Some dogs are well behaved, others not so much. A policy committee member from human resources can make a great argument for dogs, but a representative from building maintenance should have input. Is it practical? What specific rules must attend the policy to make it fair to everybody? Should we run a trial program first?

Bringing dogs to work is good for us at Airbnb, but it wouldn't work in some other businesses. At an industrial bakery, there are purity and food safety standards. Dog hair does not belong in the products, so it would be a nonstarter. In a collision of values, your code of ethics and business practices must protect the most core values.

This seems like common sense, but you'd be surprised how uncommon that can be. In accounts about the last days of Theranos, stories have arisen about Elizabeth Holmes's bizarre decision to buy a Siberian husky puppy that she appeared to believe would amuse and inspire downtrodden employees. Apparently, not only did Balto the puppy relieve himself in offices and conference rooms, Holmes's scientists worried that the dog hair could contaminate the labs. According to Nick Bilton writing in *Vanity Fair*, Holmes ignored their caution.[13] I'd call that a collision of values.

No gray zones

I do want to talk about a general concept that I would recommend incorporating into any company's code of ethics approach. This concept emerges from today's more fluid workplace boundaries. Employees work long hours, often eating and exercising in the office, but they also work at home or while commuting. They socialize together inside and outside the office. Airbnb has an urban campus with multiple buildings located within several city blocks. In this sort of fluid environment, where is "work"? And where does the code apply? We have a policy at Airbnb that I think is powerful: basically, when two or more Airbnb employees are together, you're at work, and that means that work rules apply.

When employees first hear this, some don't like it—and I get it. "What right do you have to control what I do on my time off? Are you saying I have to work 24/7?" I explain that rules aren't about a building or a nine-to-five time frame but are instead about interactions and values that apply anywhere, at any time a minimum of two employees are together, even if they did not plan on it in advance. We're not saying that when you see a colleague at the beach or a ballgame you should go up and start working. We're saying that we always expect you to demonstrate Airbnb's values of respect and nondiscrimination no matter where you are or who you're with.

Example: You walk into a bar one Saturday night and see someone from work whom you have asked out twice but who has turned you down. After a few drinks, you make inappropriate sexual remarks and try touching them inappropriately. That behavior won't be forgotten on Monday morning, and you've now created a challenging situation for that person just coming to the office and trying to work with you. The other person's livelihood depends on working effectively with others, and you have made that difficult. It's unacceptable behavior, and your conduct outside the office could lead to a legal claim—and wreck your career.

Now, let's say a manager goes to a ballgame, gets drunk, and yells a slur about a player's sexual orientation. Unbeknownst to that manager, his direct report happens to be seated three rows up. The direct report who hears this rant now has reason to believe that their manager does not respect the company's values of being nondiscriminatory after all. Neither would a customer, host, guest, vendor, or other partner if they were to hear his comments. The same would go for social media posts.

"That's a beautiful ring. So, you're married . . . any kids?"

An underappreciated value of a carefully thought-out code of ethics is that it provides an opportunity to bring attention to issues that many employees would never have even imagined were problematic. One example involves laws at both the federal and state levels that address hiring discrimination.

In the United States, federal law generally prohibits companies with 15 or more employees from discriminating against applicants by making hiring decisions based in whole or in part on age, sex, race, religion, or national origin, among other protected factors. Federal law also prohibits companies from discriminating against women on the basis of pregnancy, so companies should not ask in a job interview whether a woman is or intends to become pregnant (and state and local ordinances may extend the same prohibition to smaller companies). States have even more rules that employers must follow.

Many employees might be surprised to learn about the kinds of questions they might ask or comments they might make that can expose their company to a discrimination lawsuit. Many are not inherently nefarious. They can be conversational, friendly, and they come up all the time when you first meet people. For example, you find out someone is from your hometown: "Oh really, did you go to Central High? What year did you graduate?" You're just trying to figure out if you know people in common. The problem with these kinds of questions is that they can allow you to figure out the person's age, and it's illegal to base a hiring decision on age. So keep in mind, the more you probe, the more your questions may be construed as gathering inappropriate information to make a decision.

In California, you cannot ask a job candidate what their current salary is. Studies have shown that this practice perpetuates unequal pay treatment, and legislators have agreed. It's an issue for women and minorities in particular. In situations such as these, employers may offer a package just above an applicant's current salary rather than a salary commensurate with that of employees in equivalent positions, thereby perpetuating unequal pay for equal work.

This section of the code needs to be created, or at least vetted, by someone from your legal department. Some rules are not necessarily intuitive to otherwise ethical or reasonable people, but violating them still can create liability. Every company will need to incorporate the unique laws, regulatory reporting processes, and professional standards that apply to exactly what they are doing and where they are located.

✦

If you are driving the code process, I will warn you about a response that you may occasionally face from members of a participating group or executives outside the process. Maybe it's fear of losing control or somebody who's heard Mark Zuckerberg talk about "moving fast and breaking things,"[14] but occasionally you'll get pushback from people who often advocate for just handling many dilemmas on a case-by-case basis. I've found that anyone who brings this up tends to be fixated on rare exceptions or exotic examples. For example, "We can't have a rule saying we don't accept gifts, because someday we might do business in Japan and our partners or vendors would be insulted if I refused to accept a gift."

That's like saying, "We shouldn't have a speed limit because if you're taking an injured person to the hospital, you need to drive as fast as you can." You can have a rule, and in an unusual situation you can make an exception to the rule when it's both ethical and in the long-term interest of the business. But common sense says that we need common standards and rules of the road for the activities that occur *every day* on our roads. That's the job of your code of ethics.

CODE MOMENT 3: PAUL, SERENA, AND A DEAD DUCK

A lighting company marketing manager, Serena, enters engineer Paul's cubicle and sits down to discuss a product rollout. As Paul explains the schedule, Serena sees the top of a flyer poking out of his briefcase that says "NRA Member, You're invited to a march for gun rights." She also notices that Paul has a coffee mug on his desk that shows him wearing camo and holding up a dead duck.

Serena's niece was killed in a school shooting. She gets teary, stands up, and says, "I can't help you." She goes back to her desk and drafts an email to HR. "The gun lobby is the most unethical, immoral organization in America, and one of its members works for our company. I cannot perform my job if I am forced to work with a collaborator in my niece's murder. Our ethics code bans weapons at work, why do we allow people to promote gun ownership in our workplace?"

HR pays a visit to Paul and asks him about his interaction with Serena. Paul explains that the flyer was in his bag because he grabbed his mail on the way to work, not because he was advocating for the NRA. He says he never said—or planned to say—a word about guns to Serena or any other employee. Then he gets angry. "There is a First Amendment in this country, and I have the right to my opinion," he says. "She wears a crucifix, so why does she get to advocate for Christianity?"

Whose Code Moment is this?

For discussion, see appendix, page 237.

CODE MOMENT 4: A NOT-SO-GENTLE ETHICAL DILEMMA

NaturalCo sells clothing made from organically harvested cotton. Its advertising promotes its carefully sourced and certified green fabrics by contrasting it with environmentally damaging processes used for other fabrics. NaturalCo has never bothered with a code of ethics because obviously the company is all about integrity. Its corporate slogan: "Gentle on your body, gentle to the earth."

Samantha sources raw materials for NaturalCo and travels to remote areas around the world. In Southeast Asia, she negotiates a deal to buy organic cotton for 15 percent less than the company had been paying. The CEO sends a congratulatory email. A high bonus later reflects her work on this contract.

A year later, a national magazine runs an investigative feature on child labor practices in the region where Samantha closed this deal. NaturalCo is listed as a buyer of cotton that has been picked by children as young as seven years old from a local orphanage. The owner of the cotton farm has been arrested.

The CEO summons Samantha to his office. "This scandal could ruin us! This is obviously why the price was so low. Why didn't you ask more questions?"

Samantha replies: "I don't remember you caring why the price was low. You sent me to get a good deal on certified organic, and that's what I did."

"Yeah, well, your judgment sucks and you're fired. And we'll be putting out a press release saying we had no idea our cotton was being picked by children."

"That's simply not true—I knew and you didn't care," Samantha says. "You said it was my job to get a good deal on organic cotton and you didn't care why. Fire me and I'll see you in court."

Houston, we have a Code Moment. What should the CEO do next?

For discussion, see appendix, page 241.

5

What will derail your mission: The 10 most common integrity issues

What should the actual code of ethics cover? What are the most important ethical dilemmas and priorities that all of us face at work? What ethical lapses can tarnish—or even annihilate—your brand?

The most pervasive myth about integrity dilemmas in the workplace is that they are rare. Every single day in every single company, public or private, employees make choices with a direct or indirect ethical component.

- Should I request reimbursement for a meal with a friend where the extent of the "business" conversation was: "How is work going?"
- Should I pretend I don't know about a government regulation and plead ignorance if we get caught violating it?
- Should I have one more eggnog at the holiday party before I go back to my desk and finish answering customer emails?
- Should I ignore a discovery at the end of a quarter that a colleague improperly inflated a past revenue entry?

"No" happens to be the answer to each of those specific questions. Yet I can assure you that employees in all kinds of companies, big and small, old-school and high-tech, answer "yes" to these questions more often than they should. Why? For one reason, each of these dilemmas feels private and easy to rationalize in the moment: "Nobody will find out." Or, "The boss said, 'Do whatever it takes, and I don't want to know the details.'" Or, "They owe me this." Or, worst of all, due to intoxication or malicious intent, the person simply decides the rules don't matter—or as an anonymous employee of Facebook, who I'll tell you about later, recently wrote on an Internet board about workplace issues, "Fuck ethics."

It's also true that some individuals believe that others "get away" with these acts all the time, so why should they take the hard path? The threat of consequences or discovery seems remote. But even small acts of fraud and deceit, doing work while intoxicated, fudging numbers, violating domestic or international regulations, become compounded over time. Each concession to the easy, tempting, wrong option makes the next poor choice even easier to make, creating a culture that is ripe for what Accenture calls a "trust incident." That is too mild a term for me, as they can carry the unpredictability and potential impact of a natural disaster. I call them Code Reds.

Code Reds are catastrophic, brand-devaluing scandals that, just like a significant earthquake or hurricane, often end up remembered as the point where everything changed. Enron's meltdown, for example, was a one-company Code Red that also impacted the regulation of all public companies. People still refer to "pre-Enron" days when talking about certain rules and practices.

A Code Red brand disaster can happen at even ethical companies due to a rogue employee or unexpected events in a fast-moving world. A classic example of the latter was the famous Chicago Tylenol murders. In the early 1980s, seven people, including several members of the same family, died after taking Tylenol capsules from bottles they had purchased in the Chicago area. Police found that cyanide had been added to the capsules, and then the capsules were returned to the pill containers and put back on store shelves. Johnson & Johnson, Tylenol's parent company, had done nothing wrong. Nonetheless, there was no telling how many bottles had been tainted. Johnson & Johnson instigated a nationwide product recall and invested many millions of dollars to warn consumers not to take its own product. No suspect was ever arrested or charged for the murders. J&J later changed its over-the-counter drug packaging to make it tamperproof, and to this day J&J's overall response is held up as a model for crisis management.

But in many companies that experience a Code Red–level brand disaster, it's often the case that internal pressures had been building for some time, but the company ignored or stifled feedback that might have put it back on track. Or it may have simply tolerated bad behavior for too long. For example, employees at Theranos who raised questions or objected to the ethical or legal consequences of certain decisions were ignored or isolated. At Wynn Resorts and the Weinstein Company, senior employees covered up bad CEO behavior or lied out of "loyalty" or, more likely, concern about falling out of favor with those at the top.

My goal in this chapter is to help leaders focus on, and help employees understand, the ten most common and problematic categories of ethics dilemmas that represent the biggest threats to Intentional Integrity. I'm not going to tell you that a perfect code of ethics will prevent all problems, but I will argue that each of these ten categories must be represented in your code of ethics. So let's talk about what they are and how we can relieve small amounts of confusion or pressure as a matter of course instead of creating the conditions that trigger a scandal that registers high on the ethical Richter scale.

1. Inappropriate relationships

Just ask a salmon: biology is a powerful force. Having a blanket policy prohibiting all romantic relationships among employees in a workplace would make work life easier, but it won't work. People may be designing and creating robots, but they are not robots themselves. Even if they agree to such a policy when they join the company, some employees won't follow it. It will lead to toxic secrecy. We all know that many people meet their partners at work or doing work. According to a survey by the career-advising firm Vault.com, 58 percent of respondents admitted to having an office romance at some point in their career, and 10 percent met their spouses at work.[1] Yep, earlier in my career, I did it too (though not with a subordinate). People are social creatures who connect in unpredictable and sometimes irresistible ways. Attraction is understandable, but acting on it can be problematic. And when the attraction is one-sided or there's a nasty breakup and the consequences bleed into the workplace, you can have a full-blown scandal.

This category carries a high risk of catastrophic damage to careers as well as brands when indiscretions lead to other illegal or improper behaviors. There are few internal issues that I have seen cause more downstream angst and team disruption than inappropriate relationships.

At every stage of a reporting chain, romantic relationships cause problematic pressures. For example, if a boss proposes something romantic to a report, but the report isn't interested or sure about the advances, they feel coerced. The boss controls their pay, their rating, their job assignments, their career. What will the impact be on the report's career if they say no? Also, a relationship between a manager and a direct report *at any level of the company* will alienate or even infuriate other employees who believe they are being disadvantaged by that relationship.

In my opinion, NO organization can afford to say, "OK, go ahead and date one another, but please use 'reasonable' judgment."

The path of integrity is to have a specific workplace dating policy. For any company except a small, family-run business, the basic policy must state that managers should not engage in any form of romantic relationship with individuals who are within the scope of their control. If a relationship develops, the senior person is expected to report it and be transferred out of the reporting relationship or leave the company. Too often, as we saw with the Drummond case at Google, companies try to keep a highly valued senior executive by transferring the junior person to another department where they might not be as well suited to the job, setting that person up to fail.

A manager/direct report romance is a classic conflict of interest. Individuals tend to seek advantages for their romantic partners, consciously or not. A manager's personal relationship to a direct report cannot be artificially isolated from decisions about work assignments, expense approvals, promotions, performance reviews, salary, or anything else that should be based solely on the employee's performance and value to the company.

You might argue in the abstract that a company should "treat people like adults" and that adults are capable of managing these relationships appropriately. I promise you, many of these couples' colleagues do not agree with that. I've seen signed and anonymous letters, emails, blog posts, and voicemail messages, and I've reviewed formally reported complaints filed with human resources or ethics advisors where colleagues report an inappropriate relationship as having negative consequences for a work team. In many cases, the two people involved thought nobody had a clue about their relationship.

Conflicts also develop when a workplace relationship becomes strained or comes to an end; now the potential is there for mutually assured career destruction. If one partner manages another, the manager may now intentionally penalize their former romantic partner. In addition, the spurned employee may threaten to ruin the manager's career by reporting what was going on—or even suggesting that he or she was pressured into the relationship. What began as a violation of the "personal relationship" code can morph into sexual harassment, assault, blackmail, expense account fraud, and on and on.

Secrecy and shame may swirl around these relationships and amplify poor judgment. Acts like falsifying expense reports to cover up romantic getaways are common, and knowing about them can lead to blackmail by the involved parties—or others. I have seen situations where a manager involved with an assistant gave her virtually unlimited expense account approvals on the manager's corporate credit card. Imagine how thrilled other assistants were to learn about that. I even know of a tragic situation where a distraught CEO involved with an employee committed suicide when the relationship became public.

Not all problematic work relationships involve direct reports. For example, in my discussion of Code Moment 1 about Regina and Mike, I talk about the cascade of ethical code violations that frequently flows from work-related relationships with outside parties such as vendors or contractors. Here's a doozy: According to the *Wall Street Journal*, the head of global security (there is never a shortage of irony in the integrity scandal world) at Snapchat's parent, Snap, was fired in late 2018 after the company discovered he had not disclosed a personal relationship with a woman at a consulting firm to whom he had authorized a six-figure payment. The *Journal* reported that the woman was fired after their relationship ended. And not only did Snap fire the executive, they also fired his manager. One inappropriate and undisclosed romance, several reputations wrecked, embarrassing damage to brand.[2]

Organizations can suffer successive waves of negative fallout from relationship scandals. The dean of the Stanford Graduate School of Business resigned in 2015 following messy publicity stemming from a lawsuit filed by the estranged husband of a faculty member the dean had begun a relationship with. The estranged husband—who also had held a faculty position—obtained and made public embarrassing texts the dean had exchanged with the female faculty member that ridiculed her ex and called him a "dick" and an "asshole" and even joked about castrating him in the public square. The lawsuit was later dismissed, but the scandal was in the media for weeks, eroding morale and attracting scrutiny about leadership at the business school and even the university itself. Highly embarrassing for an institution that purports to be a leading teacher of management principles.[3]

I often say that inappropriate relationships that happen at work are as much a failure of management as an ethics violation. As a manager, any time you develop close friendships with individuals that you manage, you create an "in group" (people who hang out with the boss) and "out groups" (those who don't). Friendships can create just as many difficult situations as romances: people who hire their friends, an employee who is friends with a peer and is later promoted to manage her or him, people who went to college together whose spouses and kids are friends, etc.

I always advise: tread carefully, and be as transparent as possible. As Airbnb's general counsel I had seven direct reports who are fantastic and fascinating people, and I didn't cultivate friendships with any of them. I didn't go to their homes for dinner on the weekends or carpool with them. If I had lunch with one of them, I'd make a point to have lunch with the others within a month or so. I think they understood my message: I don't have favorites. Of course, that can change when people move jobs, and I've developed great relationships with former direct reports—after we stop working together.

Now, I'm sure that I missed out on some great times, but I'm sidestepping problems as well. What do you do if you have to discipline a friend for misconduct or poor performance? How will you choose between a friend and that coworker you never really got along with when it's time to hand out bonuses? The carefree days of bar-hopping with your coworkers after hours are now freighted with concern about letting something confidential slip, or developing relationships that will undermine your credibility as a fair, impartial leader.

More than once in my career, I have seen formal complaints and even lawsuits filed by people claiming discrimination of many different kinds—age, gender, race—that I believe were triggered by disproportionately close social relationships a manager had with some reports and not others. At Airbnb, I spend a fair amount of time talking with managers about this, because nurturing a sense of belonging and promoting diversity are so core to our mission. How do you bring a diverse group of people together and create cohesion without fostering inappropriately close bonds between selective employees? How do you make sure you're not unintentionally alienating or quieting the voices of others? Managers must think about these challenges, and I believe avoiding after-hours socialization with team members makes it easier. Intentional Integrity is not just about rules, it's about reaching for a broader spirit of inclusiveness and belonging.

2. Alcohol-fueled behavior and illegal and legal drug use

I have had to fire people for cause in my career, and many of them did what they were fired for while under the influence of alcohol. Sometimes they even blame the booze, as if it were some independent third party.

Whether a person is an alcoholic or rarely drinks, a single bad choice made while drinking can be devastating—for the person, for victims of their behavior, and for the company's brand. Some companies try to address this by banning any drinking during work hours or at company events, and they will not reimburse any business entertainment involving alcohol. An employee drinking on the job when they weren't supposed to is not typically the issue I have had to grapple with, although that behavior can be disastrous in certain industries, such as airlines or other transportation companies. But the larger problem I have observed is that excessive drinking, regardless of where it occurs or who pays for it, lowers inhibitions and clouds judgment, leading some people to sexually harass, bully, or inappropriately touch or assault others; insult customers or colleagues; damage company property or equipment; or behave in an extreme and embarrassing fashion (for example, skinny-dip in a conference resort fountain, pass out drunk, become ill).

Sadly, most of us know individuals who are smart, responsible, talented human beings but who do ridiculous and even dangerous things while drunk. At the height of the dot-com boom in Silicon Valley, one of the leading law firms there held a retreat at an exclusive golf resort in Monterey, and several young lawyers got drunk, stole a golf cart to joyride, and caused the cart to fly off a cliff. Thankfully, nobody was seriously injured, but it makes you think twice about paying for legal advice from individuals who behave so recklessly.

At Airbnb, we do allow drinking in our workplace and at events, and in fact we have open taps in our cafeteria where employees can have a glass of wine or a beer between 4:00 p.m. and 8:00 p.m. That may seem unusually liberal, but again, consider our mission and values. Airbnb's policy acknowledges that we are in the hospitality business, and a widely accepted form of hospitality is serving alcohol in a friendly, social setting. We emphasize that this puts a lot of responsibility on employees to maintain professionalism. Our policy says, "It's never acceptable to do Airbnb work under the influence of drugs or alcohol. You shouldn't come to work or be on company premises if you are under the influence of a substance that may alter your ability to think, work, or behave appropriately." If our employees violate our policy about responsible drinking and behave inappropriately, we may have to fire them.

That said, firing an employee does not relieve a company that violates the law from its liability. It's illegal in every state to provide alcohol to someone under the age of 21. In many states, laws extend liability to those who knowingly provide alcohol to individuals who are already intoxicated. Coincidentally, when I graduated from law school, I worked for a federal judge and helped him write an opinion on one of the early cases that established a precedent for what is called "dram shop" liability. Many states subsequently adopted the reasoning he did: while prosecutors or plaintiffs must prove that the individual providing the alcohol realized the person ordering the drink was already intoxicated, a bartender or liquor store owner or even the host of a private party may be the last line of defense between a drunk driver and innocent victims. There is significant social value in making the server take his or her unique role as last defender seriously before selling or giving someone more alcohol.

Now, let's be real: At the annual Christmas party who is going to tell the head of sales or a CFO that she or he has had too much? Your caterer's bartender? A junior employee who is manning the frozen margarita machine? Having a policy is necessary but not sufficient—you need employee outreach messages to reinforce responsible behavior. We like to broadcast simple, brief videos via in-house channels. And in terms of the actual parties, we de-emphasize drinking by limiting the hours when alcohol is served and making sure there is plenty of food and nonalcoholic drink alternatives.

It's also true that some who do not appear intoxicated nevertheless act out when they've had one or two drinks. They may not be staggering or slurring their words, but an otherwise pleasant, even-tempered person may make inappropriate comments aimed at colleagues, supervisors, partners, or customers. They may take a photo of colleagues drinking or dancing and post it on social media with an embarrassing comment. I've yet to see a rule that can prevent this. We say, "We expect you to know your limits and treat each other with respect." If other employees complain, we investigate—and there may be consequences.

Sometimes, by the luck of the draw or by an intentional effort of leaders, you may have a workforce that parties hard. If an unfortunate or inappropriate tone is taking over events, reassess: think about limiting amounts of alcohol and serving it over a much shorter period, and reducing the amount of hard liquor available—or not serving alcohol at all. If one or more employees lose their inhibitions in these settings, urge your managers to have a conversation with them that focuses not on their drinking but on their behavior. It can set the tone: "I was concerned by how loud you were at the department happy hour, and I wonder if you were aware that you came across as belligerent?"

The ethics team at Airbnb made a video in advance of the 2018 holiday season in which we talked about some good basic ideas for office parties:

- Always have nonalcoholic alternatives.
- Always serve food with alcohol.
- Never promote an office party for the purpose of drinking to excess—keep the parties to a few hours maximum. Serving alcohol for 6 hours straight is a recipe for trouble.
- Drinking games and excessive consumption are not appropriate at a work party.
- Don't be an alcohol pusher. Managers must not tolerate bullying or teasing of employees who don't drink or who decline to drink any more.

It's possible to both celebrate and have fun events while reinforcing a culture of responsibility and concern and care for others. When I give my integrity presentation to new employees, I tell them about a strict rule I have for myself: at a work function of any kind, including lunch or dinner with a vendor, I never have more than two drinks. In my case, two drinks does not trigger behavior I have found to be embarrassing or problematic. I encourage everyone to think about that in advance. The worst time to make a decision about how much to drink in a work setting is . . . while you're drinking in a work setting.

Illegal and legal drugs

In some ways the issue of drugs is simpler than that of alcohol, but in other ways it's much more complex. Again, begin with the law. There is no way any company should support or condone the use, sale, purchase, or distribution of illegal drugs in its workplace, or by employees who are attending any kind of meeting or event on the company's behalf. You should also draft a rule that discourages employees from coming to work if they are taking prescription drugs that interfere in their ability to think, make good decisions, treat others with respect, etc. Of course, this is all complicated by the fact that laws around consuming drugs vary quite a bit around the world; what is legal in one office might land your employee in jail if used on a business trip to another office.

That said, it's not wise to include too many details about specific drugs in your policy or urge employees to file a report if they witness any drug use. Employee A may see a colleague at a party taking a pill. Is it a legal substance or an illegal one? As an employer, you are forbidden by law to demand private medical information. Instead, rely on behavior: if a colleague witnesses an employee passing out or behaving strangely or insulting a customer, it is appropriate for them to report that behavior to a manager. The conversation changes from one about the details of a medical condition to one about workplace behavior.

Finally, what do we do about marijuana, which is becoming decriminalized in many places and legal for recreational use in some states? The law around this issue is evolving. Even if possession or use has been reduced to a misdemeanor in your state, realize that it is still against federal law. It is a judgment call whether to permit its use on your premises or at company-sponsored events.

You may have a culture that embraces marijuana, and the odds of the federal law being enforced are indeed low. You may have employees who make spirited arguments that marijuana edibles or joints deserve to be served next to the bar at company parties. Remember that a company is not obligated to serve anything. This is not a civil rights matter. The leaders of a company have to consider the culture of their workers and the impact of saying no to their requests. Many people are bothered by any kind of smoke, so your smoking rules may already make marijuana use a nonstarter.

3. Sexual harassment and sexual assault

I don't need to explain just how pernicious the threat of a sexual assault/ sexual harassment Code Red is. The challenge is communicating how unacceptable that behavior is, creating a just and safe reporting process, having a good system for handling accusations after they are reported, and assigning consequences.

For an example of a corporation that thoroughly botched every aspect of managing this issue in its workplace, look no further than Wynn Resorts. In February 2019, the Nevada Gaming Commission levied a $20 million fine on Wynn Resorts after an investigation of sexual misconduct— including both sexual harassment and multiple alleged assaults—against founder Steve Wynn turned up that the company's executives were enabling the acts. Among other things, Wynn paid $7.5 million to a former manicurist who told others he forced her to have sex. And part of the investigation showed that, on multiple occasions, executives were told about Wynn's inappropriate behavior with other women and did nothing to investigate it, much less stop it. In one case, the *Wall Street Journal* reported that an operations executive for the casino told a manager that he should comb accusers' personnel files for evidence to fire them after they complained.[4] Also in 2019, the *New York Times* reported that the Massachusetts Gaming Commission issued a 200-plus-page document that showed that "in some instances particular Company executives, with the assistance of outside counsel, were part of affirmative efforts to conceal allegations against Mr. Wynn that came to their attention."[5]

There are a number of commonly misunderstood aspects of sexual harassment. For example, the act of saying something sexual or suggestive to another person is not illegal, even if the person does not want to hear it. However, *it is illegal for an employer to tolerate that behavior in a workplace.* A company absolutely must address these behaviors in its code of ethics, but the complexity of applicable laws demands a far more thoughtful and comprehensive consideration, in advance, of how you will talk to employees about this, and then how you will handle all reports, allegations, and investigations. We'll cover this in more detail in chapter 10.

4. Data privacy

In the workplace, every single company today is challenged to create processes and policies that protect customer information. The case of Uber and its "God View" access was a chilling reminder of that.

Data privacy is a realm where a company may have no idea it has a problem until it suddenly encounters a Code Red. Data privacy in the Internet age requires a lot of technical security support, but it also demands that companies adopt a realistic, specific set of rules that acknowledge that human beings, including their own employees and executives, are motivated by messy, even crass motives from time to time. They want to spy on their lovers, friends, enemies, neighbors, and relatives or stalk a celebrity or intervene in a transaction to try to help a friend. They want to appear to be in the know or try to get attention by revealing "inside" information.

Companies that value integrity should commit to protecting customer data as a fundamental value. Facebook's aloof and somewhat confusing initial responses to the Cambridge Analytica scandal as it unfolded made the company appear to not take seriously what many users considered an outrageous betrayal of their privacy. But the issue goes far beyond Facebook. Amazon and Google also are collecting incredible amounts of data about us every day, and all three companies now have devices literally sitting in our homes with the ability to listen to our conversations. Beyond them, banks, credit card companies, hotel chains, airlines, and essentially all companies with personal customer data need to beef up their code of ethics as it applies to protecting data privacy.

The easiest part of this issue is the policy. Nobody, not the CEO, not the head of security, should access customer data unless it is specifically authorized by law and by a published policy—and is for a specific, work-related purpose. The problem is that companies must police this issue themselves, and many do not pay nearly enough attention to it. Protecting customer data privacy speaks to the essence of Intentional Integrity and has to be reinforced constantly, both in messaging and by technical systems that log who accesses data and produce reports flagging suspicious data usage. The good news is that there tends to be a digital trail of who accesses data, so publicizing the chance of being caught is a deterrent. Emerging technologies like blockchain could make identifying breaches faster and easier.

5. Expense account violations and misuse of corporate resources

In terms of actual inquiries, the most common subjects that I have seen come up over the years relate to expense account rules and the use of corporate resource policies. Questions like:

- Can I use the phone the company gave me to do personal shopping?
- Can I run off flyers for my garage sale this weekend on the office copier?
- I have a friend who is a security specialist and he'd be a good fit at our company. He loves golf. Can I treat him to a round while I try to recruit him and expense it?
- I'm swamped—can I bring food from the company kitchen to serve as snacks at my kid's soccer game?
- Will I be fired for watching porn on my company laptop or smartphone after working hours?
- I had to take a box of documents home that was too bulky for public transit, so can I expense my ride home?

These are not high-stakes dilemmas. The answer to any one of these questions may depend on details not mentioned here. But I don't consider it a waste of time for our ethics advisors to field and answer these questions. Our code of ethics couldn't possibly imagine and address all of these precise scenarios. Our accounting department has more specific rules about expense reimbursements that are specific to various job functions. Frankly, as in the case of the $200 gift card our ethics team debated, it's a positive sign of an Intentional Integrity culture when people take the time to ask questions. There are so many possible variations in this category that you need to focus on communication and transparency: when in doubt, talk to your manager or an ethics advisor. Every time you pause to ask if something is the right thing to do, you strengthen your integrity muscle for when you are confronted with a potentially career-defining dilemma.

Of particular concern to many employees today are rules governing the equipment and personal devices provided by the company, so we do get fairly specific about that in our code. Different companies have different policies based on many variables. One memorable Code Red for me occurred when a company I worked with received a threatening letter from the Motion Picture Association of America because an employee had illegally downloaded a copy of *Pirates of the Caribbean* onto his work computer using the office Wi-Fi, demonstrating bad judgment on multiple levels. It turned out that the torrent site used by the employee was a "bait" site the movie studios created to catch people stealing content. Very embarrassing. When we wrote Airbnb's code, we expressly prohibited the use of company equipment for any illegal behavior, and we specifically covered illegal downloads.

Cell phone calls are now unlimited under most data plans, so making a personal call or shopping online from your work-supplied phone does not directly cost the company money and is not generally an integrity issue. But I do feel that companies should remind employees that putting sensitive personal information on their company smartphones or laptops exposes them to potential embarrassment—or worse. Employees are wise to be concerned that if they use a work phone or laptop to send intimate messages to their spouse or partner (or go on Tinder or watch porn), what they do on the device might be seen by the company or others. The device belongs to the company, after all, and for a variety of reasons could be collected and its contents examined. Obviously, people use mobile phones to exchange sensitive material about their personal health, their relationships, their children's issues, their work frustrations, and many other subjects they would not want anyone else to see; and yet we frequently are reminded that digital data can become public. Look at Jeff Bezos, a tech-savvy guy one would imagine might be surrounded by many visible and invisible layers of security, whose personal texts to his girlfriend were made public by individuals seeking to influence his reputation when his divorce was announced.

Once an exchange is digital, there's a record. Any cell phone call log or record of a string of texts is fair game for a subpoena if a crime has been committed or is being investigated by law enforcement. That applies to your personal phone or your work phone. The carrier has the information on the calls you made and received, and the text data is stored with them as well.

A company might have to legitimately review emails or texts from or to you, perhaps to respond to discovery in a lawsuit or confirm that you did not discuss a bribe with a vendor or make an offensive comment to a customer. In the process, investigators might see private information you'd prefer we not see. If you're willing to take that risk, that's fine. If you're not, you'd better carry a personal phone to discuss sensitive matters like your health.

As a risk to the company's success or brand reputation, inappropriate use of resources and expense account improprieties generally do not rise to the top of my worry list. But the importance of addressing it can vary by the type of business you're in. If you run a private security business, you would need extremely specific rules about employees' use and storage of weapons and uniforms, for example. If you own several jewelry stores, you might want a detailed policy about employees being allowed to borrow jewelry for a personal occasion. You might see that as a marketing opportunity, but it would need to be done in a documented, and insured, way.

The customs of certain roles dictate policies as well, and line managers can generally police expenses without resorting to the ethics process. Sales traditionally spends money to entertain and spend time with clients. If an engineer wants to be reimbursed for "recruiting" meals twice a week but never delivers candidates, her manager needs to warn her that her expenses are going to be denied if the practice continues.

One important consideration is that a rising level of small-time cheating can be a barometer of discontent or frustration. Some employees who aren't bought in to the company's mission and culture, or who feel they deserve more money or attention or responsibility than they're getting, sometimes behave in ways that sabotage integrity as a corporate value. For example, they may frequently run their personal mail and packages through the postage meter in the mailroom. The dollar impact may be small, but perpetrators of this kind of behavior like to claim that "everybody is doing it" and recruit others.

That's corrosive to Intentional Integrity. Ripping off the company can become a toxic and infectious form of bonding. It can start over mischievous acts or petty thefts, but it can escalate to something like a group of employees sneaking into a vehicle fleet lot at night and joyriding in a delivery truck. When the "cool kids" look like they're getting away with something, others may want in as well.

You have to be alert for indicators of growing stress or ethical threats in your workplace. Evidence of small but persistent abuse of corporate property can be one of them.

Especially regarding the actual rules and language that address expense account and company resources, I again encourage you to avoid relying on vague descriptors like "best judgment" that put the onus on individuals whose own "best judgment" may be clouded by personal desires. Here's a true story that I think explains the importance of specifics.

Two years ago, a tech company agreed to transfer an executive from California to Asia to manage an office there. As part of the move, the executive negotiated a contract that called for the company to pay "reasonable" expenses for shipping his car from the United States to Asia. Months later, the executive sent the company a bill for $931,000. It turned out the car in question was a Lamborghini Aventador, and the charges included shipping, insurance, and tariff and inspection fees the receiving country had attached before it would release the car to him. The company rejected the ridiculous expense report and paid only a modest sum for actual shipping. It was still a time-consuming mess.

Again, vagueness sets an integrity trap. The company should have had a simple policy saying either that automobile shipping costs must be approved in advance or that a limit must be determined beforehand by getting an estimate for the vehicle to be shipped.

As you tackle different issues in the workplace, you'll often find situations that seem tedious to address but that "reasonable" people should be able to figure out. When you need that kind of judgment, the better solution is to require one or more management or ethics team approvals or to design integrity into the process. What's reasonable to someone like Lamborghini guy is not at all reasonable to, well, a normal person without unmitigated gall.

6. Conflicts of interest

Generally speaking, a conflict of interest is a choice that prioritizes personal benefits or loyalties above the best interests of an organization whose rules and values you've pledged to uphold. Conflicts of interest are common in all aspects of life. They can be found when the Little League coach plays and praises his child more than other players. They appear when a resort-area newspaper gives limited space to stories about crime because it knows the local advertisers don't want to scare off tourists.

Often, the person with the conflict likes to use the excuse that they did what they did out of loyalty, as if that absolves them of blame. Of course the coaching dad is loyal to his son; and of course the newspaper wants to be a good community member. I coached my son Cliff's Little League baseball team, and we had to work through the challenges of how to treat him at practice and whether I could nominate him for the city's all-star team. You can begin these experiences with very good intentions, but if you give yourself permission to play favorites, you can easily step into an integrity trap. What did you commit to doing? What did you say your mission was? A youth coach is supposed to encourage and develop all players, not just his own son. Similarly, if you promote your local newspaper as an objective eye on the community, covering up crime violates that mission and potentially gives a false sense of safety to residents and visitors, even making it harder for law enforcement to get support. Both of these choices lack Intentional Integrity.

Some employees conflate personal loyalty with integrity. I've been asked, "Are you actually saying you expect us to put the company's interests above a friendship?" And, "If I'm the kind of person who has no loyalty to my manager, why would you even want me working here?"

Personal loyalty is admirable. Standing by friends and family is always important. Loyalty in the workplace is a more complicated idea.

Some companies really talk up loyalty. The idea is to motivate employees to thoroughly embrace a mission and even call out others they perceive to be disloyal. In the early days of eBay, some leaders grumbled when they noticed employees picking up Amazon packages from the company mailroom. The message was clear: Why are you buying from our biggest competitor?

A friend once told me a story about a Pepsi executive who was leaving work late one evening and saw a Domino's Pizza delivery person outside the company's locked doors trying to deliver a pizza. Since Pepsi owns Domino's rival Pizza Hut, the idea of a Pepsi employee ordering from Domino's so annoyed the executive that he opened the door, offered to take the pizza to the employee himself, walked to the employee's desk, and made a show of shoving the pizza in a wastebasket and stomping on it. I get it. As an executive, you want your employees to feel deeply attached to their company and its mission, so much so that they would not dream of preferring something as innocuous as a competitor's pizza.

However, when loyalty among colleagues or to a manager takes priority over company rules and policies, that is not a desirable trait—it is a conflict of interest. Both as a prosecutor and as a legal executive, I have seen individuals first ignore, then cover up, and eventually get sucked in to inappropriate and even illegal behavior, all the while telling themselves that they are doing the right thing because they are showing loyalty. I once prosecuted a CIA agent who became a spy for a foreign government; after being caught and jailed for the crime, he recruited his own son to the scheme, which eventually ended in the son's conviction and imprisonment. That is toxic loyalty.

In companies, I've seen toxic personal loyalty motivate executive assistants to falsify expense and travel records and lie about their bosses' whereabouts. I've investigated colleagues who concocted fake stories to cover up a buddy's inappropriate behavior. I've heard of perpetrators playing the loyalty card with another employee when they're caught stealing equipment or defrauding the company with kickbacks: "Don't rat me out, I'll owe you."

Toxic loyalty is one form of conflict of interest, but there are many others. In our code of ethics, we try to help employees understand the wide variety of behaviors that can be considered conflicts:

- Taking a kickback from a vendor or material supplier in exchange for recommending them or making a decision to do business with them.
- Making any business decision or corporate purchase that involves a romantic interest, close friend, or family member without revealing the connection.
- Using market research or other intellectual property belonging to your company to start or help another company.
- Advocating for an acquisition of a company in which you have a personal and undisclosed ownership stake.
- Basing a business decision on your desire to maintain a relationship with a vendor who provides gifts you value, such as concert tickets.
- Making business decisions about travel on the basis of your personal travel agenda. For example, your sister now lives in Boston, so you exaggerate a marginal business case to visit Boston or even specifically start working with Boston vendors so your travel is paid for (conflict of interest and misuse of corporate resources often overlap).

In tech companies, a common conflict can be moonlighting as a consultant for another tech company, or even starting your own company while working full-time. The barriers to starting a software company are very low: a programmer with a laptop can invent an app or program just about anywhere, including at her desk during the day where she's supposed to be working on projects you're paying her to code. For these types of situations, we at Airbnb reinforce the importance of discussing any potential conflicts with an employee's manager and an ethics advisor. The worst thing is for the company to discover an unreported conflict of interest from outside sources.

For example, we don't want to find out from a vendor that they paid the conference expenses for one of our employees at a resort destination or other desirable location. We want employees to talk to us about serving as a consultant to a company that is even remotely connected to our business, because we may have plans to expand into that space in the future. I've handled a case where an employee hired their spouse's company (at a premium price) for warehouse maintenance without divulging the connection. It's not that any or all of these were necessarily inappropriate actions, but clearly the decision about that should not be left to a person who benefits personally. A rule of thumb is to ask, Does any action—a decision, an expense, an investment, an explanation, a trip, a gift, an assignment to work with a customer, an outside project or consulting relationship, or an accommodation like working at home—go against the best interests of the company or a work team in order to benefit an individual? If so, it may be a conflict of interest.

7. Fraud

Fraud is a misrepresentation of information. Lying. At Theranos, Elizabeth Holmes was charged with fraud for claiming to investors as well as doctors and patients that the company's medical devices were capable of providing accurate diagnostic data when she knew they didn't work.[6] At Enron, the company had a dizzying chain of accounting entries that inflated its actual revenues by several times. VW deliberately loaded its cars with software whose specific purpose was to allow the cars to appear to pass emissions tests, when in reality they violated federal standards. All these scenarios conform to the definition of deliberate and intentional fraud.

Personal fraud by individuals within an organization can span a variety of situations. When you apply for a job, misrepresenting your education or work history or forging recommendation letters is fraud. More elaborate frauds can include falsifying research or testing results in a development laboratory or deliberately misstating a unit's financial results to paper over a bad quarter. One person taking credit for something someone else did is a form of fraud. Creating fake invoices for friends and shipping them products they haven't paid for is fraud. I've seen a customer service rep try to divert money that belonged to a customer to their own account. He assumed the "mistake" would not be traceable to him; he assumed wrongly and lost his job.

Fraud overlaps with other ethical dilemmas. Any deliberate effort to get reimbursed for expenses you didn't incur or that you know aren't truly work expenses is a form of fraud. Falsifying credentials or exaggerating the strength of the references of a job applicant who also happens to be your girlfriend is both fraud and a conflict of interest.

Fraud is almost always a crime of some kind, although the specific crime committed in business is often "wire fraud," or basically transmitting lies over public communication networks to gain a financial or other type of advantage. In the federal college cheating scandal indictments, some parents paid money to obtain the assignment of special SAT proctors who actually corrected their children's answers before the test was turned in—or even just took the test themselves.[7] Because these arrangements were made over email and telephone, many of the parents were charged with wire fraud. It can take many years to discover a fraud, but the bad news for fraudsters is that the statute of limitations for prosecuting criminal fraud begins with the fraud's discovery, not when it was committed.

You must address fraud in your code of ethics, but also be realistic. Fraud does not result from vague rules and confusion. It's a deliberate, and sometimes devious, criminal choice.

One of the most interesting frauds I've been involved with occurred at eBay. A seller posted a painting for sale that resembled the work of noted artist Richard Diebenkorn. It was listed with an elaborate story about how the owner found it at a garage sale and his young child damaged it with his Big Wheel. It later came out that the buyer was a con man who prowled flea markets and garage sales looking for any cheap work he could try to pass off as a famous artist's.

When he listed the painting, the seller never mentioned Diebenkorn's name, but he forged a signature mark on the painting to look like the artist's. The seller also set up two partners with shill bidding accounts so that it appeared that art collectors had "discovered" a valuable find and were slowly bidding it up. The seller later told *Wired*, "My description of the Diebenkorn painting was just a complete fable to make me look like a hapless everyman rube."[8]

A fan of the artist fell for the con and eventually bought the work for over $135,000—only to discover that it was a forgery. The FBI investigated, and the seller, an attorney, lost his legal license and pled guilty to felony shill bidding. I doubt a code of ethics or community standards document will ever matter to a criminal mind responsible for elaborate frauds like this—but it is a good reminder that companies must invest in technology and other process controls that flag certain behaviors so that human beings with integrity can intervene. Otherwise, a company can find the integrity of its whole value proposition harmed by this kind of activity—and by the media fallout.

8. Sharing confidential information and trade secrets

All codes of ethics should include a provision that prohibits employees from sharing confidential information and intellectual property. Sounds simple, but this is a huge challenge for most companies. There have never been more technology tools or media options than there are today, making it much easier for employees to break this rule. In the age of transparency, confidential information should never be put in group emails or distributed on paper as "internal use only." The odds are low it will remain confidential.

The confidentiality dilemma is an almost daily challenge for employees of high-profile companies that are in the news. They are constantly getting asked by reporters (who troll for sources using sites like LinkedIn), family members, friends, vendors, clients, and customers for the inside story. So it's essential to keep reminding employees and vendors and contractors how important it is that they protect your company's intellectual property and confidential information. Make it a policy that anyone outside the company who has access to confidential information to do their job must sign a nondisclosure agreement. And you must make clear that you will enforce those agreements and there will be consequences if and when they are broken.

The release of confidential information can include the malicious exposure of embarrassing company secrets about misbehavior or conflicts, but it can also pertain to many other topics and categories. Recruiting plans, product and marketing strategies, proprietary algorithms, data analytics, patent applications, and confidential employee or data information that the company cannot legally disclose are all fair game. Protecting confidential information and IP is distinct from protecting customer data privacy, but as an ethical breach, one incident can overlap both categories.

For example, one of the most sobering abuses of confidential information I have ever read about was a 2011 story in the *New York Times* about an accidental release of the detailed emergency room records of

20,000 patients who had been treated at Stanford Hospital. Stanford had sent a spreadsheet with this data to a bill-collection consulting company it had worked with for years.[9] The company had requested the data to create a new strategy for improving collections, and the transfer of the data was covered by confidentiality agreements. There was nothing wrong with that—patients upon admission agree that their personal data can be accessed in a bill-collection process.

However, a consultant to the bill collector who was looking to hire a new data analyst had access to the spreadsheet. He made a copy and gave it to one of the job applicants he was considering, challenging her to convert the data to charts and graphs as a demonstration of her skills. Although not malicious, it was a hugely inappropriate abuse of confidential data and a classic integrity trap: the consultant wanted to hire the best person to work with this kind of data, so he rationalized exposing 20,000 people's records to achieve that.

But the story continues. The applicant later said she did not realize the spreadsheet contained real data about real patients. She had trouble completing the project, and so she went to an online resource where students can pay to get help with various programming or analytic problems. She posted the live data along with a request for help. On that website, personal medical information about 20,000 patients sat in an unsecured project bin for over a year.[10]

That's how easily vast amounts of sensitive data can be released and even distributed in the digital age.

And don't forget that many confidentiality issues are analog, not digital. At the extreme end you have industrial espionage, a deliberate, and criminal, form where a competitor pays an employee to reveal secrets of many kinds, including insights on competitors' fears or weaknesses. A not-so-extreme example could simply be one employee speaking too loudly in a bar or telling tales at a party, actions that can have damaging consequences as well. Putting confidential papers in the trash without shredding can also be a problem.

When you're developing your code, you have to think about three different kinds of employees (and vendors and consultants) in your policies about confidentiality.

First, you must consider existing employees. In any company, there are general categories of confidential information everyone needs to keep private: project launch calendars, commonly accessible customer lead notes and databases, all new product designs. And there are specific instances when a piece of information needs to be kept confidential, such as when a company is going to file a lawsuit or announce a product recall.

It's also a good common practice to implement a policy that directs all media inquiries and requests for interviews related to your company to the communications team. That does not just mean that employees must ask for permission to be quoted, it means that they agree not to speak to a media representative, including on background or off the record, until the situation is discussed with the communications team. Leaking confidential information to the press can be corrosive to the company, although it is illegal to interfere with or retaliate against a legitimate whistleblower.

Second, you must consider employees who are exiting the company. As an element of their severance, they should sign another confidentiality agreement, which may be amended to reflect specific information that would be damaging to the company if they revealed it. Obviously, an employee with information about a company's current plans is going to be a target for competitors and reporters. It's essential to make clear that revealing trade secrets or confidential information will violate the employee's original agreement with the company as well as any exit agreement, and could even be grounds for a civil lawsuit.

Third, you must consider new employees to your company. Intentional Integrity demands that your company's managers not ask new hires for any trade secrets or confidential competitive information they are not legally allowed to share, nor should they make any hiring decisions based upon that type of information. It's sort of a "golden rule": you wouldn't want a competitor doing this, so you shouldn't either. Not only is it patently unethical, but theft of trade secrets is illegal. For some managers, the temptation is too great, and they'll come up with clever (in their minds) attempts to gain information ("If you were still at Other Co. working on Project X, at this point would you be able to plan a celebratory vacation in July?"). Don't play games with this. If you act on information hounded or coaxed out of a new employee, both your company and that employee may incur serious liability.

9. Bribery and gifts

There are important differences between bribery and gifts. I've already talked in some detail about gifts, so I'll be brief here. I get a lot of questions about gifts from employees. I feel strongly that every company needs a policy about gifts to remove any ambiguities about what employees should accept or offer.

Bribes, on the other hand, are without question a potentially disastrous source of brand damage to a company. In the United States, it's a crime 100 percent of the time to pay a public official to act outside of established channels to benefit a company, whether it's a building inspector or a mayor or a U.S. senator. Don't pay bribes. Find legal paths to success or to speed up progress.

It's also true that companies operating on a global basis must face the fact that in some countries, bribes to public officials are so common as to be considered the price of doing business at all. A colleague of mine who worked at Amazon told me a story about his meeting with a group of 100 employees in India before the company launched operations there. He emphasized repeatedly, "We do not, and will not, pay bribes." Visibly upset, a female employee stood up in front of the entire team and told him, "That policy is not possible. In India, you cannot move trucks from one state to another without paying the border guards. They have the power to turn you around and not let you cross." She felt that the company was setting her up to fail: if it stuck to this policy, she would be out of a job.

My colleague was empathetic but firm: "We will not operate that way. Tell all of the truck drivers—if they're stopped and asked for a bribe, pull over, park, and take a picture of the station where the bribe is being solicited. We will go to the Indian government with the evidence and demand action. The government says it wants us here; they will need to help us make this work." The border guards got the word that Amazon trucks were not going to pay bribes, so they stopped asking for them. That ended the matter. Of course, very few companies have this kind of clout, and some employees in country may be tempted go along with bribes unless you specifically train them that this is prohibited.

And you should do just that. Bribes are expressly forbidden in the Foreign Corrupt Practices Act, which is one of the most aggressively enforced and prosecuted federal laws on the books. Companies face enormous fines, sometimes hundreds of millions of dollars, for violating these laws. Any company expanding overseas must take the FCPA seriously and ensure that all of its vendors do as well. Violations can bring your company down and even result in the imprisonment of your employees. It might seem like everybody in country is looking the other way about bribes, but you cannot take that chance. A former employee or local competitor might be only too happy to report you.

10. Employee use of social media

"Morale is super high. We are paid a ton. Looking forward to my yearly bonus of $100k. Fuck ethics. Money is everything."

—Post on the website Blind from an anonymous but self-described engineer at Facebook[11]

That post makes me wince.

In January 2019, Mashable ran a story about Facebook's latest troubles. Apple had just announced that it was suspending some Facebook certificates in the iTunes store, because it found out Facebook had violated a policy about collecting data-using apps. The reporter went to the anonymous job gossip site Blind and looked for comments about the breaking news from Facebook employees. The writer found more hubris than humility.

I am not trying to pile on Facebook's woes. Many employees from many different companies post discouraging, depressing, snarky, and many other flavors of negative comments on these discussion boards. But the reason that "Fuck ethics" quote hit me so hard is that it exemplifies exactly the new sense of transparency that pervades the reality of business today. There are many aspects to it. Whether a name is attached to a post or not, your employees have instant access to a world of social media where anything they say will reflect on your company's brand, whether it represents a majority of employee opinions or it's the caffeinated outburst of one person.

A policy alone will not prevent this. Reinforcing the policy openly and promoting your values constantly is your only hope. You must treat this as a teaching moment, a challenge to employees to make sure they understand and think through what they post on social media. An arrogant, aggressive comment, when described as coming from an employee, can explode. It can attract copycat grandstanding by other employees and distort the real emotions inside the company. It may anger various stakeholder communities and partners. It may become the evidence regulators or politicians cite for introducing restrictive legislation. It could be a last straw for somebody who loves the good things about Facebook but is just fed up with its perceived arrogance—which could lead to them deleting their account. We all have bad days and say things we regret. And some tiny percentage of any company's employees may truly have no regard for ethics. But as leaders, we have to keep reinforcing that we value our reputation and that the world is watching. Think before you type.

Social media is a minefield for those who care about Intentional Integrity. There are so many different kinds of issues that play out on the pages of Instagram and Facebook or sites like Blind where people seek the "real story" about working at a company from users whose employee emails are verified but whose identities are not revealed.

All companies today need to have a policy about their employees' use of social media. And when your company makes those rules, you can expect some questions and even resentment: These are my personal accounts! How can you limit my speech? Well, we aren't interested in what is truly personal, but by definition social media is not private or personal. It's a problem for your company when you agree to act in a manner that reinforces your brand—then do the opposite on social media. It has become so easy to connect anyone's ostensibly private, personal page or account to where they work, usually via LinkedIn. Employees might hold passionate views about controversial subjects that have nothing to do with Airbnb, but anything they post can be connected back to us.

Remember the example I gave in the last chapter about the manager who goes to a ballgame and yells slurs at a player or ref? In a public place, that person has (or should have) no reasonable expectation of privacy. If it occurs in the presence of another employee or a stakeholder, like an investor or even a host, the offending manager may be reported—and we at Airbnb would take that behavior very seriously.

It's the same logic on a social media page. At Airbnb, our ethics code notes that if coworkers, vendors, contractors, or other members of the Airbnb community "are in your Personal Social Media Channels, your online interactions with them are essentially workplace interactions. Comments and posts that disparage, abuse, insult, or convey bias against others based on protected characteristics severely undermine an employee's ability to effectively represent our brand and manage or work with others." Consequences can include termination.

CODE MOMENT 5: THE GAME IS ON, THE VIBE IS OFF

A company's CEO encourages employee team backpacking trips and outings to promote communication and teamwork. Most employees enjoy these activities, and they seem to be good for morale. Trip highlights become the basis of lots of inside jokes, weird nicknames, and friendships.

You're an operations executive and you get an email from an employee two levels below you: "Last weekend I finally signed up for my team's backpacking trip to Yosemite. I avoided the last several, but it's all everybody talks about for two weeks. Ten of us had a nice hike. But around the campfire after a few glasses of wine, one guy said let's do 'the game.' He said we should go around the circle and talk about our first sexual experience and what it taught us. I was freaked out. I don't feel I need to share something that personal with colleagues. I said I was not comfortable. Our manager said, 'We can start with other folks, and then you can decide if you want to play. It's actually fun.' I went to my tent and heard them snickering. The next morning, I felt isolated and humiliated. Since when is something like this part of our job description? I would like to discuss a transfer to another team."

Is this an overly sensitive employee—or a Code Moment?

For discussion, see appendix, page 244.

CODE MOMENT 6: JUST ANOTHER TEQUILA COFFEE BREAK

Work has been really tough, so on behalf of your team you ask if you can build a fun themed bar area in the corner of your workspace. The team manager, Meredith, loves the idea and personally donates her neon Jose Cuervo lights. She also approves spending $500 on margarita ingredients and plastic glasses with the company logo. Meredith makes it clear, however, that this is your project and you need to manage it. Everyone on the team agrees that they won't actually use it before 4:00 p.m., unless it's a special occasion.

Do you prefer your code dilemma with salt or without?

For discussion, see appendix, page 247.

CODE MOMENT 7: MARTY AND THE MEDIA QUANDARY

Marty worked for five years at BigCo, a large, well-known public company that makes skateboards, bikes, and other recreational equipment. He was recruited to NewCo. He left BigCo on good terms and he signed an exit agreement with BigCo saying he would not compete or share secrets for two years.

The day after he arrived at NewCo, which has a code of ethics that says all media inquiries must be cleared through the communications team, a reporter that Marty knows from a business magazine sends Marty a message through LinkedIn: "Hey, congrats on the new job—how about coffee, would love to catch up." Marty respects the reporter's work. It's flattering to hear from him. They meet, and Marty realizes that the reporter wants to talk about the rumor that BigCo's motorized skateboards are being returned in droves by unhappy customers. The reporter says that some of the skateboards have malfunctioned and caused serious injuries. "I know you had nothing to do with that division, but what's the scuttlebutt on how this happened? I've heard a teenager is in a coma after an accident on the new Xmodel, and there may be a lawsuit."

When the reporter mentions the injury, Marty groans out loud. He'd heard rumblings internally that the BigCo engineering team had issues with components used in the skateboards but that management overruled them to hit a shipping target. Clearly, he knows something.

What's the right thing for Marty to do here?

For discussion, see appendix, page 249.

CODE MOMENT 8: DEFINE "ACADEMIC"

You are a marketing executive for a global restaurant chain that is making a big push in Asia. You hear through the food grapevine that at a local university, a group of hospitality school professors have done insightful research about the differences of marketing food to different Asian cultures. You reach out to the professors and ask for a meeting to discuss marketing in Thailand, but also their work in the larger region. You also say you would consider creating a consulting relationship between them and your company.

They respond that they are open to the idea and anxious to meet, and that it happens that they have been trying to raise money for a research trip to Japan, where they plan to meet with regulators to discuss the hurdles foreign companies sometimes face when trying to open restaurants there.

You have plenty of funds in your budget to send them to Tokyo for a few days.

Consulting relationships are usually straightforward, right?

For discussion, see appendix, page 252.

6

Mix it up, blast it out, repeat: Communicating the integrity message

Developing a code is only part of the solution—you need to drive it into the culture of your company. How do you send a message that being ethical matters? You want to inspire a way of thinking—a desire to take the high ethical road even when it's difficult and nobody will know if you don't. Try to make your messages memorable, and reinforce them in multiple channels. Don't bring a checklist mind-set; think like a coach. The good news is: science is on your side.

Communicating expectations about integrity to employees is essential. But as the pages of history and literature would suggest, even the clearest of messages often fall short of achieving the desired behavior. Moses tried to create a roadmap with the Ten Commandments. Nathaniel Hawthorne's *The Scarlet Letter* was about enforcing morality with the threat of public shaming. When I attended the University of Virginia, the penalty according to the honor code for lying, cheating, or stealing *for any reason* was expulsion. Violations of the Mafia's code of silence, *omertà*, are punishable by death. None of these efforts lacked enthusiasm, significant threats, or even divine endorsement. And yet . . .

So let's begin by acknowledging that Intentional Integrity does not assume that perfection is possible. One thoughtless act can frustrate the most determined leadership and blow up sincere efforts to inoculate a brand from scandal. And researchers have determined that the majority of individuals, in fact, are capable of rationalizing dishonest and unethical behavior.

Dan Ariely, a behavior scientist at Duke University, has been studying why people lie and cheat for decades. In the film about him and some of his research, *(Dis)Honesty—The Truth About Lies*, Dan says that dishonesty is actually "a deeply human experience."[1] It's not helpful to think of people as "good" or "bad," Ariely told me when we sat down to talk in his office in the fall of 2019. We are all capable of dishonesty. One of Ariely's experiments shown in the film is particularly troubling. The subjects are given a sheet of paper with math problems and a limited time frame to complete the test, so that no one can finish all the problems. When time is called, subjects come up to the front of the room, put their test in a paper shredder, and then tell the proctor how many problems they completed. They are immediately given $1 for each problem they say they completed.

What the subjects don't realize is that the shredder cuts only the outer edge of each paper test; Ariely's team can go back and determine who told the truth about the number of problems completed. The results after more than 40,000 people have taken this test? Nearly 70 percent of people lie, most by just a little. Ariely refers to this as the "fudge factor." Most people can lie just a little and still feel good about themselves. And this tendency to misbehave actually increases if the subjects believe that others around them are probably misbehaving a little as well.

Ariely says that frequent fudging can condition the brain to lying, making it easier for people to rationalize unethical behavior. Once you lie in one area of your life, it's easier for you to lie again in that same domain. Interestingly, research suggests that people who are creative have a tendency to lie more than noncreative people. Ariely believes that this is because they are better storytellers, so they can more easily rationalize their lies to themselves and others. When people are in a creative mind-set, there are "no bad ideas." When encouraged to abandon traditional thinking and go outside the box, creative entrepreneurs trying to disrupt industries—Uber, Theranos, and WeWork come to mind—can sometimes push the boundaries of ethical behavior. Most of this is likely unintentional, Ariely explains. Creative entrepreneurs who went astray often convinced themselves and those around them that what they were doing was so important and so groundbreaking that they had to break some rules along the way.

This shouldn't be a surprise. The bigger the brain, Murali Doraiswamy at the Duke Institute for Brain Sciences points out in *(Dis)Honesty*, the larger the capacity to rationalize and lie. That should be thought-provoking for any workplace that looks to attract the most creative talent.

However, there is reason to believe that these tendencies can be overcome. Ariely's research also shows that when subjects are given a talk about integrity prior to taking the same math test noted above, cheating virtually disappeared. Ariely says that people are far less willing to "fudge" if they are reminded of the importance of integrity, and if they believe their peers are being honest. Reminding people of their own moral fiber changes behavior. Ethics can easily erode under the wrong circumstances, but Ariely's work suggests that there are ways we can help ourselves act better at home and at work to protect and build up trust and integrity, with intentionality and effort.

Reinforce the message. Repeat.

What I take from this research is that integrity, regrettably, is a fragile human attribute even for people who value it. I can think of moments in the course of my life when telling a white lie or fudging an explanation came embarrassingly easy to me. But I truly believe that Ariely's research is correct: companies can shore up integrity and honesty in the workplace by deliberately talking about it a lot and reinforcing its importance. If employees believe that ethical behavior is the norm and others are following it, they are more likely to adhere to that type of behavior as well. As NBA commissioner Adam Silver told me about the league's ethics programs, "You have to keep repeating the messaging in multiple channels. It's like television advertising. You need repetition to get your point across. But if you create an environment where this sort of messaging is consistently being delivered, it will soak in."

It also matters when the message comes from the top. When I was a federal prosecutor, Eric Holder was in the U.S. Attorney's Office in Washington, DC, and we occasionally interacted over drug prosecutions. We have kept in touch through the years. Later as attorney general, Eric was known for visiting each of the local federal prosecution offices in person—93 of them—to deliver a message directly to the thousands of federal prosecutors who worked for him. "I wanted to set out, not a moral code, but a code of what was expected from people. And I think that's important because I've worked on the private side and I've seen that [ethical leadership] comes from the top. What a CEO or leader of a company does, how they conduct themselves, what it is they say really matters."[2]

This concept is so important, and yet conversations about ethics and high expectations are too rare across today's business landscape because some CEOs believe they will come off as preachy, or because they worry that the conversation is a distraction from delivering bottom-line results. "I can name on one hand the large technology companies who are serious about ethics," Donald Heider, executive director of the Markkula Center for Applied Ethics at Santa Clara University, told me recently. The Markkula Center explores ethical issues in corporate governance, global business, leadership, executive compensation, and other areas of business and also offers training programs to companies. He believes passionately that "you have to build a culture where it's OK to talk about it."

So yes, there will be frustrating setbacks. A boss may fall in love with a direct report and act on those feelings regardless of the rules. There are always going to be good people who rationalize terrible choices, and there are going to be employees who try to circumvent the rules no matter how much you reinforce them. What I think I'm telling employees may not be what they hear or want to hear. But I say, let's talk anyway, and I challenge myself constantly to try to change up how I talk about these subjects so the message doesn't just become background noise.

✦

When I worked as general counsel at the textbook rental company Chegg, I once put several senior executives on a stage in front of 200-plus employees and acted as the emcee of a gameshow-style quiz about our code of ethics. I would pose ethics dilemmas, and the executives would answer, and I would either make a "Buzzzzzzz" sound if I thought the answer contradicted our code of ethics or give an enthusiastic affirmation if I thought the answer was solid and consistent with our code. I posed mostly hypotheticals, similar to the Code Moments I've included in this book. Initially we went back and forth in a joking way, and our chief technology officer, Chuck Geiger, missed a few on purpose so I could make specific points (I had worked with Chuck at eBay). But as I drilled in on some of the questions, the room got quieter. Sometimes the executives did not agree, or they weren't sure what the answer was.

That's what I wanted to see—people realizing that the answers were not always obvious, that there were trade-offs and gray areas. But that does not mean that we should turn away from discussing them. In some cases when I buzzed Chuck's deliberately wrong answer and explained why I disagreed, I could see that other folks in the room realized that they would have given the same answer he did.

Then, I read a question that came from a real complaint from a male employee who said that his female colleagues had been talking a lot about Sheryl Sandberg's book *Lean In*. In fact, they seemed to be discussing it so much that he said it left him feeling ostracized and uncomfortable. What should he do? Should he report this to human resources, or was he just supposed to "act like a man" and suck it up?

The room was dead quiet. The question suggested a reversal of the cliché of women feeling left out by guys spending half a Monday morning meeting talking about a football game or some new car model they were all coveting.

Chuck took his time, then he answered: "I think the point is that no person in the workplace should feel ostracized. It doesn't matter the reason, if they feel excluded, they should address it with a manager, and if they want to go to HR to report it, that also is appropriate."

No response in the room. They were waiting for me.

"I think that's correct," I said.

Chuck still recalls how this exercise created discomfort, but also that it was a memorable forum. "The questions were not black and white. Some of them were 49–51, and some of them had answers that were highly debatable."

I give a lot of credit to Chegg's CEO Dan Rosensweig for letting me put on this event and not stopping it even when it got tricky. He was always a staunch supporter of my efforts to make sure we were communicating our values. Dan told me recently, "It was a little scary. But I figured if we weren't willing to stand up and put ourselves out there in situations we see every day, how would we show the employees how to live these values? It was a chance to get together and show we're all human, we all make mistakes."

In other words, it was a teaching moment for everybody. Adds Dan, "I believe we need to be willing to talk about our values. We don't want to assume people are bad because they made a mistake, and we don't want to be afraid to ask, 'Hey, why did you do what you did in this situation?' You can do that if you don't attack people."

My purpose for this presentation was to show, first, that the executive team was supporting the importance of talking about integrity. I also wanted to emphasize that making an ethical choice isn't always easy or automatic—it may be highly dependent on key details or context. But I also felt that the experience pushed a little humility into all of us. I am certain some employees later pulled up the code of ethics to review and make sure they understood the rules in dispute. Some of Chuck's answers even made me rethink how I had been communicating certain ideas within the executive team. I've been working on that ever since, and what follows are the principles I've landed on in this journey.

Start with humility and enthusiasm

Successful communication is always a two-way street. That means you need to approach any conversation about integrity with an open and receptive mind and a humble attitude. A general counsel can explain legally defensible rules as well as processes that represent the lowest risk to a brand in a given situation. But displaying the "Moses syndrome" I mentioned earlier—acting like you've had a revelation and now you're going to lead everybody to the promised land—turns people off real quick. So does behaving like a preacher or a "my way or the highway" sheriff.

As you think about communicating the integrity message, it's essential to have an enthusiastic ethics champion. It's also essential for the CEO to support the effort, but a CEO usually won't have time to get into the details. Somebody has to be the face of integrity when it comes to grappling with its complexity, and it has to be a senior leader. At Airbnb, that's me. I enjoy this challenge, not because I like catching people doing something wrong but because I like thinking about what it means to be ethical. I like trying to figure out the best way to prevent problems. I take pride in working with others and trying to figure out, and then do, what's right. In a complex situation, I want concerned employees who think there may be an ethics issue to stop and reflect and seek advice *before* they act. The more transparent everyone is in making these decisions, the more thoughtful and intentional employees are in seeking advice, the better the outcome will be.

This is the ethos among our ethics advisors as well. They come from all corners of the company and include technical employees with advanced degrees and experience in computer science or engineering. They think about and solve problems differently than I might. What they tend to have in common is that they are intellectually intrigued by this subject and they like thinking about the culture they want to support.

Our communication plan basically boils down to four main components.

1. **Make sure you deliver a message on the importance of integrity to every single employee, as early as possible in their career, at your company.**

Our Integrity Belongs Here 75-minute program is part of the Week 1 orientation we have for new employees in any of our locations, from San Francisco to Ireland. When we first developed our code of ethics after I arrived, I gave the same basic talk in small-group sessions to all our employees, as well as to our executive team. It has taken time and travel, but I figure I've given this talk over 100 times in 20-plus countries. Once in a while I may be traveling on business and assign a team member to give the new employee talk, but I always do it myself when I'm in town. I was inspired to do this by Meg Whitman, who for years insisted on speaking to every new hire class at eBay herself. She had a crazy schedule, but Meg recognized how important it was for new employees to hear directly from leaders right up front about what was important to the company. Like Eric Holder, she knew that her endorsement of eBay's values mattered more than anyone else's if she was to appear serious about maintaining our integrity.

At my talks, I start by projecting a slide plastered with recent media headlines of tech company scandals. I have already listed many of them in this book. They speak to embarrassing and even outrageous lapses of individual and institutional judgment, and I don't pull my punches in talking about them. It's sort of like those short, bloody driver's-ed films I remember seeing as a teenager; they were designed to scare us a little bit to get our attention about driving safety. The headlines I display are also designed to get the room's attention; they cover topics like data breaches, sexual harassment and assault, bribing foreign officials, inappropriate social media behavior, buying the silence of victims, lying about company policies and behavior. I have more examples than room to put them on a slide, sadly, but I always tell our employees, "I don't want to see Airbnb go through this."

I remind them that they received a copy of the code of ethics on their first day and that they have already electronically signed and agreed to abide by the code. (I doubt that more than half have actually read it carefully.) Then we dive in to what it means. I try to bring it to life.

2. **Use real-life examples. Paint a picture of actual situations where conflicting instincts may collide or where intentions may be misinterpreted.**

I don't just talk in my presentations, I also pay attention to what our employees are worrying about, reading about, and thinking about. I go down a list of real cases that have occurred inside the company and refer to the relevant provisions in our code of ethics. We have a conversation similar to the discussions I have provided about the Code Moment examples where I point out the issues, the options, and the realization that there is not always a perfect answer, but that our goal is to plot a course based on the unique details of a situation and exhibit an intention to be ethical.

I also get questions. For example, when I first began giving the integrity talk, a group of customer support employees alerted me that Airbnb hosts occasionally offered them gifts like free weekend stays when they felt the employee had been particularly helpful, and they asked whether they could accept these generous offers. Alarm bell! Every single host should receive excellent service. We would never want our service reps to hint about or ask for a gift, implying it's the way to get better service. We have since incorporated a rule about this into our code of ethics, and we emphasize this incident in our training of customer support employees. In this sense, my presentation occasionally functions as a laboratory where I collect data and later plug it back into the actual code.

When I began giving these talks just a few years ago, I would occasionally see a male employee in the audience rolling his eyes when I mentioned thinking twice before touching someone in the workplace. Those eye-rolls are becoming increasingly rare. The #MeToo movement and the incredible numbers of CEOs and others who have left their jobs in disgrace have made that kind of reaction uncool. Our entire culture has shifted on this.

Another unexpected insight for me came when I was asked about whether there are any places that are "off limits" for employee get-togethers—for example, strip clubs. I now discuss this dilemma in my new-employee integrity talk because it helps me raise the broader topic of exclusionary behavior. Holding a meeting or an off-site at, for example, a strip club is not an appropriate setting for team bonding or for work. No person should feel like they have to be in a sexually charged environment unrelated to their work as a condition of their job, or feel like an outcast if they object. Employees have the right to go where they want on their own time, and they can certainly choose their companions, but they should never organize outings or talk about them at work in a way that excludes others.

When we wrote the code of ethics, I never anticipated having to address strip clubs. Nobody in San Francisco, where we are headquartered, has ever mentioned this as a workplace issue, nor has it come up in the almost two decades I've worked in Silicon Valley. But there are regions of the country where some companies are OK with their employees meeting at or even taking customers to strip clubs. Now, I mention the example in most presentations because it highlights the fact that while there are differences between people, regions, cultures, and points of view, we have to look at any integrity issue through the lens of our company's values, not what is cool or square in the abstract or in a specific location. Airbnb is about making people feel they belong anywhere. You could substitute another activity for strip clubs—maybe golfing or marching in a local political protest—that might appeal to some members of a team but not others. Deliberately nurturing off-site activities that appeal only to some members of a team or workplace is in conflict with the values of inclusion and belonging.

The more relatable your examples are, the more your training becomes interactive—then you can engage better with employees in determining the right answer. Force folks to think about the dilemmas and questions you pose, and you will prevent passive listening. Talk about the whys behind the rules—for example, I bring up why we allow gifts up to $200 while Walmart does not allow any at all.

I deliberately raise issues and cite examples that involve ambiguities, unclear motives, and context. I make a point of saying that I appreciate that there isn't always a right or wrong answer, but there are instincts and hunches to pay attention to. It makes me feel a bit like a legal hero of mine, Supreme Court justice Potter Stewart.

Stewart, in an opinion related to obscenity in a film, once said that while it was difficult to define hard-core pornography, "I know it when I see it."[3] It became one of the court's most famous quotes. He was expressing a sentiment that in my experience is relevant to many matters associated with sex, including harassment, normal attraction, flirting, casual touching, and compliments. Sometimes it's hard to define the clear boundaries of what is or isn't any of those things. It's not just the words used that matter—the context matters, intention matters, vocal inflection matters. For example:

- You can say "hey" like you're identifying what's growing in a pasture.
- You can say "hey" like somebody just stole your parking place.
- And you can say "hey" like you're auditioning for *The Bachelor*.

In my presentations, we talk about sexual harassment and hostile work environments. Women are now coming forward to report abuses they once thought they had to suffer in silence. Men have a range of reactions, from being glad creeps are getting their due to feeling paranoid that they can't joke around like they used to.

One of the questions I ask during ethics training is, "What about compliments. Are they OK?"

"Some," somebody usually calls out.

"OK," I say. "Which ones?"

"Nonsexual."

I reply: "Like, 'THAT'S a nice sweater!'"

"Yes."

"But what about "Baby, that's a NICE sweater?" (I say this in a lounge lizard voice.)

Most people laugh, some shake their heads.

"Ah, so same thing said a different way, not OK?" I ask.

Now I see frowns. Feet shuffle. Uh-oh. Yes . . . right?

I turn to someone in the front row and say, "Nice boots." The person squirms. I say, "Seriously, I like those. Where'd you get those?"

I look up. "Was that OK what I just did there?"

"Yes."

"Boots are OK, sweaters aren't?"

"Boots are not sexual," somebody will offer.

"Maybe not to you," I say.

I try to use a little humor in my presentations—it doesn't have to feel like you're getting your teeth cleaned. I'm trying to convey that intention does matter, no matter how slippery and murky it may seem. Generally speaking, I say to be careful when offering compliments in a way that suggests a sexual attraction. But *how* you say something can be as important as *what* you say. Is that frustratingly subjective? Well, yes, but respect is based on thinking before you speak. Err on the side of caution. Consider how others might respond to jokes or comments or physical descriptions. Put on your ethics goggles and look at both the details of a dilemma and the larger issues it raises and how it might look to someone unaware of your personal point of view or intention.

It's a myth that valuing integrity creates an uptight, rigid, police-state culture. Yes, some people are more sensitive than others. But common sense and manners are good, easy rules of the road. If you show up at work with a gaudy, lights-flashing holiday sweater like one I once wore to make one of our videos and somebody laughs and says "Nice sweater," we both laugh. We're enjoying the joke together. But suggesting after the fact that you were "just kidding" when you asked a woman if she painted her pants on that morning—sorry, that's not a joke, that's either an insult or a trial balloon.

Intention always matters. A female senior executive I worked with who was the general counsel of a public company once had this happen to her: prior to a meeting, another executive leaned over to her and said, "May I give you a compliment?" Slightly confused, she said, "OK?" He replied, "That's a very attractive bra you're wearing."

Wow, ick, but wait, didn't she give him permission to . . . uh . . .

Of course she did not give him permission to say something inappropriate. How could she possibly have known what he was going to say? He might also have said, "The notes you sent around from the last meeting were well done." Instead, this was just one of a series of inappropriate comments the executive had made to her and others, and he was let go not long after this occurred.

I go through similar scenarios about issues like inappropriate access to customer data.

"How many people here have family members who believe you should now be their personal Airbnb customer service rep?" I ask.

Many hands go up. And then I explain that while it's tempting to want to resolve an issue that your friend may be experiencing, it's not your job to resolve it . . . and you have a conflict of interest. Rather than logging in to the database to figure out the issue yourself, the right thing to do is get your friend to a customer support representative whose job it is to help. We don't want any confusion about how customers, and their data, are treated.

3. **Call out specific issues in multiple communication channels— including employee newsletters, message boards, posters, emails, and—this is very important—brief and entertaining videos.**

One of the great surprises to me at Airbnb has been the success of our cheap, quick, and easy-to-make videos about subjects ranging from responsible drinking to bribery in foreign countries. These aren't masterpieces. We literally shoot them with an iPhone and a $10 table tripod. We push them out in emails, and it is incredible to me how positive the response is. We get fan email for them, thanking us for clarifying certain rules. We get employees asking to be in the next video or suggesting a topic for future videos. They're a topic on Slack channels. I get stopped walking down the street, in offices all around the world, after I have appeared in these videos.

It's exciting to me that they seem to prompt serious reflection, even though they're short and fun. I received an email from one of our engineers from China who wrote after viewing one of our integrity videos: "I like to read Warren Buffett, and he always talks about ability *and* integrity. I have been thinking that . . . I've got the ability part, but how do I get the integrity part . . . how do I *acquire* integrity?" That kind of email really inspires me to keep at this. It's why I feel so strongly that companies advocating for integrity have the power to influence the world well beyond their own walls.

I was having lunch one day in the office when a woman walked up to me, apologized for interrupting my lunch, and said that she had to know the truth behind one of the videos. "Sure," I said.

"The last video, the holiday party video, when you were talking in front of a video screen that had a fake fireplace on it."

"Yes," I said, wondering why that caught her attention.

"Were you trying to be a 'Chesnut roasting by an open fire'?"

One of our most successful videos was one we made where a manager is conducting an interview with a job candidate, played by me. He's friendly and upbeat. He asks if I'm married and have kids. As I sit down, he says, "You're limping? Is your back OK?" We succinctly point out the issues with some of these questions. For example, asking about a person's family and childcare situation can make it seem like parents might not be welcome at Airbnb. That's not OK.

He asks me in the video, "You have an extensive resume . . . what year did you graduate from college?" He asks about my background: "Where did you grow up? Chesnut—what kind of a name is that? You're from Virginia—you're not a Republican, are you?" I later learned that many employees watching the video were surprised at how routine small talk during an interview might later be interpreted as ageism or the desire to probe for medical or other information, which are illegal according to federal and state discrimination laws and inappropriate to use as a basis for hiring.

In another video, I show up in my notoriously ugly Christmas sweater to a room where a team is setting up for a holiday party. They try to tell me they are looking forward to getting drunk. I look around and ask questions, such as, If I don't drink, am I still welcome? In this case, we want to emphasize that office parties are about socializing and enjoying each other's company, not about excessive drinking. Parties and other festive events need to have nonalcoholic alternatives, food, and a welcoming attitude.

People who are working hard occasionally need a laugh, a way to bond with others. I think the videos tap into that. I credit my daughter, Bianca, a college sophomore, for helping me understand just how ineffective some other approaches to teaching about integrity subjects can be.

After getting a new job in a restaurant, Bianca was required to complete a sexual harassment training program. She said it was awful; it was a video consisting of boring, wordy slides that had to be viewed on her laptop while she clicked through each page. She did it in an airport, and the main thing she remembers was that it helped her pass the time. Later, she talked to friends who had been required to take a similar online training course for their summer job, and they told her they all sat down and clicked through it together, making fun of how bad it was and not getting a thing out of it.

But my daughter had a previous experience with sexual harassment training when she enrolled in a summer program at Carnegie Mellon University, and she had a completely different view of how training can be approached. What was different? I asked. It also centered on a video, one called "Consent; it's as simple as tea," which is available on YouTube and has been viewed more than 7.6 million times. It knows its main audience—young people. As such, instead of using text slides, it features stick-figure animation and a guy with a pleasant, slightly snarky voice. Its message is: if guys thought about sexual consent in the same way they might think about asking a woman if she'd like a cup of tea, they could avoid getting into trouble. If you substitute "have a cup of tea" for "have sex," the narrator says, and she says "I'd like to have a cup of tea," by all means, pour her a cup of tea. But if she says she thinks she would like tea, and when you make her a cup she changes her mind, she is not obligated to drink—so don't try to make her! If she is unconscious, do not pour tea into her mouth—"Unconscious people do not want tea." And just because she wanted tea last Saturday does not mean she wants tea every day . . . or ever again.

The topic is serious, but the messaging does not have to be boring and severe. Using humor made it engaging and memorable to its target audience. The same studio that made "Tea Consent," Blue Seat Studios, made another video specifically about workplace sexual harassment that was directed by Rashida Jones and narrated by Danny Glover. Once again it's short, the animation is funny, but the messages are clear and memorable. It addresses the confusion and concern that the #MeToo movement has created in the workplace for people who don't have nefarious motives, but who like to give hugs or compliment other people or touch in ways other people have the right to object to.

If you make videos related to your code of ethics, keep it short and use some humor. Make it relevant. Throw in something unexpected. If folks like the first one, they'll look forward to the subsequent ones regardless of topic. A little creativity keeps the messaging process from feeling stale, hackneyed. And I prefer to involve lots of employees so as many people as possible own the message and have an interest in spreading the word about it.

4. **Appoint and train a team of ethics advisors who will represent your company's most accessible face of integrity.**

As enthusiastic as I may be about integrity, we have over 6,000 employees, and I need help addressing their questions about expense reimbursement, gifts, and potential conflicts of interest. That's one reason we created ethics advisors.

I first worked with ethics advisors at eBay and witnessed firsthand how effective this kind of peer consulting could be. At Airbnb, after we wrote our code of ethics in 2016, we started with three ethics advisors, and now we have over 30 around the world. If you are writing or updating a code of ethics, I would recommend choosing folks from the appointed committee as your first group of advisors, as they will already have a greater appreciation of the goals of your program. At Airbnb, we regularly get inquiries from employees asking to become ethics advisors. It involves about four hours of training and an annual trip to San Francisco for a meeting to inform everyone of new policies. The only additional compensation is a very cool jacket with an ethics logo on it that many wear proudly.

Advisors have two main tasks. First, the entire ethics team is copied on and is expected to read any email that goes to our general ethics email account. This is a valuable resource for employees with questions, and it's a great way to keep the team engaged and thinking about questions of real concern to our employees. Sometimes I answer the employee's question, and sometimes I wait for our team to suggest an answer. The emails span a lot of different topics, from trivial ones to more serious issues:

"A vendor wants to give me *Hamilton* tickets, is that OK?"

"Can I sell wrapping paper for my kid's school fund raiser in the office?"

"You need to talk to Mark Manager about his confrontational style. He's a bully."

The team's second task is in-person conversations. We make sure our advisors are distributed geographically, as well as in different departments. We want these folks to be an accessible, friendly, and knowledgeable resource about what is in our code of ethics and how an employee might want to think about a dilemma. We want them to listen and give feedback consistent with our code of ethics.

The main point is to encourage the employee to find their own answers. For example, sometimes an advisor will be asked about whether moonlighting for another company is OK. The response can be more questions: Is the other company a competitor . . . or might it be in the future? Would the person's potential workload be limited to weekends or personal time? How does the other company intend to handle the person's involvement in its communications—for example, will it imply that working with the person means they're working with Airbnb?

Our ethics advisors' primary role is to be educational and informational, and to act as ethics coaches. They are not tasked with being undercover agents. But, that said, I caution ethics advisors—and anyone who launches an ethics advisor program—to remember that the team members should not see themselves or present themselves to employees as confidential counselors. An employee consulting an ethics advisor is not having a privileged, confidential conversation any more than a senior executive seeking the general counsel's advice about his or her personal behavior should think it will remain confidential if the GC perceives any kind of threat to the company or the brand. The general counsel is the company's lawyer and must elevate the client's interests above those of any individual.

In my experience, this is not a major issue; those who seek advice from ethics advisors tend to do so proactively, not as a confessional. But to be clear, if an employee relates information about a matter that is illegal or potentially a legal liability to an advisor, the advisor must report it, which then becomes a job for our investigation team—but I'll talk about that in the next chapter.

To sum up, here are the key elements of a good ethics communication program:

- **Leaders and advisors need enthusiasm and a sincere interest in the topic. The higher level the executive is who talks about ethics, the more impactful it will be for employees. The seniority of the person who delivers new employees' first exposure to a company's ethics signals how seriously the company takes ethics.**

- You're a coach, not a preacher.
- Use real-life examples, and talk about gray areas.
- Use multiple channels, humor, videos; mix up the message so it doesn't get stale, but keep repeating it.
- Use advisors to spread ethics throughout the company.
- Point out that the goal is not handbook-clutching, it's empowered employees who are proud of their culture.

CODE MOMENT 9: TORY AND THE TEN SHEETS OF COPY PAPER

Tory works in data analytics for SportsCo, an e-commerce company that puts sports team logos on items like backpacks and coffee mugs. She loves her job and gets high marks from her manager. Tory just finished an analysis of winter clothing purchasing patterns from the SportsCo customer database, including a spreadsheet of the top 1,000 buyers by spend in cold-weather states, along with their addresses and emails. Marketing plans an email campaign selling team logo parkas, gloves, and hats.

Tory's sister Katy in Minneapolis has started a home business knitting beautiful, bulky sweaters with an unofficial version of football team logos. Katy is struggling to make ends meet.

After she sends her report to marketing, Tory prints out a copy, and three days later an envelope arrives at Katy's house. Tory has written on the cover, "Thought this would be helpful, and you can target these folks with an email to get sweater orders." Katy calls Tory. "This is awesome—you won't get in trouble for sending this, will you?"

"Of course not. I had to do this report anyway, and nobody cares about ten sheets of copy paper. I saw my boss's poker party invitations on the copy machine last week."

Is there a flag on the field for Tory?

For discussion, see appendix, page 254.

CODE MOMENT 10: WIN-WIN-WIN, OR NO GOOD DEED GOES UNPUNISHED?

You are the president of a midsized bank and active in your community. Your friend and neighbor wants to get his house set up with new A/V equipment and Internet. The neighbor asks if you know anyone good. "I know exactly who you need," you tell him. "I've got a really terrific IT support person on my team, and I'll check with her about when she might be able to do it."

"Fantastic!" your neighbor says. "I'm happy to pay her, I just want someone competent."

"No charge, happy to help you out," you say, although you intend to pay the IT tech yourself.

Moonlighting brokered by the boss. What could go wrong?

For discussion, see appendix, page 256.

7

The welcome mat for complaints:
A clear and safe reporting process

Reporting an integrity violation can feel fraught with risk. Companies must create a sense of trust so that if and when an employee reports a violation of the code of ethics, the reporter will be treated with respect, and management will investigate the accusation fairly rather than sweep the issue under the rug. Employees always worry about retaliation for reporting; the company must make clear that retaliation is unacceptable, and encourage those who report violations to alert the ethics team if they believe retaliation is occurring.

Early in my tenure at Airbnb, our COO, Belinda Johnson, and I were talking about ethical violations and how it was important to encourage reporting. After I left our meeting, she turned to her laptop and began searching our intranet for the existing options employees had if they experienced or witnessed something that appeared to be a violation. She knew we had online resources, but after about fifteen minutes, she still could not find an option or link that seemed like the obvious place to start. She called me back in and said, "Rob, if I can't find the right place to report an ethics violation, how can we expect employees to make these reports?"

Belinda was right. We had posted resources and recommended a reporting process, but it was buried in other material from the human resources department and difficult to find. We immediately went to work fixing that, and we prominently placed a box with large type at the top of our internal company home page so employees could see exactly where to go.

A very simple exercise that can help both leaders and employees think about the topic of this chapter is to go back and take a look at the list of the most common integrity violations. Now, ask yourself, If I was victimized or if I observed one of these violations, where would I turn? Whom would I call? What resources would I have?

Every employee of your company should be able to immediately answer these questions. The path to reporting a violation should be worked into all your communication messages on integrity.

Practically speaking, however, the answer to where an employee should turn will depend somewhat on the size and age of the company, and whether the company is private or publicly held. For example, a start-up may not yet have an in-house legal team or even a formal human resources function. But just because all employees are within sight of one another in the apocryphal "garage," that doesn't mean you won't encounter ethics issues or behavior that is inappropriate or even illegal—and that can ruin your chance at success before you even get going. Fraud, misrepresentation of the company's technology to investors, skirting regulations, sexual harassment, and other potential problems can materialize at any stage of a company's growth.

Part of the exhilaration of joining a start-up is that employees tend to have a "do what it takes" mind-set. That's great if the sentiment refers to working long hours, pitching in on tasks and projects outside your strict job scope, and doing more with less. I have a ton of respect for companies who have changed the world with aggressive thinking and lightning execution. But part of the risk of working for a start-up is the need to assess whether the CEO or founders have sufficient maturity and integrity to "do what it takes" when difficult ethical dilemmas develop. Will they act in the best interest of both the company and employees like you when crises erupt?

Sadly, Theranos once again is a poster child for how not to establish trust. Its leaders had a "shoot the messenger" posture toward employees surfacing issues. John Carreyrou's book about the company suggested that paranoia and secrecy ran so high in Theranos, and the CEO seemed to hold the board in such thrall, that employees could trust no one and couldn't share their concerns with anyone until journalists got wind of the story. This culture allowed the deceit to continue long past the time that any impropri-eties otherwise might have been exposed. Theranos also demonstrated that it's not just about "Will someone get caught?" or "Will outsiders find out about integrity violations?" but it's also about the culture you're building. High-integrity employees who perceive a tolerance for bad behavior on a leadership team will be eliminated or will choose to leave, as a number of Theranos employees did. "Many people did speak up and found it did not make a difference. They were overlooked, shut down, or terminated," ob-serves Ann Skeet, senior director of leadership ethics at the Markkula Cen-ter, which has devoted considerable attention to the Theranos case because of the lessons it teaches on a number of important integrity issues.[1] These explorations are important, and devoting serious attention to understand-ing the conditions that create Code Red scandals may be paying off. Adds Markkula's Donald Heider, "We're hearing from VCs that they are starting to look at ethics among founders as a predictor of success."

◆

As a company matures, it will add a legal team and human resource lead-ership, two obvious functions below the CEO level where employees can turn to report something overtly illegal, questionable, or related to the health and safety of workplaces. But just knowing you *can* file a complaint with HR or legal is very different from having the company explicitly en-courage you to report something inappropriate and giving you a specific path to do that.

At Airbnb, after Belinda's frustrating attempt to find our reporting process, I spent hours and multiple meetings with the team that designs and maintains our intranet to ensure that there was a prominent link to our ethics resources on the front page of our web portal. I wanted the largest font possible and a clear design for presenting our hotline (which offers an anonymous option for reporting issues) and our email address for ethics, which I review personally along with a team in legal and all of our ethics advisors.

This reflects my belief that companies that want a culture of integrity must make the process of getting timely guidance and reporting viola-tions of the code easy, straightforward, safe, and clear. You cannot just say, "It's your job, employees, to tell us what's going on," but then ignore the barriers to them doing that.

In the case of a public company, there are some other required layers of regulation and process, although thoughtful private companies are also adopting these best practices. First, public companies must maintain a hotline that allows employees to report inappropriate behavior in a confidential, anonymous way without going through their manager. The obvious reason is that when a manager is an employee's only resource and it's the manager who is behaving inappropriately, it puts the employee in an impossible position.

We have a hotline at Airbnb, and we get a wide variety of reports, some anonymous, some not. As I said, these reports address a range of issues, from accusations of conflict of interest to a manager having an inappropriate relationship with a direct report to whether a gift might violate the rules. We take each and every one seriously.

One frustration for me is that while I respect the intention, I don't think anonymous hotlines are a sufficient solution, standing alone, for employees to report sexual harassment. If you are a victim of sexual harassment and you report it anonymously, the company is now on notice, and its only avenue to investigate is to talk with the accused, who in most cases will deny that the harassment has occurred. So now what happens? Well, the accused knows who he or she has been interacting with and may retaliate immediately against the victim (negative performance reviews, transfer to a less desirable project, or even personal threats); however, the company doesn't know who the victim is, so it can't intervene or prevent that type of behavior.

Companies are beginning to explore other means to learn about inappropriate behavior in the workplace. For example, we at Airbnb are experimenting with a new app-based system for employees called Vault Platform that allows them to create a record in real time of what they're experiencing. Initially, it is just for them to use to collect details that might be helpful later if they decide to report the harasser. The app gives the person an option, however, to release their record to the company only if they're not the first or only ones to be reporting the same harasser. The technology "connects the dots," enabling people to have strength in numbers, and companies to be notified of repeating patterns of harm. Victims of harassment are often terrified of getting into a he said/she said situation, but once they learn that corroborating evidence of the person's behavior exists, they are more willing to go forward.

At the NBA, Adam Silver is making sure his reporting process does not insulate powerful figures inside team management. He has created a league-wide hotline for any employee anywhere to report workplace misconduct. Complaints are reviewed by an independent party who reports directly to the NBA's audit committee, not to team presidents or owners. The point is to make sure leaders who themselves may be engaged in misconduct are not in a position to shut down an inquiry or retaliate or threaten the reporter and block an investigation before it even begins.

Other companies have addressed challenges with reporting by creating an ombudsperson's office that employees can call or visit to talk about these same kinds of issues. This is intended as a confidential resource for the employee. The company pays for the service, but it does not by design have access to the identities of employees who seek advice or report a violation. There is a very important reason for that confidentiality, so I want to unpack several of the issues here.

Today, once a company learns (from any avenue) about a situation that represents a threat to its reputation or the integrity of its brand, it must investigate the situation and resolve it. The general counsel is the company's attorney and provides legal advice to executives, managers, and employees for the purpose of advancing the interests of the company and protecting the company from liability. But to be very clear, the GC is not the company's *employees'* attorney, and it would be unethical and unprofessional for the GC to have an "off-the-record" conversation with any employee to advise them how to proceed if they felt they had been harmed in any way at work.

A number of times in my career, colleagues have come to me for advice, saying they would like to speak to me confidentially. In my role as GC, I had an ethical obligation to stop them and remind them that as an attorney for the company I cannot promise confidentiality to any employee of the company. In theory, I have a duty to protect the company's interests by acting on anything that represents a threat to the company that any employee, even the CEO, tells me about.

A few have replied, "Oh, don't worry, this has nothing to do with the company or my work, this is a personal issue." Same answer: "I can talk with you, but I can't promise you confidentiality or that I won't take action based on what you tell me." It's my duty to broadly interpret what protecting the company's interests means. Anything that might be embarrassing or call into question the integrity or judgment of any senior executive or person associated with the company in any way could impact our brand. I might be obligated to recommend that the CEO or board take serious measures, including termination and publicly disclaiming prior corporate knowledge of an act or certain behavior.

Sadly, there are many examples I could cite of supposed non-work-related personal behavior with enormous impact on a brand. Remember smiling Jared Fogle, the former Subway spokesperson who assured people they could lose weight by eating sandwiches? As I write this, he is serving prison time for distribution of child pornography and sex acts with minors. Subway's high-profile brand spokesman's criminal "private life" caused a full-scale Code Red for the company.

◆

So, with some of these issues as a backdrop, here's a hypothetical example to explain why the idea of an independent third-party resource or ombudsperson has some appeal to me.

Let's say a marketing manager, Kristen, heads to a bar with three friends on a Saturday night. She walks in and immediately sees a male colleague, Kevin, doing shots with several guys playing darts. Kristen believes Kevin is her boss's favorite on their work team.

Kevin sees her and literally stumbles over, wrapping her in a big, sloppy hug. "Krish, come meet my frennns." Kristen takes a step back. "Ah, thanks anyway, Kev. I'm with some friends, too. Good to see you though, have fun." Kevin frowns, "Now see . . . see . . . that's what I was juss sayin' the other day to Bill [their manager]. I'd ask you out—but, well, you're kind of stuck-up. See yaaaaaaaa." He turns and rejoins the dart game.

Kristen is offended and angry. Kevin was not only insulting and physically inappropriate—he referenced their manager Bill in a way that suggests they talk about her. Should she report him? To a manager he's friends with? She's conflicted. She's worried that taking action could backfire on her in terms of her performance review or assignments. Should she just let it go?

Sunday morning, she gets an email from Kevin. "Kristen, I had way too much to drink last night and I was out of line. I should never have spoken to you like that. I apologize."

Is Kevin sincere or just trying to avoid getting in trouble? Did he already discuss what happened with Bill? What should she do next? She makes a list of her options.

1. Do nothing.
2. Confront Kevin at work and tell him what he did was offensive and if he ever does anything like that again, she'll turn him in.
3. Talk to Bill about Kevin's behavior in the bar.
4. Call an ethics advisor to get help figuring this out.
5. File an official complaint with human resources or legal, describing exactly what happened in the bar.
6. Report Kevin anonymously on the company's hotline for "being verbally disrespectful and inappropriately touching a colleague."

Sexual harassment is not only an emotional and humiliating incident for a victim, but the whole mess is compounded by the challenge of navigating through the right response. It's Kristen's right to accept his apology and do nothing . . . or tell Kevin she was offended . . . or turn him in. It's appropriate to talk to her manager—but also understandably intimidating if she believes he and Kevin are friends, and worrisome since the manager would have an obligation to report the matter to HR. What should she do? To whom should she turn for advice?

If the company had a neutral, third-party reporting resource like an ombudsperson, someone who understands the code of ethics, the law, and can be sympathetic to her situation . . . *and who does not have the same duty the company has to act on what she reports,* Kristen could discuss her options and fears more freely. Together they might create a plan for her to go forward that fully considers the possible consequences. The resource can help her understand her rights and what will likely happen next if she files a complaint. Since this interaction does not represent official notice to the company, it creates some breathing room and space to think. If she does not wish to proceed, she does not have to. If she does, she will go into it eyes wide open.

✦

Reid Hoffman's venture firm Greylock Partners uses a third-party reporting mechanism to handle reports about sexual harassment. Reid explained to me that he is sensitive to sexual harassment issues based on an experience he had early in his career when he was a senior executive at PayPal. He tells a story about how a work colleague asked if she could discuss a situation with him, with the caveat that he must explicitly promise her he would not act on it. He agreed. She then related that an employee at the company was being sexually harassed by her manager—the manager was sending sexually explicit texts to her, asking her to come over to his house naked. She showed Reid a copy of the texts, and Reid was both concerned and angry, but he felt powerless to do anything because he had given his colleague his word that he would not act on it. He ultimately decided to put a note in the manager's file saying that he had a bad experience with the manager and not to promote him. "In retrospect, of course, that was a mistake. I realized going forward I can never agree to accept information in complete confidence like that, and looking back on it now, I actually wish I had broken my word and fired the manager."

These days, Greylock contracts with an independent organization that receives calls or complaints about sexual harassment or any kind of ethics issue from a hotline. An employee does not have to give his or her name, but after receiving the details of the report from the third-party organization, Greylock commits to investigate the matter and report findings back. If the third party does not feel the company has done an appropriate job investigating or acting on the information after a certain amount of time, it is free to release the existence of a report publicly. Says Reid, "That holds our feet to the fire."

I respect Reid's commitment to leaning in and grappling with solutions to these difficult situations. Reid took an additional step in 2017 and called on venture capitalists to take what he calls a "Decency Pledge,"[2] which holds adherents to the same standards a company's executive should in terms of, for example, prohibiting the pursuit of sexual relationships with entrepreneurs the VC is engaged in a business relationship with. It was controversial, with some VCs suggesting that existing law was sufficient and that it was impossible to codify character, but I support any effort to stimulate conversations about these difficult subjects.

Going forward, I suspect we're going to see a number of creative new ideas for making it easier and less risky for employees to report inappropriate behavior of many kinds. It's the right thing to do—and it's easier to try and solve problems before they blow up and get much worse. Which leads me to one consequence of *not* creating a good reporting process: whistleblowing.

Whistleblowing

An important motivation for creating a respected and trusted reporting process inside your company is to avoid "whistleblowing." Whistleblowers tend to report their concerns outside the company, perhaps to regulators or as part of a civil lawsuit, or to the media. For a company, an aggressive whistleblower who has bypassed your internal process or tried it and found it inadequate can trigger a Code Red.

Society has a vested interest in encouraging certain kinds of whistleblowing. If you work for an aviation contractor and discover that the company is skirting safety standards for engine parts or is falsifying inspections, then it's in the public interest that you come forward with that information. You may have signed confidentiality agreements at work, but as a society we want to encourage reporting matters where there is a serious and immediate risk to public safety. We are seeing whistleblower cases in the data arena as well, such as employees reporting that their employers are using private customer data improperly.

For example, in July 2019, the global consumer goods company RB Group entered into a $1.4 billion civil settlement and a non-prosecution agreement with the U.S. Department of Justice. Six whistleblowers had filed a report stating that the company was using illicit tactics to promote its prescription drug Suboxone, including a special "Here to Help" hotline whose real purpose was to send patients seeking help with addictions to doctors willing to prescribe their drug to more patients than allowed by federal law. The company, which denies allegations of wrongful conduct, spun off the division responsible for Suboxone, and now that entity is facing criminal charges in a trial scheduled for 2020.[3]

I support principled whistleblowing. It's an important check on devious and dangerous practices. But what I'm focused on is encouraging companies to behave in a more ethical manner to employees who raise legitimate issues so they can be addressed and solved before whistleblowing is the only option that's left. A common lament of whistleblowers is that they attempted to report a problem but were shut down, transferred, retaliated against, shamed, or ostracized for doing that.

However, just as there are no perfect ethics officers, there are no perfect whistleblowers. Some individuals have complicated agendas for wanting to report certain acts, or they have incomplete information, or it's not clear whether their accusations are correct. Whistleblowers in the Suboxone case, for example, are due to share 15–25 percent of the settlement paid by RB Group.[4] One legal strategy some companies use to defend themselves is to impugn whistleblowers' intentions and suggest they exploited the situation for personal benefit instead of trying to resolve it using proper channels. That's why you need more than just a reporting process—it must be yoked to a thorough and fair investigation. Together, they will improve the odds that the behavior in question will be fairly examined and that individuals with legitimate concerns will not have to publicly air their complaints to initiate appropriate action.

When an employee shines a light on an ethical violation, your company's fundamental values will be tested. Focusing on discrediting a whistleblower is generally not the path of integrity. Remember: even an imperfect person may have identified a legitimate problem or issue that should be fixed, not papered over. What is the right thing to do? Can you resist shooting the messenger in favor of fixing the problem? In my opinion, a company with integrity will seek the truth, not a cover-up. And it will look for opportunities to celebrate employees who raise ethical and legal issues in good faith.

Investigations

So, you've received a report of an ethics violation. Now what?

The thought of a formal investigation at work is scary to most people, whether they are reporting inappropriate behavior or accused of it. Stressful scenarios run through their heads—that time they texted their partner an intimate joke or photograph using their company phone . . . the fear that a colleague competing for a promotion will exaggerate facts to suit his or her agenda . . . the concern that an email or a comment in a meeting will be taken out of context. What will investigators find? Will there be a chance to explain?

Once an accusation is made, the company must investigate it. Depending on the size of a company, an investigation can take different forms. My first rule is that the investigation itself must have integrity. In a ten-person start-up or small business, it will likely fall to the company's CEO or owner to sit down with involved parties and directly discuss an accusation. That is a difficult and distracting conversation nobody wants to have. But if you ignore the issue or take a side without looking at the evidence, you are undermining your culture before you've barely begun. At a larger company, the CEO or GC may hire a team of investigators to look into an accusation, especially if it represents a significant brand threat. My advice is: take all accusations seriously and make an effort to seek the truth, not jump to conclusions.

What will the investigators look at? How will they proceed? Trained investigators will mine different sources: the digital trail and personnel files for any red flags from past complaints or reports; suspicious expense account or budget items; and, eventually, in-person interviews. But in any given case, how they proceed depends on the offense. An anonymous tip that a senior manager in an overseas office bribed a local official would, if true, be catastrophic for a company. Before confronting the manager, the investigating team would look at emails, the manager's progress reports, the feedback the manager has given her or his manager, and any unusual budget or expense account items that seemed related to cash, for example. Then the team would likely call in the manager to discuss the accusation while simultaneously talking with the manager's direct reports so that there is no time to craft a common story line.

Alternatively, another report may be about something that is not illegal, but, rather, offensive and in violation of company policy. For example, a company may learn that some employees are online friends with an executive who regularly posts jokes and photographs that denigrate women, such as female political candidates, in his social media account. An employee who has seen the posts reports that she is offended by images ridiculing women candidates as shrill or clueless.

Wait, isn't this a free speech issue?

If all employees in a company must agree to abide by a code of ethics, which states that they understand that the company does not allow gender-based discrimination and that speaking in a disrespectful way in public violates the code, then the executive has broken that compact. If the company doesn't have permission to view the account, it should talk to the executive and ask if the report is true. If the executive denies it but refuses to provide access to the account, that would not bode well for his credibility. If the company determines with certainty that the accusation is false, on the other hand, it should then investigate the accuser and try to discern his or her motives. A false accusation is an integrity violation. However, if the executive opens the account for review and the reported behavior is true, there would be serious consequences.

This example is reasonably straightforward. But I would be lying if I said that all investigations are so easy to sort. Sometimes an accusation is serious but speaks to behavior that is somewhat vague, or the only evidence hinges on the testimony of other individuals who may be friends or in competition with the accused. Sometimes, an anonymous accusation is made with very little evidence at all, just a voicemail left on a recorded line like, "Ronald in transportation is getting kickbacks from our fuel supplier." In difficult cases, it comes down to keeping an open mind and investigating in a balanced way.

Suppose a company receives a report that a manager is a bully, that she ridicules employees, insults their intelligence in meetings, and pits team members against one another by isolating them and grilling them about other employees' loyalty and work habits. An alleged victim of her bullying, who recently received a poor performance evaluation, reports the situation and says her confidence has been ruined by a deliberate effort by the manager to try to make her unhappy so she'll quit.

Most codes voice the value of a respectful workplace. Bullying is disrespectful and involves public shaming and criticism, ostracizing an individual from group activities, perhaps even conspiracy to sabotage someone. The trouble is, in an intense workplace where employees sometimes are not performing to expectations, where does constructive criticism end and bullying begin? What feels like bullying to one person is considered "enforcing high standards" or "blunt feedback" to another. Perceptions of bullying can be tied to race and gender of the alleged perpetrator. There can be cultural issues around bullying that complicate a person's perception of an insult.

Considerable media attention has been paid in recent years to bullying in schools. The workplace is not the playground, however, and managers expected to deliver results may be terse or critical or even visibly angry if a team is not performing to plan—reactions that, on their own, are not integrity violations. Also, because bullying is subjective, the whole concept creates ambiguity that inspires other undesirable behavior. Colleagues may already have taken sides. In interviews with investigators, they may exaggerate or make assumptive leaps that aren't based on much evidence. They may deliberately use what they say in an investigation to curry favor with the team leader or undermine a colleague they didn't like anyway.

This is a difficult subject, and each case demands a full and fair investigation, but even that may not produce concrete evidence to act on. It may be that a manager needs some coaching in how to motivate and create a productive and supportive environment, but that is different from committing an integrity violation.

You also need to balance rigor with humanity. The scandals that have plagued tech companies have revealed that employees who believe in their companies' missions and have been working hard to make the company a success sometimes put on ethical blinders. They want to believe that accusers are not "team players" and have suspect motives or that an indiscretion involving a trusted and valued performer is less virulent than it appears. They want to blame the media for "stirring up trouble." These responses have led to stacked investigations designed to exonerate someone, not to illuminate a situation; they also can prompt a rush to judgment that there is no problem. Using the letter of the law to get an outcome you know you wanted going in, or "going easy" because you like the accused, undermines trust and faith in leadership.

Investigations are serious and stressful for all involved, and sometimes they may need to be deployed quickly. A large corporation will likely have on-staff investigators, managed or directed by the legal department. Even smaller companies would do well to think in advance about the resources they have to conduct an investigation in an emergency, which could be as simple as identifying or retaining an attorney who could be consulted to recommend a trained investigator available for hire. What you don't want to do is assign a company insider who is unskilled at investigations, as you run the risk of a biased, clumsy, or incomplete effort.

You may also need to instigate an investigation if there are external accusations of unethical or improper behavior. I recently had an interesting conversation about investigations with a former director at the fast-food chain Wendy's, which faced a Code Red in March 2005 when a customer eating in a Northern California Wendy's claimed she had opened a container of chili and, after she began eating, found a human finger in it.

A lapse of food-handling safety of that magnitude threatened catastrophic damage to Wendy's brand, and when the item the customer said she found in her chili was confirmed to literally be a human finger, sales did initially drop. Over the next month, Wendy's said it was losing $1 million per day in sales, with Northern California franchises seeing drops of 20–50 percent.[5]

To Wendy's operations executives, the scenario the customer described seemed impossible. The company announced a $50,000 reward for any evidence of where the finger came from, and later doubled it. But Wendy's also assigned a team of investigators to comb every step of the supply chain that delivered chili to the specific store, beginning with the ingredient suppliers, through transportation providers, packagers, chefs, and store employees. The team tracked back every possible step, and it administered lie detector tests to employees.

After a thorough investigation, Wendy's team was confident: no employee or supplier anywhere along that chain had lost a finger. It was impossible for this to be a work- or process-related contamination. Meanwhile, after the customer who ordered the chili retained a lawyer, reporters looking into the accusation discovered that the accuser had a history of lawsuits and had previously filed claims against another fast-food chain for supposedly contaminated food. Police investigators eventually discovered that the fingertip belonged to someone the customer who said she found the finger knew. It had been accidentally severed at work by a truck tailgate. The accusing customer and her husband, who had been part of the scheme, eventually pled guilty to conspiring to commit fraud and attempted grand theft, and they went to prison.

No company could ever prepare for every possible con artist plot or employee indiscretion, but as the chili hoax shows, anticipating that you may need a full and fair investigation on short order is a good idea.

CODE MOMENT 11: ON THE GLASS

You manage the ethics advisors at your company. First thing on a Monday morning, an advisor comes in and shuts the door. She says that she overheard a conversation between two women she could not identify while she was in a bathroom stall. One said, "I went to make a photocopy today, and on the glass was an agreement between Trevor Jones [a high-level executive], and

Louise Crawford [his administrative assistant]. He is loaning her $100,000 with repayment to be 'mutually agreed upon over the next five years.'" Then the other said, "Are you kidding me? Louise is late every morning and he never seems to care, but when anyone on the team is late, he always makes a comment. Trevor is such a jerk. I'll bet you 20 bucks he is sleeping with her."

Well, that sounds messy. What should you do?

For discussion see appendix, page 258.

CODE MOMENT 12: BLAME IT ON RIO

Elliott runs international operations for a pharmaceutical firm based in Miami and has always traveled extensively. It turns out that Elliott has two families: a wife and twin daughters who live in Miami, and a companion and a son in Brazil. Brazil companion knows about Miami wife. Miami wife does not know about Brazil companion.

Elliott has legitimate business reasons to travel to Brazil, but lately he has been advocating that his company expand its operations there even more. He's said he wants to spend half his time there. He's made a good business case to do that, and the plant there has been productive and efficient.

Elliott's longtime rival Stewart gets a tip that Elliott has a second family in Brazil, and that Elliott's U.S. family is in the dark. Stewart has also learned that a small group of Elliott's direct reports know about his two families and are covering for him. Stewart arranges a meeting with the general counsel, to whom he suggests that Elliott's first priority is having a business excuse to fly to Brazil and support his second family on the company's tab, and that there are better expansion opportunities elsewhere.

Carnaval is much more fun than sorting this out. Now what?

For discussion see appendix, page 261.

8

When the other shoe drops: Creating appropriate consequences for integrity violations

The consequences for an ethics violation must reflect a thoughtful and intentional process that employees perceive as fair. Both "looking the other way" when a high-value employee makes a mistake and unrealistic "zero-tolerance" policies can undermine a company's integrity.

My legal career began at the age of 22 when I went to work for Judge Richard L. Williams in Alexandria, Virginia. The late Judge Williams was a federal trial court judge who ruled the courtroom with a husky southern drawl and a colorful, opinionated demeanor. "I'm not going to let you punish my juries with long speeches," he'd warn lawyers. Repeat a question, and the judge would cut off an attorney with a fast "Asked and answered—the jury heard it the first time." And if the defense or prosecution tried to argue with one of his rulings, Judge Williams would tell him to "head out the door and take a left," referring to the road outside the courtroom that led to Richmond, Virginia, where the Fourth Circuit heard appeals. Judge Williams was smart, and I admired his deep understanding of trial courts and his commitment to justice.

That isn't to say that I always agreed with him. On Friday mornings we handled criminal motions, and there were always a few sentencings on the docket. Sentencings were stressful for everyone, with victims, case agents, and families of defendants all in court together. Prosecutors often recited unpleasant details and consequences of the crimes and pushed for sentences sometimes exceeding 10 or 20 years. Defense attorneys tried to emphasize a defendant's limited criminal history and good deeds. There was a powerful silence as the judge would announce: "I hereby sentence you to serve a term of imprisonment of . . ." Somber federal marshals would lead away the defendant as family members sometimes cried out or slumped against each other, devastated.

Toward the end of my year with Judge Williams, he faced a white-collar defendant one Friday who (at least in my eyes) had committed a serious crime related to national security. But Judge Williams only gave him probation, which was startling to me. I saw the prosecutor clench his jaw, while the defendant's lawyer turned to his client with raised eyebrows. Neither attorney saw this coming, and neither did I.

When we went back into chambers, I casually asked the judge, "Why did you only give probation?"

"Because I'm not some mean, hard-assed son-of-a-bitch," he growled. We had a great relationship, but his body language suggested that the conversation was over.

On that day, Judge Williams, someone I had tremendous respect for, did something that I didn't understand at all. He never told me what triggered that particular sentence or his reaction to my question. I fully understood that there were good reasons for judges to have some discretion in sentencing—two defendants convicted of the same offense may have had very different motives, mental capacities, or prior criminal records. But as a young and still idealistic lawyer, it bothered me to think that the system could be that capricious.

My judge was not alone in delivering punishments that people found too lenient or too harsh at times. And soon after my clerkship, Congress created federal sentencing guidelines. They scored crimes and limited judges to choosing punishments within a range. The concept made sense to me and was designed to ensure the fairness and integrity of every element of the process, including investigations, interrogations, the handling and presentation of evidence, court procedures, and impartiality of judges and juries.

So did the guidelines correct injustices? Some. But later, as a federal prosecutor, I saw many individuals suffer unfairly because those same sentencing guidelines were too rigid. That frustration in part is what drove me to the corporate world—where I'm still committed to finding the right balance between strict rules, mitigating circumstances, business brand protection, and a culture based on Intentional Integrity that everyone can be proud of. It's not easy.

A ladder of possible consequences

In the corporate world, disciplining an employee for a code violation is a necessary part of the integrity process. And I'll be honest: it's my least favorite part. While it's fun and energizing to write a code of ethics and feel like you are shaping a great company where everyone will be proud to work, it can be infuriating, frustrating, and sad when someone violates that code. Sometimes people, for a wide variety of reasons, can make consequential mistakes that cost them their jobs, put their families' financial stability in jeopardy, and create a permanent stain on their reputations—and the company's as well. But you have to respond, or your code will have no credibility. You'll fail as a leader, and the people who follow the rules will suffer.

Companies have much more discretion than federal judges. There is a basic ascending ladder of disciplinary actions most HR teams recommend: verbal warning, written warning, suspension, demotion, termination. But the company is not obligated to start at any one step—or do anything at all unless the offense violated certain laws. Occasionally, in the midst of trying to sort out a violation of the rules, a company will even deem an outdated policy to be inappropriate for the current business or cultural climate or its stage of growth and decide to change the policy or omit it completely from the code.

That said, if the consequences assigned to an integrity violation are not themselves perceived to have a fundamental integrity and fairness, it will undermine the entire system. If you can't explain the rationale for why two employees received very different consequences for the same mistake, your employees will become disillusioned—and you may end up in court yourself.

Different contexts

There are important differences between the criminal justice system and the system in place for enforcing company rules. For one thing, with limited exceptions, American criminal justice happens in public; all interested parties, including the media, can observe a trial.

Conversely, most corporate investigations and the assignment of consequences happen in private. When organizations publish a code of ethics, they lay out rules and policies. During an investigation, employees who are questioned get a sense of what the company is trying to figure out, but even witnesses to an incident may not know the whole picture, and they may never know it. There are typically no transcripts of interviews or depositions that the company ever makes public.

Once the facts are collected, someone from either the general counsel's office or HR now has to consider, often in consultation with the affected employee's manager, what to do next. The code itself usually says something ominous but vague like "Violations will result in consequences up to and including termination." It is unlikely that individuals in a position to make decisions have the wisdom of a seasoned judge. They may try to be fair, but they are not impartial. Managers who feel their team's success depends on the employee who's in trouble may plead for leniency. In fact, as already noted, certain leaders, such as the general counsel, must explicitly put the good of the entire company first. In a company with Intentional Integrity, upholding the company's basic values is always the right thing to do, because the long-term good of the company depends on an ethical and honest culture. Companies with a shorter time horizon do not often see it that way.

In any event, leaders must make a decision. Perhaps the result will simply be a verbal warning. Perhaps the result will be termination. Perhaps it will be a transfer to another location or job. Perhaps the accused just returns to work, absolved of any culpability. There is no formal appeal process, but there may be additional consequences. For example, a victim of sexual harassment may be displeased with the outcome of an investigation and sue the company or insist on arbitration of a complaint. Or someone who is terminated for violating the code of ethics may be enraged that she or he has evidence that other employees received only a warning or a suspension for the same offense—and that person may file a formal complaint with the Equal Employment Opportunity Commission (EEOC). If there is an arbitration, the parties in many cases may be prohibited from discussing the settlement. That could mean that someone accused of a violation might be back at his desk and unable to talk about why an arbitrator found that an accusation was without merit. That may also mean that a devious predator who was exposed during this process could leave the company citing "personal reasons" and go on to a new job with a new employer who has no idea what has occurred.

I won't sugarcoat this. This process can be difficult and legally complex. There are companies that have used confidentiality clauses in what I would consider an unethical manner. And it can be even more challenging if you're the leader of a small business that might not have an HR department. You're the investigator, the judge, and the jury—and in a small company, everyone is watching.

Predators and devious actors may also exploit confidentiality elements and the current state of the law in challenging ways. I'll get to some ideas I have about how to inject more integrity into the process, but for right now, let's deal with the existing rules.

Seek the high ground

The primary guidance I have for those who find themselves in a position of having to work out appropriate consequences is: put on your ethics goggles and be intentional. At every stage of this process, every leader involved should strive for fairness and honesty and be able to understand how decisions come across not just to those involved but to other employees. Don't just do the minimum the law requires, and don't look for technicalities to fire difficult employees. Have a rationale for what you do and communicate that rationale. Let's work through a fictional example that will ground some of these ideas.

Milo has spent the last year working as a logistics manager for a family-owned furniture company with 150 employees. The company has a code of ethics that includes a $100 limit on gifts. Milo's administrative assistant, who is the nephew of the owner, mentioned to his uncle that Milo accepted a pair of Stanley Cup playoff tickets worth $500 from a shipping partner.

Clearly, Milo broke a rule.

The owner calls Milo's manager and learns that Milo is an excellent employee who has never had any other complaint lodged against him. Next, the owner talks to Milo, who says he realizes that he was supposed to read the ethics statement but he never got around to it. He relates that at his last company, there was no policy about gift limits, so he did not think to check when the tickets arrived. He apologizes and appears genuinely upset to learn that he violated this rule. Not only was Milo contrite, he offered to call the vendor who gave him the tickets and reimburse the value. His admin, the owner's nephew, admits that he didn't mention the policy to Milo when he saw the package arrive with the tickets. He's a hockey fan and was jealous. He says he has never seen Milo accept any other high-value gifts.

Milo screwed up here, no question. He was careless . . . but, far as I can tell, not devious. Based on these facts, I'd probably advise the owner to give Milo a stern verbal warning. I'd be sure to say if he did this again, there would be serious consequences. I'd reinforce that he must read the code of ethics. I would remind Milo that he should not retaliate in any way against his admin, who had every right and arguably a duty to report his violation. If he's already used the tickets, Milo probably should reimburse the shipper and explain that he made a mistake, in part so that the furniture company is not seen as a partner where high-value gifts are expected or appropriate.

This may seem lenient. The company has every right to "throw the book" at Milo . . . but he seems like a very good employee who made a mistake. Remember, he has not broken a law, he has only violated a private rule. The ball's in the employer's court. Ignorance of the code is no excuse, but Milo seems genuinely sorry, and I think he deserves a second chance.

Demonstrating compassion and thoughtfulness in this case might create an opportunity for the owner to remind everyone to reread the code of ethics, and thus prevent more problems. There is no mandated confidentiality involved in a verbal warning, and so Milo and his admin can talk about what happened, and others who might have questions can raise them as well.

So, let's call that scenario one. Now, let's alter the facts a bit.

What if Milo gets angry and defensive when asked about the tickets? What if Milo's admin says that this is the third or fourth time the shipper has sent Milo tickets for a sporting event or a concert and that he has warned him several times that accepting the tickets is a violation of company policy? What if Milo's manager says that Milo suggested the company shift more business to this shipper . . . just a few days after the shipper sent him the tickets?

In the second scenario, the results of the investigation suggest that

Milo has engineered a relationship with the shipping partner that is a conflict of interest. So here we have two identical offense reports, but the details elevate the second scenario to a much more serious level. They may suggest a deliberate bribe by an employee of the shipper, and they may be significant enough to warrant terminating Milo immediately.

Wow, harsh. Terminating an employee can be catastrophic for that individual, and it can hobble a work team. It should never be done lightly, but some offenses, like sexual harassment or fraud or bribery, are so serious that once you have established that they occurred, you must act decisively and signal that this is unacceptable behavior.

I have experienced this firsthand. I've worked with companies where a small number of employees have taken advantage of their position for their own enrichment—for example, issuing coupons intended for customers to themselves in some cases, giving them away to friends and family, and even changing coupons intended as small discounts to "50% off" and more. Unlike Milo in scenario one, these individuals did not "forget" to read the code of ethics, they deliberately and deviously exploited a program designed to encourage customer engagement and used it to benefit themselves. It was a betrayal of trust and corrosive to the company's values, and the punishment in these cases was harsh. They also led to internal work to strengthen controls and a communication effort to prevent future abuse.

The broader message

As Milo's example shows, the facts and details always matter. Intentions are important. Mistakes are different from premeditated acts. Investigations must be fair and full, approached objectively. But here's another example that shows how it's also important to properly set other employees' expectations following a code violation and punishment.

Joe works at a warehouse for a major electronics distributor. One evening, he forgets to lock the door, and the warehouse is robbed. You're in HR, and you investigate. Has Joe done this before? No. Is there any evidence he colluded with the thieves and deliberately left the door open? No. Turns out he came to work all week out of dedication even though he was battling a fever and a splitting headache. On Friday he was exhausted, left early, and forgot to ask someone else to lock up for him. Nonetheless, the act violated the company's policy about security, and there was a significant negative consequence to the company.

Joe's manager would have the right to suspend, demote, or fire Joe for leaving the door open. But under the circumstances, the manager argued that those responses were way too punitive. Joe was ill; this was an accident. Punishing Joe would not make sense. Joe got a warning to be more careful.

Fair enough. But every consequence delivered sets a precedent.

A month later, Katy forgets to lock the door. There is no robbery, but the manager discovers the mistake on his way home. The manager is furious and suspends Katy for a day without pay. In the manager's mind, this escalation of consequences is due to the need to drive home that employees must lock the door. But to Katy, and possibly to other employees, this seems unfair. Joe "only got a slap on the wrist" when he didn't lock up. Katy may view getting suspended as the final straw in a string of situations where her male employees have been treated better or suffered less severe consequences for making a mistake. She may file a complaint alleging workplace discrimination on the basis of sex. Another employee may cite the situation in her EEOC complaint about a supposedly sexist manager as well, saying the company habitually treats women more harshly. Attorneys for the plaintiffs in these cases may demand that the company hand over all files involving disciplinary actions so they can scour them for evidence of inconsistency.

One of the reasons I talk so much about inclusion being an important value in a workplace is that I believe it creates a healthy and empowered workforce. Diversity creates a breadth of thinking and experience that leads to better decisions and more open-minded assessment of opportunities. But when employees perceive unequal treatment, feel exclusion from an "in group" of popular employees, or perceive inconsistent consequences for the same mistake, they may feel that they are victims of discriminatory decisions and treatment.

That is why any significant personnel decision like a warning or disciplinary action should involve putting on those ethics goggles to imagine how the decision will look to all the relevant stakeholders—the employee or employees directly involved, the manager, work teammates and bystander employees, company partners, possibly even customers. One by one, as you review other possible perspectives, ask: How have we handled this in the past? Have we been thorough and fair in our investigation and analysis? Might we have any unconscious biases? Did we set expectations properly, or does the organization bear some responsibility for this mistake? If you do those things, I believe that you are building a high-integrity workforce with a strong sense of trust. If you ignore those factors, there will be negative consequences, including the possibility of being sued.

Let's go back to the warehouse. One reason there was a security breach is that one person was responsible for locking the door and setting the alarm. For a high-value facility, that strikes me as a flawed plan. After Joe's mistake, the manager could have called a meeting and asked for team input in terms of creating a backup plan. Perhaps the actual security team should double-check the locks within 15 minutes of closing each day. Perhaps a second person should confirm with the assigned person that the door is locked and notify security if that can't occur. Perhaps the warehouse needs an automatic system that locks the doors at a preprogrammed time.

In any case, given the threat of failing to secure the facility on an ongoing basis, the manager also should have said to the team after Joe made his mistake, "OK, folks, we're going to handle this with a warning, but the next time someone forgets to lock the door, the consequences will be much more serious." If he had done that, the unequal punishments would not seem like a mystery to other employees—the more serious consequence would have occurred regardless of who forgot to lock the door. In any punishment less than termination, always lay out how consequences will escalate if inappropriate behavior does not change. Even the appearance of inconsistently applying consequences can trigger mistrust, paranoia, or the suggestion that a code is being weaponized against employees for other reasons.

Ok, but what about . . .

The violations involved in the examples featuring Milo and Joe are fairly straightforward. Now I want to tackle two difficult issues where multiple corporate priorities conflict when you're trying to deal with a violation of the code of ethics. These kinds of cases can really test a company's commitment to integrity—and we've seen many, many companies fail that test.

I mentioned in chapter 3 that no company should have a provision in its code of ethics that it's not prepared to enforce against its most valuable employee. This idea must be incorporated into your value-setting exercise, and it applies to both the actual rule you write and your plan to react if the rule is broken. In that same chapter I talked about the "golden" employee phenomenon—the employee whom a senior leader likes and tends to shield from criticism or even consequences for violating a rule. One of the most difficult integrity dilemmas for a company is when that person exploits their status in full view of others. They essentially dare their manager or other leaders to look the other way and ignore bad behavior or acts that violate the code of ethics.

Let's explore this with the fictional outfit ThriftyCo. In its early, scrappy days, the company saved money by insisting that all employees, including the CEO, must fly coach for domestic travel. It's ten years later, and ThriftyCo is now global with over 2,000 employees. One of those employees is a sales executive named Jane, who generates the most sales revenue of anyone in the company. Jane regularly flies around both the country and the world, running from airports to sales presentations and back to airports. Jane has multicity serial trips, sometimes a mix of international and domestic flights, and she values the ability to catch up on sleep when she can so she is rested for meetings that occur shortly after landing. And by the way, Jane is five feet, eleven inches tall. Coach seating is literally painful for her, and after a year on the job, she began ignoring the rule. She books exclusively business-class seats at the company's expense, and her manager ignores it. Jane, after all, is a superstar.

However, another sales rep complains. The manager calls in Jane and says, "Jane, the time has come. I've looked the other way but now we've had a formal complaint. You have to go back to coach or pay for your own upgrades." Jane can't believe he's hassling her about this. She responds: "Well, our competitor's sales team flies business class. Maybe I should go work for them."

What's weighing on Jane's manager is that the CEO often tells reporters and Wall Street about how all ThriftyCo employees still fly coach. Because of that, the rep's actions technically undermine the brand. But he should have surfaced this issue, not just ignored it.

In theory, holding the line and insisting Jane fly coach might seem like the high road now. But it's also a dumb hill to die on. If you're tall, trust me, trying to sleep in a coach seat is not just unpleasant, it's painful. And if the manager loses this star producer over a few thousand dollars in travel expenses and preserving an old anecdote for the press, the entire company suffers.

On the other hand, if there are no consequences for breaking this rule, Jane may break other rules when it suits her. Plus, other employees will copy that behavior. By my reckoning, this rep is a valuable asset, and her request is not outrageous. I think that means the company should exercise the flexibility to pivot—either remove this rule from the general code and give managers the freedom to selectively approve upgraded travel or get creative and reframe the rule as an incentive. Perhaps it should make traveling business class a perk for employees *who exceed specific business goals.* Now instead of a code violation, Jane's travel perk is a reward and an incentive to others rather than an exception undermining the company's integrity. And if the marginal reps increase their sales to qualify as well, their productivity more than pays for the incremental cost.

The CEO may not like reframing what she says about coach travel, but she'd probably prefer it to losing this star sales rep. A rule that's right for one time and situation can outlive its utility. Changing it doesn't mean you lack integrity. At the end of the day, this blanket rule no longer advances the business goals of the company, and so the company needs to admit that and rethink it—not put on hypocritical blinders.

10X

Now, let's push a similar dilemma even further.

In Silicon Valley, you sometimes hear an expression: "He's a 10Xer" or "Pay her whatever you need to—she's the ultimate 10X." Steve Jobs once said that the dynamic range between an average software engineer and the best software engineer is 50–1, maybe even 100–1. What that literally means is that this computer programmer is more productive than 10, 50, or 100 average programmers. It's not just work ethic. A tiny fraction of coders have the unique combination of intelligence, focus, (sometimes) obsession, problem-solving skills, creativity, and determination that delivers extreme value. These unicorn-rare individuals demand, and receive, astronomical salaries.

I have a friend who has had a successful career managing and turning around tech companies. Many times, she has been brought in to "fix" teams at start-ups that have gone off track. More than once she has discovered that managers at these companies have been covering up accusations of inappropriate behavior, including sexual harassment—by a 10Xer.

Why? She explains: "10Xs are 10Xs because they're usually high IQ, low EQ; they're often incredibly socially awkward. Not all but most are men. They're not typically like the 'bro' partiers or trying to be jerks—they are often guys who don't know how to interact with women. They say and do inappropriate things, like they get fixated on somebody and won't stop bugging her." There is no question in her mind that women on the receiving end of this attention have every right to report the "bugging" and sexually charged comments as inappropriate. And there is no question that if a sexual assault occurred, she would immediately fire the offender. The problem for lower-level complaints is, "When companies have a 10X they bend the rules."

That's a candid insight you won't find many companies talking about in public. My friend admits that even she sometimes will work very hard to create a solution where the employee who has been victimized is supported and protected but the 10X stays and completes the project. "When you have a 10X, all bets are off. Their value is so high you figure out how to make it work. That's the reality when you're in survival mode."

Many companies just put on blinders or look the other way as long as they can. If the leadership of the company has Intentional Integrity, this scenario is a true nightmare. Any ethical person reads this and thinks, "That person should be fired immediately if they continue to behave disrespectfully to colleagues."

But here is what often happens in real life: The law says that the company cannot tolerate sexual harassment or foster a hostile work environment, but it does not say someone accused of inappropriate sexual overtures must be fired. In some start-ups, a 10X is the difference between success and failure. Firing that person could spell the end of the company, and everybody, including the target of the harasser's attention, could lose their jobs. However, the risk of keeping the harasser around is persistent discomfort and continued harassment of a victim, who could file a complaint with the EEOC or sue.

How do you go forward? I believe you have to be intentional and, I would argue, collaborative. You talk to the person who's been harassed; if the investigation supports it, you can issue a serious warning to the offender that the behavior must stop and the price of ignoring that will be termination (although this option does come with challenges). Meanwhile, you validate the victim's experience by saying, "Here is the situation, it was wrong, you should not have to put up with that. We are not going to do anything that harms your career or inconveniences you by moving your desk or office. We will move the harasser away from you. Is that a reasonable response and accommodation? What if we commit to watch his behavior closely for any sign that he is not appreciating the seriousness of what has happened? Yes, this employee is valuable, but so are you, and you have the right to feel safe and not be harassed at work." Going this route means that you risk criticism for being lenient toward the top employee, but it also commits you to acting if the bad behavior occurs again. There is risk regardless of what you do, but there must be a line that, if crossed, means the harasser has to go.

I haven't experienced having to manage a 10X problem in a company whose future depended on that person, but my friend who told me this story explained that in her experience very often the victim does not demand that the person be fired, she just wants the harassment to stop. She doesn't want to see the company go under. But even if you move the 10X as far away from her as possible, she also doesn't want to face the discomfort and sometimes awkward distraction of interacting with the 10X in the breakroom, the parking lot, or the hallways. Sometimes, my consulting friend says, she has made future bonuses or stock awards or other compensation for the accused harasser contingent on behaving appropriately. In most cases, she says these methods work, but sometimes they don't, and if the company truly is wholly dependent on one person, it often becomes clear that it's going to fail anyway.

Nobody feels good about this. It's a volatile and unpredictable situation involving individuals who are valuable assets but who themselves can be volatile and unpredictable.

These dilemmas are not just about sexual harassment. A friend of mine at another company was telling me about a truly genius 10X programmer there who nonetheless demonstrated a slew of distracting and bizarre personal behaviors in the workplace. For example, his phobias about fire were so extreme, he walked around his second floor office every day with a 25-foot length of rope coiled around his neck. He would tell anyone who would listen that he carried it so that if there was a fire he could lower himself out of a window—and they should not even think about asking to borrow his rope.

In a department store or a bank, an individual exhibiting that kind of behavior might be encouraged to seek counseling but would have to either stop distracting and upsetting colleagues or find another job. But the entire future of the software company rested on their 10X's talents. So the software company accommodated the behavior. I get it, but imagine if another employee—not a 10X—announced that she was so afraid of the birds outside her office window that she either needed a new office or had to work exclusively from home. If you go down the list of possible accommodations people might request, it may never end. And accusations that you're not being fair can tear your teams apart.

Can you move forward in these situations with integrity? It's not easy. But shareholders expect you to try. The most ethical course of action is to recognize areas of your company where the exceptional talent there could create difficult ethical dilemmas down the line. Be proactive—make special efforts up front to talk to that group about ethics and the rules. It's the proverbial ounce of prevention, and Duke behavior scientist Dan Ariely's research suggests that constantly reinforcing the importance of following the rules and being ethical increases the odds that employees will exhibit that behavior. It really does matter for an organization to connect the self-image of its employees' as good people to behaving with integrity.

What you don't want to do is just cross your fingers and hope it turns out OK.

Zero tolerance

One point I want to make about consequences involves a communications strategy that I would NOT recommend. Especially now in the #MeToo era, when there is a scandal, some companies will make a dramatic, public commitment to "zero tolerance" about integrity violations. These sorts of statements are tempting when a company wants to be seen and credited with opposing a certain type of improper behavior, and I understand that. But I caution against using language like this lightly because it can be hard to deliver on down the line, particularly in more nuanced situations. Too often companies make big, strong statements *instead* of taking immediate, serious steps to solve the problem.

In September 2018, hundreds of employees of McDonald's walked off their jobs during a busy lunchtime period to protest what a group of #MeToo activists said was McDonald's widespread tolerance of sexual harassment in both company-owned and franchise restaurants and offices. Although the corporation's code of ethics says it will "not tolerate" sexual harassment, and spokespeople have repeated that, women employees had filed EEOC complaints filled with graphic details of being harassed verbally and groped on the job by male workers, often as managers watched or chimed in. Some said they had been cornered in bathrooms and pressured to have sex. And when they made formal complaints, they said that not only was nothing done to the harassers, but the employees who reported the incidents were retaliated against and given reduced hours or more abuse. Subsequently, another 25 cases against McDonald's alleging similar abuses have been filed.[1]

McDonald's responded in an email about the walkout to *The Nation* that "there is no place for harassment or discrimination of any kind at McDonald's."

What does that mean, exactly? Corporate spokespeople say that the company has invested in additional training, is setting up a new hotline, and is reinforcing that managers should not allow harassment, sending out anti-harassment posters to all stores. The American Civil Liberties Union is supporting the employees in these suits and has been critical of McDonald's for not doing more.

Does putting up posters sound like not tolerating sexual harassment, or a firm commitment that there is "no place" for it? Workers say the abuses they've reported occurred at the time McDonald's says it was instituting new training—and that those same workers never heard about any sexual harassment training. So, what does "not tolerate" mean? Unless it moves to create real consequences for managers, McDonald's does not appear committed to eliminating harassment.

Maybe the complexity of franchise arrangements or other details legitimately limits what McDonald's can do quickly to respond to reports, but here is my point: regardless of whether your company is full of 10X unicorns or minimum-wage workers, employees have the right to expect a safe and harassment-free workplace.

If companies accept that it's meaningless to reach for quick sound-bite responses emphasizing "zero tolerance," they must conduct appropriate investigations and deliver meaningful consequences to those who break the rules. In my opinion, you must admit that this is a tough problem and commit to fixing it. You have to take concrete steps to investigate and act to protect your workers. Unless you fix the problem, you will still have furious employees walking out and taking their case to the media. This is not just a philosophical issue, it's a bottom-line threat. In the cities where McDonald's employees walked out, customers inclined to support #MeToo issues might happily discover they like Burger King's Whopper just as much as a Big Mac and never come back.

The long game

Companies can earn the trust of employees by enacting forward-looking changes to their approach to bad behavior in the workplace. One obvious example is in pre-employment agreements around dispute resolution. Historically, many companies have insisted that employees agree when they are hired that they will not file a lawsuit if they have a dispute, but rather commit to binding arbitration. Every company where I've worked, including Airbnb, insisted on agreeing to arbitration as a condition of employment.

Arbitration is typically a more cost-effective way to resolve disputes, and its less formal procedures can result in faster decisions than you would find in crowded court systems. Arbitration is also private—trials are informal and held out of the public eye, and that confidentiality often suits both the company and the complaining employee. Companies do not want their internal decisions dissected in court, potentially exposing them to embarrassing stories and ridicule; and depending on the issues, a complaining employee may appreciate the chance to avoid discussing private or embarrassing matters in a public forum.

But the #MeToo movement has exposed the other side of forced arbitration—it keeps sexual harassment cases "under wraps," and legal clauses prevent the victim, the accused, and the company from discussing the facts publicly. Even if the perpetrator is terminated, the details almost always are confidential. Sound familiar? This trifecta of confidentiality then releases the perpetrator back into the job market to find another position—and perhaps another victim, beginning the cycle anew.

In early 2019, Airbnb announced that it would no longer force employees into arbitration in sexual harassment or discrimination cases. Instead, the company simply asks that employees with a grievance in this area make a good-faith effort to resolve the matter with the company informally, and if they are not satisfied, they have the right to choose between arbitration or court. Months later California enacted a law banning these forced arbitration clauses, and although this law is widely believed to be unlawful as it conflicts with federal law that favors arbitration, it's clear that change is coming in this area.

There are several dynamics motivating the change in perspective about this. First, one of the persistent issues that has dogged institutions like the Catholic Church and the Boy Scouts of America is that accusations of illegal and inappropriate behavior were not only shelved and hushed up, but confidential dispositions meant that perpetrators were allowed to move on to other assignments or roles where they had the opportunity to victimize others. We have to come to grips with the fact that secrecy has enabled many accused of sexual misconduct to go to a new workplace and do it again.

Second, people need to be accountable for their actions. And companies need to be accountable for their actions. If we settle with a victim in our workplace, the victim deserves to be able to talk about it. While a public airing of a harassment case obviously will be disconcerting and perhaps embarrassing, there will be benefits associated with transparency. I actually believe it will deter harassment going forward.

Finally, doing something that's not in your immediate short-term interest builds trust, and, in my opinion, that is important. A company might have to publicly defend some lawsuits as a result of this move, and perhaps even take a hit if some bad behavior goes public. In the long run, I think, you're sending an important message to employees that they matter too, and that the company isn't going to take advantage of its leverage to force a concession around something so important.

Good cause

A second consequence-related shift I'm advocating for across business is focusing more attention to personal behavior clauses in employment contracts and board agreements.

High-value employees with clout—and high-powered attorneys—sometimes negotiate unusual clauses into their employment agreements related to many variables, from base salary to performance bonuses to parking spaces to idiosyncratic compensation like access to personal trainers. Sometimes the clauses, or negotiated exemptions from standard contract elements, can come back and bite a company.

For many years, for example, it was standard for employment contracts to include the stipulation that any severance payment due an employee would be voided if the individual were "terminated for cause," which is defined as committing acts of violence, abusing drugs or alcohol in public, committing sexual harassment, or engaging in other behavior embarrassing to a brand. In one of the most dramatic recent examples of termination for cause, in 2018 CBS's former CEO Les Moonves was denied $100 million or more in severance compensation after CBS announced that an investigation showed that he repeatedly and over many years violated the company's sexual harassment policies, which constituted termination for cause.[2]

But references to termination for cause have become watered down or removed entirely in many cases when highly sought-after employees and consultants refuse to sign contracts containing them. In part, the move away from those clauses, sometimes called "morals clauses," was a response to fears expressed by some men that it makes them vulnerable to false accusations by women who might blackmail them. Over the last twenty years, I've seen venture capitalists refuse to agree to morals clauses when they sign on to a board seat at a company. As a result, the VC can engage in all sorts of inappropriate behavior that, if made public, could be terribly embarrassing to the company. But contractually, the company is powerless to remove the director and may be stuck with the relationship unless the director agrees to step aside. I'm concerned that the main effect of losing these provisions has not been an increase in protection against false accusations but rather an empowerment to behave inappropriately without serious consequences.

We've seen executives receive a significant buyout when they're fired or when they leave a company after being accused of inappropriate behavior, though it appears to other employees as if they've suffered no consequences and in fact have been rewarded. As for boards, how can companies enforce a code of ethics—that in theory ultimately falls to the board to enforce—if board members won't agree to abide by its provisions themselves? There have been numerous examples of inappropriate behavior by venture capitalists toward entrepreneurs seeking funding as well as in other situations. In his "Decency Pledge" article, Reid Hoffman notes that "on a structural level, venture capitalists unfortunately have no HR department to prevent predatory and inappropriate behavior, and so try to characterize (falsely) their actions as innocent flirtatiousness or banter."[3] What's more, the structure of VC firms themselves means that powerful partners cannot easily be fired or removed without restructuring the entire firm.

I can appreciate that some fear liability, but as leaders, VCs and all board members need to commit to demonstrating the same integrity they expect to see from executives and employees of companies.

In the next chapter I'll explain another novel step we at Airbnb are taking that reinforces the importance of a code of ethics, transparency, and the consequences of violating it.

CODE MOMENT 13: PASSWORD PIRACY

Terry's a new hire to the security team at ProCo. One afternoon, Tina, the company's chief technology officer, invites Terry to join her in a conference room. Tina hands Terry a wallet card with a list of a ProCo competitor's customer database server addresses, as well as a username and password written on it.

Tina smiles grimly: "We have seen some posts on Blind that suggest these guys have been hacking us. One of our sales guys found this card. He did not steal it or buy it or ask anyone for it. That makes it fair game." She pushes a laptop toward Terry. "I want you to find some diner or coffee place on the other side of town with Wi-Fi. Use this laptop, and see if you can get in these databases and let me know what you find. Download anything that might be related to us, and also copy any directory you can find. Don't use it for anything else, and bring it back to me."

Terry stammers, "Have we called the FBI?"

"We will, but we need evidence. And we need to get it before they go in and seize everything." Tina stands up: "Don't let me down, Terry, you have a bright future. And don't talk about this with anyone; this is a highly confidential assignment. Not even your manager—you got that?"

Nobody said protecting the company's data was going to be easy . . . but how should Terry handle this mission?

For discussion, see appendix, page 264.

9

Check the canaries:
Monitoring the company culture
for signs of trouble

Intentional Integrity does not run on autopilot. Company leaders must embrace an ongoing process to make sure that Intentional Integrity policies are being implemented and interpreted in the spirit in which they were envisioned. They should monitor complaints and be proactive about investigating what might be ethical "hot spots" in a company. Companies also should consider involving employees in a feedback loop about ethical dilemmas and resolutions.

The expression "canary in the coal mine" dates back to the early twentieth century, when British coal miners brought tiny cages holding canaries deep into the mines with them every day. Why canaries? Apparently the birds need lots of oxygen while flying at high altitudes, and they have evolved special air sacs that give them a boost when they inhale and exhale. That means they also double-dose any poisons they may breathe in. Miners were said to like how the birds talked and whistled to them as they worked. If a canary's tune changed or it passed out, it was an early warning that CO_2 or methane levels were rising—and the miners should run for their lives.[1]

Smart companies are always looking for alarms like those canaries that can tip them off to and fix ethics challenges before they reach toxic levels. I've talked about some of the specific resources companies use:

- an anonymous telephone hotline where employees can report ethics issues without giving their name;

- an internal email address where a company can receive questions, reports of issues, and other communications about its policies;
- a cadre of volunteer employee ethics advisors that serves as both an information resource to employees and a feedback mechanism to help the company understand where it needs to invest more time and attention in education about the rules;
- software programs that are used by security and investigation teams that flag inappropriate access to customer data or prohibited websites or other behaviors that involve a company's platform and systems;
- and, of course, just normal complaints filed by employees to a human resources team member.

Together, the data from these systems can help you assess the integrity climate in your company. If the hotline receives an anonymous tip of drug dealing in a manufacturing plant, you face a huge brand threat, not to mention potential harm to rule-abiding employees as well as the alleged drug dealers. If several different individuals on a work team are asking questions about whether they can accept gifts from a specific vendor, you need to look into this "hot spot" before the vendor finds an employee who doesn't bother to ask about the gifts and secretly begins pushing the vendor's interests. If one manager is reported by several different employees who've experienced or witnessed inappropriate, sexually harassing behavior—well, that's a fainting canary.

The increase of less dramatic code violations can be an important integrity climate sensor as well. For example, I talked about the importance of not dismissing small acts, like using the company postal meter for personal mail. The excuse: "I work too many hours as it is, the least the company can do is save me half an hour I'd have to spend going to the post office to buy stamps." The cost may be insignificant in the great scheme of things. And it actually may make business sense for a *manager* to authorize suspending a specific policy in a given case. But there is a psychic and cultural cost when an individual decides he or she is going to use a personal calculus to balance out their frustration or unhappiness with the status quo. That's a slippery slope, and it can lead to more than just additional inappropriate acts by that person—it can also spread to others. Next thing you know, she or he tells a colleague, "You've put in 14 hours for the fifth day in a row—if I were you, I'd call my girlfriend and go have a nice meal and claim reimbursement for recruiting a candidate."

An individual or a team that adopts the rationalization of such unethical behavior is headed for trouble. Project commitment, compensation, working conditions—all of these things are legitimate and negotiable issues to discuss with a manager, but solving them with secretly subversive behavior is not OK. It violates the letter and spirit of the code of ethics. And by the way, this is not just a low-level problem: I am aware of a promising company that recently fired its CEO because, among other things, the individual hired a "special assistant," one of whose key deliverables, it turned out, was to buy artwork for the CEO's home. The excuse: the company would not exist without him and it has a vested interest in his happiness. Well, he was told, guess what: that is what salaries are for—so you can afford to buy things that benefit you and you alone.

✦

It's not hard to collect integrity-related data, but it takes courage to act when the data canaries start singing songs with ominous notes. Seems obvious, right? But as so many companies have shown, that's not a given.

One of the precipitating events that led to Uber spending many unhappy months in the headlines was a lengthy 2017 blog post by a former engineer named Susan Fowler titled "Reflecting on one very, very strange year at Uber." In it she wrote that on her very first official day on her team, her manager sent her a stream of messages that had zero to do with work. He was in an open relationship, he said, and his girlfriend was having an easy time finding new partners but he wasn't. He was trying to stay out of trouble at work, he said, but he couldn't help getting in trouble, because he was looking for women to have sex with. "It was clear that he was trying to get me to have sex with him," Fowler wrote. She thought that was inappropriate, and so she took screenshots of the messages and reported her manager to HR.

> Uber was a pretty good-sized company at that time, and I had pretty standard expectations of how they would handle situations like this. I expected that I would report him to HR, they

would handle the situation appropriately, and then life would go on—unfortunately, things played out quite a bit differently. When I reported the situation, I was told by both HR and upper management that even though this was clearly sexual harassment and he was propositioning me, it was this man's first offense, and that they wouldn't feel comfortable giving him anything other than a warning and a stern talking-to. Upper management told me that he "was a high performer" (i.e., had stellar performance reviews from his superiors) and they wouldn't feel comfortable punishing him for what was probably just an innocent mistake on his part.

Fowler says she then was told that she either needed to go find another team to join, or, if she chose to stay on her current team, she had to understand that her manager would likely retaliate against her by giving her a poor performance review. And by the way: "there was nothing they could do about that."[2]

Fowler goes on to say that in the weeks and months after she reported this individual, she met other women who had also reported him to HR for harassment before she joined the company. Through it all, she contends that HR would always insist that each report was the manager's first offense and the victim would be told nothing was going to be done. Not long after the head of HR purported to be "shocked"[3] at Fowler's position that harassment was widespread, a firm hired to investigate the company said there were 215 accusations of sexual harassment, and 20 people were fired.

Separately, former U.S. attorney general Eric Holder was retained to study the culture at Uber. Among other recommendations in the public report he prepared, it was noted that "senior managers should be able to track whether certain organizations or managers give rise to multiple complaints such that intervention with the manager is needed."[4]

It's obvious they should be *able* to track those complaints. But for that ability to matter, they need to *want* to track those complaints. This is yet another example of why leadership from the very top is so important.

Flying blind

Blog and social media posts represent another challenge to companies, as they offer opportunities for employees to publicly air grievances when they feel their concerns aren't being addressed. And as Uber learned following their response of shock and disbelief that Fowler's experiences represented a larger pattern of behavior involving other women (in spite of their knowledge to the contrary), the truth has a tendency to come out.

Fowler's post is relatively rare in that it contained such meticulous detail of her experience and that she released it under her own name. She did not name other people involved, but I'm sure many of those she interacted with saw themselves in her post. I thought it was incredibly courageous. Employees understandably often fear that they'll have trouble finding new jobs or be blacklisted by companies for speaking up.

However, other platforms have evolved to concentrate employee commentary about work issues, and that commentary is less like a canary's specific song than a flock of magpies squawking at one another on a telephone wire. I'm talking about company discussion sites like Blind and Glassdoor, social media job platforms where participants are identified by the company they work for but not usually by their real names.

The idea behind these sites is to provide authentic, uncensored information and feedback by and for employees of companies. To have, as Blind says, "meaningful and trusted conversations." Anyone can read the threads that talk about tech, social media, relationships, women at work, and all sorts of other issues. To register and be able to post on Blind, however, you need to provide a verified work email, and then, Blind explains: "Our patented infrastructure is set up so that all user account and activity information is completely disconnected from the email verification process. This effectively means there is no way to trace back your activity on Blind to an email address, because even we can't do it. Our patented infrastructure ensures your work emails are encrypted and locked away, forever. Your user activity on Blind is stored in a completely separate server. It is impossible to match your user activity to any profile or email information provided upon sign up."[5]

So, to unpack that: You initially sign up with your ostensibly real company name and verified email address. Then you put on your anonymous disguise and post anything you want with no accountability.

Even the operators of the site don't know who you are. With anonymity guaranteed, users, can—and do—post all manner of information they would be hesitant to share on the record: salary and bonus information, comparative perks (great gym, but cafeteria sucks!), interviewing advice, speculation about IPOs, insults about the boss's breath.

Is there value in such a platform? Absolutely. Unvarnished information can be very useful. Companies recruiting a candidate always put their best foot forward and may not mention looming negatives, from accusations of racism in certain divisions to an office's physical proximity to a toxic waste dump, to rumors that the CEO is about to leave. And to be fair, sites like this do give employees an avenue to ask questions about their own companies that they might be afraid to ask because they don't want to look dumb.

For example, a newly hired employee might note that a new strategic initiative announced by the CEO seems to contradict the roadmap the employee's manager recently laid out. The employee might post some questions: Should I be concerned? Is my boss just out of the loop? Does the company often change direction like this? Am I understanding what the new initiative really means? A conversation like that seeking context and historical perspective could be productive and helpful to an employee whose intentions are not at all bad.

These sites can also give employees an avenue to vent frustrations without fear of retaliation, and that can be healthy too. Getting validation that you're not the only person who finds the company's HR portal hard to navigate or that, yes, five days working without air conditioning is unacceptable releases emotional steam. And who knows, maybe somebody at the company in a position to do something will read it and then actually do something.

But sometimes anonymity can bring out the worst in human nature. I've seen bullying and other vicious, racist attacks on other employees posted on these sites. I've seen contempt expressed for whole classes of people, whether ethnic groups or certain teams or alums of certain universities. Someone might "leak" a rumor about an improper romantic relationship or discuss proprietary information or post internal documents or trade secrets about expansion plans or a lawsuit. Some post crude, sophomoric comments like this one I recently read: "I'm drunk and worth 5M." Someone else will post that they've heard the VP of X is on his way out. From the anonymous duck blind, users sometimes take aim at reputations and attack their colleagues' honesty, competency, and intentions, occasionally by name. Is it true, false, fiction, fact? Who knows? If you're the target, how do you feel?

Though it's a bit beyond the ken of this book, I'll say that from my point of view, there are serious flaws in this model. You may have been an employee of the company you registered with when you joined Blind, but Blind doesn't track your career. You may leave in a huff but keep your login and post highly critical comments of your old enemies. Or you might give your login to a reporter to monitor the supposed "real story" at the company. A friend of mine who's a CEO shared with me his view that "these sites are incredibly unethical. If you want to fix something, put your name on it. Then the company can look into it, do something. So many of these are people mad they didn't get a raise or a promotion. I've seen accusations that are absolutely untrue."

I understand his frustration. There is no question that some of these posts can damage both individuals' and a company's reputation. I've had some agonizing conversations with individuals who have been targeted by vicious anonymous attacks. Within hours of going up, a post full of inaccurate information may go viral and get tweeted out to thousands of followers and colleagues before I or anyone else in a senior leadership position even knows they exist. Some posts have triggered investigative stories into companies by mainstream media; others just contribute to an overall bad impression of employees that may not be fair at all and lead to distracting and demoralizing gossip.

All that said, we can't ignore these sites. They surface information that can offer a window into problems or misunderstandings that must be addressed. Yes, some of the posts are sour grapes or ad hominem attacks. But some clearly seem to spring from frustration and carry details that make me think the person has tried other avenues and been ignored. Many posts I've seen are from employees frustrated about workplace ethics violations. They don't believe their companies do enough when problems are reported. And sometimes being ignored triggers a mean-spirited desire for revenge. Let me give an example.

In mid-July 2019, I went on Blind, and a topic title caught my eye. It simply said "Ethics complaints." Here is what an employee who ostensibly works for a very large, publicly traded defense contractor wrote:

I'm in the process of leaving my current company due to some major issues with director level staff and a super shady retribution-type termination of my mentor and a well-respected senior level team member. Several of my coworkers have filed ethics complaints around the termination and the subsequent fallout and have urged me to do the same. The more complaints the more seriously they have to take the charges, at least that's the going theory.

Has anyone had a company actually take action due to ethics violations reports or did it just further contribute to the animosity and bad blood?

I wasn't going to bother with a complaint because I didn't think it would make any difference. Would a complaint be taken more seriously if a formal complaint is filed while I'm on staff or done during an exit interview?[6]

I had several immediate reactions to this. First, this sentence: "Has anyone had a company actually take action due to ethics violations reports or did it just further contribute to the animosity and bad blood?" The idea that the poster has to ask if "anyone" has ever seen a company respond to an ethics violation report is sobering. Corporate America, we have a problem. Every single public company in the country must have a code of ethics, and it must outline a reporting process, and yet this employee at a major public company seems perplexed at and mistrustful about whether a company is likely to respond to a report at all.

Nonetheless, I read this post as a sincere, legitimate effort to get advice and resolve an unethical situation before it hurts an entire team and the company's reputation. My impression is that the person wants to do the right thing—which I truly believe most people do! And I can appreciate that having members of the community's identities shielded is more likely to produce much more candid answers than an official corporate website might produce, or even social media where people are using their real names.

Most of the replies to this post were pretty measured, some urging the person to report, others matter-of-factly urging the opposite: "Won't work. just move on and find a new job and stop stressing. so many shitty managers that are ruining this industry . . ." said one.

Another Blind member wrote: "Put it in a blog and tweet it to Tech Crunch, then grab 👜 and watch what happens next. Big company?"

Another posted: "Remember, HR doesn't work for you; they work for the company. Being a manager, have seen ethics complaints being taken so lightly and thrown out of the window. So much for annual ethics certification and other ceremonies."

A fourth said: "I reported . . . a suspected affair between my ex manager and other team member during my exit interview. Nothing happened. The team member is not worth a penny and was rejected by the interviewer. Manager vetoed and hired him and defends that stupid to the point the entire team started dismantling. In less than a year, team shrunk from 10 to 3 developers. I am the only one who made the allegation during the exit interview but the entire team talks about them."

◆

I perceive deep cynicism and mistrust in these posts. Clearly, these individuals have little or no faith in their companies' commitment to ethics, and it appears some believe their leaders routinely disregard their own ethics policies and reports of problematic behavior. If I were the general counsel at the companies these posters purported to be from, I would look into this from a systemic point of view. It's hard for me to imagine that these companies make an effort to show that they value integrity. But even as an outside observer, these kinds of sentiments in the business climate more generally amount to a national Code Red, and they have motivated me to do something different at Airbnb.

At Airbnb, we're trying to double down on internal reporting media channels, specifically reports we circulate to employees about what our ethics issues are and where they exist and, most importantly, what we are doing to resolve them. I've talked about how we track reports of toxic behavior and grievances, where they occur, what the issues seem to be. But so far, these reports have been mainly for the ethics team's use so that we can respond effectively.

In the future I think that companies need to address the concern, which clearly came through both in Fowler's blog post and in the responses from the Blind commentary, that many companies receive reports of ethics violations and simply ignore them. Because there have been issues of privacy and confidentiality surrounding the consequences of ethics investigations, I can understand why employees sometimes believe a company may put on a show of responding but in practice do nothing. In the case of Uber and the overhaul it has experienced in the wake of the accusations against it, it's possible that that's what happened. But I will tell you that in the companies I've been involved with, that is certainly *not* the case. The fact that we can't talk publicly about what we did in detail does not mean that we did nothing.

One approach that companies might try is to publish annual summaries about ethics code inquiries and also reports on how violations at the company have been handled. At a minimum, boards should get these reports. But somehow, companies need to find ways to inform their employees about how cases are handled. Of course, for privacy reasons, the general employee population could not see the same reports as the board might get, but I think employees need to know more information, in some redacted format, about how hotline reports are handled. In the absence of any information, it's not surprising that employees sometimes might suspect that complaints are just swept under the rug.

A more open approach flies against the traditions of most companies, which historically have tried to keep this kind of data quiet. They may be willing to post internal metrics about safety records or sales targets achieved, but reports of bad behavior and what happened to perpetrators? Not so much. Some worry: What if it gets out? What if it's misinterpreted? What if we find out that some of the allegations are impossible to prove or resolve? What if we're sued and we have assembled the very data the plaintiff will use to prove we knew about issues in the workplace?

In my view, focusing on those fears is an integrity trap. As we've established, ethical violations represent an enormous threat to brands. It would be great if employees were perfect and just read the code of ethics and never made a mistake. That's not real life.

Specific industries have long grappled with issues about sensitive information and how to present it. Restaurants are often required to post scores from health inspections. Of course they don't love doing that, but most reasonable people realize that no restaurant is likely to be permanently 100 percent free of ants or keep its refrigerators at the perfect temperature 24/7. It's also a given that the very best hospitals will often report the highest death rates for certain kinds of risky procedures. That's not because they secretly don't deserve their good reputations, it's because

physicians in other hospitals respect their skills and refer the most difficult cases to them. Addressing certain challenges publicly is a reality of
doing business in demanding and transparent times.

◆

Some reported ethics issues have a geographic or cultural component.
For example, work groups in urban locations near lots of bars and dance
clubs may find they have more issues with employees going out in groups
and drinking heavily, leading to reports of inappropriate and disrespectful behavior. Or, in companies with culturally diverse teams, employees
cooking certain ethnic foods may end up in conflict with others who dislike the smells that then permeate the communal kitchen and surrounding work areas. That might not seem like an ethics or integrity issue, but
when your company's basic values include belonging and mutual respect,
anything that brings people into conflict in the workplace is an integrity issue. Are folks working through the issue in a thoughtful, respectful
manner? Are the cultural practices of an underrepresented group being
dismissed or disregarded by the majority? Can you create a physical accommodation so that all parties' needs are addressed? This is the price of
a diverse workforce and it is worth paying, but it does require thoughtful and informed management aided by data that helps you figure out if
it's an isolated issue or if there are common threads. In rolling up your
sleeves to understand and address and resolve these conflicts, you will often arrive at solutions you end up exporting to other regions, to challenges
that might initially seem unrelated.

◆

A concern some leaders raise is that just because there are reports of certain violations, it doesn't mean that they are true, so isn't it inappropriate
to publicize unproven allegations? Well, if we are getting multiple reports
of violations that don't involve much evidence or may be proven untrue,
then we have a different kind of problem that is also worth solving. Do reporters not understand the code of ethics? Do we need to clarify the rule?
Is there some kind of resentment or revenge issue in a specific group?

Also, what should we conclude from reports of specific violations going up or down—or not coming in at all? Just because there are no reports

of violations from a division does not mean they are not occurring (although that might be the case). Once again, if we choose more transparency at the outset, we can put the data up and see what happens. Maybe we can crowdsource better ideas than we have thought of as managers. If a work group that has not used ethics advisors much or may even have been subtly discouraged from reporting violations sees how other teams are using these resources, it might motivate more accurate reporting.

In the ideal world, my measure of success would be that we're seeing a steady increase in questions about our code of ethics but that reports of serious violations are declining. We have to try new ideas, put transparency to work for us. Let's not stubbornly operate within the same parameters that we know are not solving the problem.

The process never ends

We've now walked through the Six Cs for building a culture of integrity. Common feedback and questions I've had in response to my Intentional Integrity presentation suggest two more areas that require a deeper dive: The first is sexual harassment in the workplace; the second involves a broader notion of community standards and integrity, and even the idea that a company sometimes needs to set behavioral standards for its customers. I'll tackle those next.

CODE MOMENT 14: THREE BLIND MICE

Rick hates conflict. But he has strong views about many subjects, so he goes to the anonymous website Blind and lets it rip. For example:

"Our recycling fixation is BS—we spend all this time separating paper from cans, blah blah blah, and I've seen our maintenance folks just dump it all into the trash. More phony lib-speak that means nothing from our PC execs."

"Sure have been a lot of 'high'-level meetings in Building 4 after hours this month. I hear the new GM of the Orion project grows his own premium weed and will share. And by share I mean sell."

You're the general counsel of Rick's company, and you've received an anonymous tip on your ethics hotline that Rick is the employee who posts harsh, sometimes inappropriate comments under one of three different usernames. The tipster claims to be a colleague of another employee in IT who created the fake emails for Rick so he could register different names to use on Blind.

Do you rip the mask off the poster?

For discussion, see appendix, page 266.

10

Dude, you're not just "bad at dating": Sexual misconduct in the workplace

For far too long, women victimized by sexual harassment and other predatory behaviors have suffered in silence. The issue has been compounded by company leaders and bystanders who failed to act, and as a result sexual misconduct remains an ever-present threat in the workplace. The old formula for dealing with sexual harassment— hotlines and canned training—doesn't work. We need new ideas.

My wife, Jillian, and I like to take long evening walks through the hilly streets of San Francisco. One evening several years ago before we were married, we were making our way through Chinatown, past tiny cafes serving steaming bowls of noodles and shops displaying exotic jade carvings. Jillian's phone rang. She answered, and for the next hour she mostly listened, now and then interjecting "Oh my God, no" and "Aaagh—you need to be strong." I'll never forget her gently saying, "Killing yourself won't solve anything—it's not your fault."

This was the first time I'd heard her side of what she calls the "911s"; it was riveting, sad, and scary.

Jillian has had a range of interesting careers in multiple industries including banking and media, which she remembers as "playgrounds for predators." She is presently a partner in a Silicon Valley venture fund. She is also an active and generous philanthropist who supports homeless shelters, food banks, and other impactful nonprofits.

In her twenties, Jillian was homeless for a time herself. Although she had a comfortable childhood and later high-level jobs, she became involved with a physically abusive man. Eventually he injured her badly, and she was so broken by the experience that she did not want to reconnect with her family until she found herself again. It took a year of living in shelters and a challenging reentry to society, but she emerged stronger than even she expected and became a committed protector of women.

When the #MeToo movement erupted, Jillian had many conversations with women and men in venture capital about these issues. As we've now discussed, it's an industry where some wealthy and accomplished men have exploited their power by demanding sexual favors of women founders, executives, and fellow board members in companies. The more Jillian spoke with professional women, some of whom seemed strong on the outside but on the inside were in deep pain from their traumatic experiences, the more frustrated she became. She often gave them her phone number and urged them to call her anytime. This evolved into her 911 or "SOS" phone number for women facing #MeToo dilemmas and experiences; soon women she had never met started texting, asking for her help.

In the space of three years, Jillian estimates she has received nearly 2,000 texts and calls. Hundreds of people have watched an interview with her on YouTube where she talks about sexual harassment in the VC world. Over and over women entrepreneurs would tell her chilling stories: sometimes that prospective male investors had propositioned them for sex with the not-so-implicit threat that they would not get any financial support and might even get blacklisted if they did not comply. Sometimes women executives would tell her they'd been cornered and groped and pressed for sex by a boss or colleague at a company party or while traveling.

"Around the holidays, the calls go way up. People get drunk. I had one call from a woman who had a senior executive tell her repeatedly at a party that 'You're right on the edge of getting that promotion I know you want.'" After the woman excused herself to go to the bathroom, she told Jillian, this guy managed to pry the bathroom door open and come in; he put his hand over her mouth and raped her over the toilet seat. Then he said to her, "OK, now you've gone over the edge. You'll get the promotion."

By now, I'm used to these calls. Jillian mouths "911" and I know she'll be tied up for an hour. Some women call once, speak anonymously, and never call back. Others become her friends. Jillian says in about two dozen situations, the calls have been about repeat offenders—men she had already heard about from another woman. She offers to connect the victims if both agree. Jillian says that once victims realized that others had experienced the same abuse, they often connected and gained the strength to file official reports and complaints—leading to their abusers being outed and losing their jobs, and more. After receiving an SOS about a venture capitalist she knew who was trying to pressure a female founder into giving him oral sex for funding, Jillian took matters into her own hands. She alerted his partners. And confronted him directly.

"I'm almost never shocked, a lot of these things have happened to me. At first the women blame themselves for being alone with the man or putting themselves in this position," Jillian says. "But when they start talking to other victims, they realize these predators engineer these situations. When the women connect, they feel less dirty. They realize they did not ask for this treatment. These should have been business meetings, period."

Jillian says that her goal is not personal therapy, it's to help the women who've experienced these incidents regain their confidence in the workplace. "I always say you must keep calm and not break down and lose your temper. You have to become proactive instead of reactive. Never let them see you cry." But that doesn't mean do nothing or ignore the offenses. She also once received a call about a man she knew and had considered a friend. After hearing an account of something he did, Jillian called the man and said, "I know what you're doing and it needs to stop. You need to get help."

Jillian keeps all the details confidential; she's never uttered a name to me. But the stories are powerful and haunting, and I've learned a lot about the consequences of sexual harassment through Jillian's eyes.

"Out of context," huh?

Obviously, this subject matter is not new to me. As an in-house attorney and advisor to other tech companies, I've been involved with a number of sexual harassment investigations in my career. I've received specific reports of the kind of behavior that Jillian describes. I've terminated leaders. I've looked into the eyes of men accused of inappropriate comments, propositions, and even physical overtures or assaults. I've heard denials. Sometimes there's corroborating evidence such as inappropriate emails or cell phone logs showing hundreds of texts over a few days' time. Some guys still won't admit what they've done, insisting it's all "playful back and forth" or "out of context." In other cases, there is no evidence beyond the claim of a victim.

I've also not been a stranger to sexual harassment scandals in my personal network. I've invested in a company that was destroyed by a sexual misconduct scandal. And another CEO, a former colleague whom I had advised at a previous company, left his company in disgrace after getting drunk at a holiday party and pressing up behind a woman, grinding his pelvis into her in front of others.

Jillian still gets many texts and calls from women, but the mix is becoming more complicated. She's had men call her SOS line, for example, to suggest that they were being blackmailed by women threatening sexual harassment allegations unless they invested in their companies. She also sees a consequence of #MeToo that she feels is hurting women in the workplace: "The actual number of acts may be decreasing, but some men are using this alleged fear of #MeToo to justify not working with women. They say they're terrified of being falsely accused. They don't want to have private meetings. They think they'll be reported for telling a joke. Some are sincere, others are using it as an excuse." I've heard that argument myself, and not only is it not the right ethical response, it is flat-out illegal to exclude women from meetings on the basis of their sex.

Shocking numbers

I don't know if the number of #MeToo-related acts has begun to decrease in light of the increased attention, but I do know that they are still occurring in unacceptable numbers, and sexual harassment remains a simmering and explosive threat to women and their companies. In October 2018, the global business advisory firm FTI Consulting partnered with a women's advocacy group called Mine the Gap to survey nearly 5,000 professional women and 1,000 professional men. These individuals worked in technology, finance, legal, energy, and healthcare. Among the report's sobering statistics:

- Over the past five years, 38 percent of professional women have experienced or witnessed sexual harassment or misconduct in the workplace.
- More than one in four professional women (28 percent) have experienced or witnessed unwanted physical contact in the workplace in just the last year; nearly one in five have personally experienced it. By industry: 34 percent of women who have experienced or witnessed physical contact at work in the last year are in technology, 29 percent of women in energy, 27 percent of women in legal, 26 percent of women in healthcare, and 25 percent of women in finance.
- Approximately 55 percent of professional women surveyed are less likely to apply for a job, and 49 percent are less likely to buy products or stock from a company with a public #MeToo allegation.
- Of the professional women surveyed, 43 percent did not report the behavior they had experienced or witnessed. Of the professional men surveyed who reported experiencing or witnessing it, 31 percent did not report it. Both sexes cited the same primary reasons for not reporting: fear of negative career impact, being viewed as "difficult," and retribution.[1]

It doesn't take a genius to see that despite all the media discussion, despite all the prominent men who have lost their jobs and reputations for sexually harassing colleagues, and despite all the supposed "zero-tolerance" policies that companies have announced, the way most companies are handling sexual harassment is still failing. Generic, mandatory HR videos are not adequate to dissuade some individuals from harassing others, and many people still have no interest in using anonymous company hotlines. Employees at many companies have no confidence that reports will be taken seriously, and they believe that reporting is futile and can result in "career suicide."

I want to dig a little deeper into some of the complications of addressing sexual harassment in the workplace, but I also want to advocate for a couple of changes to the status quo. I don't accept that these levels of inappropriate behavior are just "human nature" that can never be solved.

I think we need to start a larger conversation—"we" meaning men, women, executives, nonprofit organizations, media, basically everybody—*about driving sexual harassment out of our culture.* We need to motivate and clone the Jillians of the world, whether they are ethical change agents or just bystanders who witness harassment and are willing to speak up and support victims and shut down harassers. Business leaders need to set a tone and say that sexual harassment is not just inappropriate but also distasteful, disgusting, and uncool. And then they need to walk that talk.

The status quo

Let's quickly review some of the legal realities that shape how companies deal with sexual harassment and assault. For starters, terminology matters. Many cases that have been in the news in recent years have been lumped under the term "sexual misconduct." That includes both sexual assault and sexual harassment, but it's important to realize that there are very specific differences between the two categories of crime.

Sexual assault is a felony. It refers to intentional sexual contact, characterized by the use of force, threats, intimidation, or abuse of authority, or when the victim does not or cannot consent. Sexual assault includes rape, forcible sodomy, and other unwanted indecent contact (e.g., kissing against another person's will) that is aggravated, abusive, unwanted.

In the United States, sexual assault is a crime whenever and wherever it occurs. Every victim has an absolute right to report a crime to law enforcement. Companies with integrity don't interfere with that process, and they support law enforcement's efforts to investigate it.

There is a loathsome hall of shame involving workplace sexual misconduct where individuals have been accused of repeated sexual assaults and those complaints were ignored and in some cases covered up by others. As we referred to in previous chapters, two companies exemplify the problem most prominently: Wynn Resorts and the Weinstein Company.

Wynn Resorts was fined and its executives accused by government regulators of enabling, ignoring, and covering up multiple complaints about founder Steve Wynn's behavior over many years.[2] This at a company that supposedly had a "zero-tolerance" policy about sexual harassment in writing since 2004. Harvey Weinstein, meanwhile, has been charged with rape, criminal sex act, and predatory sexual assault for behavior involving women he was ostensibly meeting for business purposes.[3] Further, many actresses and other women have come forward alleging Weinstein behaved inappropriately with them as well, often manipulating them to meet with him privately in hotel rooms where he would try to intimidate them into having sex. Both men deny their behavior involved anything other than consensual encounters.

The bottom line on sexual assault is this: a company must investigate any claim of a sexual assault as fully and fairly as possible. If a preponderance of evidence suggests an employee has committed a sexual assault, the company must remove that person from the workplace. And I would add that the decision to remove does not require the person to be convicted in court. Companies can act with a much lower burden of proof than the jury in a criminal trial must apply.

Sexual harassment is a more complicated term, and it's often misunderstood. For one thing, many people are shocked to learn the actual crime is not committed by the harasser but by an employer who allows it to occur (realizing that sometimes the employer is the harasser). According to the Equal Employment Opportunity Commission, sexual harassment involves two specific kinds of workplace violations: **Quid pro quo harassment**, which is a request for sexual favors, or **hostile environment harassment**, which is creating a hostile workplace that interferes with performance.[4]

Media accounts sometimes get this wrong. It's usually not a crime for a peer or even a boss to make comments, proposition another person, tell dirty jokes, etc., but it is a violation of the law for an employer to tolerate this behavior in the workplace. Also, a company is liable if its supervisors use sex in a threatening way or as a condition for a woman to receive a raise, an assignment, or a promotion.

If you think about this, it makes sense that the law has evolved this way. Adults initiate romantic or sexual relationships or interactions in many ways, ranging from catcalls from construction ladders to swiping right on Tinder, to sidling up to someone in a bar, making eye contact on a train, or going on a singles-only vacation. A provocative comment one person finds offensive is charming and sexy to another. Romantic attraction is far too complicated for the law to reasonably insert itself in regulating this kind of speech. Further, a truly consensual relationship between colleagues that starts at work isn't unusual or necessarily problematic, as long as there is no "control," where one person manages or controls the other in the work hierarchy.

The onus has fallen on employers because employees are essentially under their control when they are in a workplace. People need to work and earn a living, and they need protection from inappropriate behavior that interferes with that basic human need. But workers often don't get to pick who they work with, where they sit, how much interaction they have with any given person. At a party, if a guy says he likes your hair and asks you out and you don't want to go, you can say no and walk away or leave the party. If a colleague in the next cubicle has invited you to dinner at her home eight times and you've refused each time, and now she's emailing you articles about threesomes and bondage, it impacts your ability to focus and feel safe. The law agrees that you should not have to quit your job or ask to be moved to restore your peace of mind, and so if you report this behavior to your employer, the employer needs to figure out how to protect you (and others) from this harassment.

That said, however, it's also true that the law surrounding a hostile work environment is inconsistent across federal, state, and local jurisdictions. In New York, for example, the standard for assessing a hostile environment is whether a "reasonable person" would call the working environment in question hostile. The federal standard is whether the behavior at issue is "severe or pervasive."

Given these considerations, and without minimizing the discomfort and even trauma that victims of assault and harassment experience, what this complexity says to me is that companies can't train to a legal standard (or many legal standards for companies with offices in different states). Employees need practical, specific guidelines on what is and isn't allowed—legal principles aren't good enough. For example, Airbnb and Facebook have an "ask out once" rule: if you ask a coworker out and the person refuses, you're done, you may not keep nagging or pressing the point, or you are violating the code of ethics.

Another important fact is that the line between sexual assault and sexual harassment can be very thin. In the FTI survey, for example, note that one question involved "unwanted physical contact." Depending on how intense the contact was, it could be either sexual assault or sexual harassment. Grabbing a woman's breast, pushing someone against a wall to kiss them, and obviously busting into a bathroom and raping a person are clearly sexual assaults. If an allegation of this sort of behavior is credible, the perpetrator ought to lose their job . . . and be prosecuted.

However, making contact as someone brushes by you in a crowd, or lightly touching someone on the arm or upper back may be unwanted contact, but is it deliberate? Sexual? Did it happen once, or several times? Was there malevolent intent? Working through the dynamics of each situation can be complex, and your decision on how to handle a complaint might depend on your findings.

You might ask, if these issues have such a high risk of triggering Code Reds, why wouldn't you fire the person on the first offense? Wouldn't that create a powerful deterrent to similar behavior? In theory . . . maybe. But people can be clumsy and distracted. Accidental contact can occur. It may be that someone walking behind someone else, perhaps in a tight space, did not mean to touch the other person in a sexual way. It would matter to me if the accused seemed indignant to have been reported, or apologetic and embarrassed that the contact occurred. The person who was made uncomfortable has every right to report this act, and the accused deserves a fair and humane hearing.

Another element a company has to consider when it weighs a response to a situation like this is that an employer who fires an alleged harasser for an act without sufficient proof could be reported or sued for wrongful termination or discrimination against a protected class—in essence accused of using a fake harassment charge as a pretext for another form of discrimination.

It's complicated, so here's a fictitious case to illustrate the often difficult reality for companies who end up with all the liability and the harassers avoid it. Let's say Harold, age 59, is infatuated with his assistant, Judy. But he's only inappropriate when they're alone; he's too clever to leave a trail. He's never threatened to fire her or hurt her performance ranking. There are no witnesses or emails or texts. Judy can't even privately record her meetings with Harold for corroboration, because that's illegal in her state. Judy files a complaint with HR that Harold tried to grab her in his office when they were alone, saying that it was one of many inappropriate overtures from him.

HR investigates and can't find proof. The CEO considers herself a zero-tolerance leader. "I believe Judy. Let's fire Harold."

Is that the right call? The CEO is legally within her rights to fire Harold even without outside corroboration if her decision is based on reasonable evidence. What would that be? Well, for example, Judy may have no witnesses or outside evidence, but in three interviews her account of what she said Harold did and said when they were alone is completely consistent. Harold, on the other hand, changes certain details of his explanations for exchanges with Judy that he insists she "took out of context" or "read too much into." That could be sufficient legal protection for the employer to fire him—but that may not be the end of the story.

Harold may have a defense already prepared suggesting the deck was stacked against him from the start. He says, "None of this ever happened. Judy made it all up to try to ruin me because she's been slacking and is afraid of how I'll review her performance. I know why you're really firing me, it's because of age discrimination."

Now the GC's office investigates. The GC learns that the CFO wrote an email that someone forwarded to Harold that says, "We need to get rid of some old timers who are just resting in place, get some fresh young energy in here." Harold threatens a discrimination lawsuit.

So the bad news is there is no hard proof of what Harold the harasser did to Judy, and if you fire him, Harold has concrete evidence that the company is inclined to make personnel decisions based on age. In many cases like this, both the victim and the company lose. Or the company negotiates a substantial settlement and lets Harold announce that he's leaving to spend more time with his family. The details of all this are confidential, and maybe he can keep his job or go to a new company where details of his behavior won't follow him. Arguably, the person responsible for the bad behavior suffers the least.

Companies deserve serious consequences and criticism if they promote or ignore a culture where harassment is open and pervasive (such as in a "bro" culture). When that's the case, there are often multiple improper sexual comments that have been witnessed by others, or an assault, or even an email trail to corroborate or disprove claims.

But too often, misconduct happens in a quiet corner, an elevator, a hotel corridor where there are no witnesses. The alleged victim has one story, the alleged perpetrator another. Assuming both are reasonably credible, a company is then placed in a very uncomfortable position just as Harold and Judy's employers are here. I've set this example up and made clear Harold is at fault, but the available evidence isn't clear.

We need policy solutions to resolve these tensions. We need to figure out how to provide appropriate support for victims and, in my opinion, extend personal liability to harassers as well. Companies that tolerate harassment and a hostile work environment deserve what happens; companies that are dealing with devious harassers who leave few clues are put in the difficult position of assuming all the liability for a situation they didn't know anything about. How do we move forward to a better, more just culture surrounding sexual harassment issues?

I think progress will rest on three fronts—leadership, the larger legal framework, and the culture more broadly.

1. Remember the 1st C: Ethics starts at the top—executive leadership shapes workplace culture

Leaders must set the right tone on appropriate workplace behavior. If a leader uses inappropriate, sexually charged language, others will as well. If sexually explicit discussions or jokes are tolerated by leaders of either sex, by the way, bad behavior is more likely to occur. A leader sets the tone not only by what they do but by what they tolerate—if the bad behavior isn't called out and stopped, it will likely get worse.

In response to the stories of bad behavior by powerful men, I've heard other men (including leaders at well-known public companies) complain that they now feel like victims. "I feel like I can't say or do anything anymore, it might be taken the wrong way—I'm just going to stay away from women." Or "I'm just not going to go to dinner with female colleagues at all because it might make me vulnerable to a false claim of misconduct."

That's exactly the wrong approach, and if followed, it perpetuates discrimination (and violates the law). If you're doing business over dinner, you can't limit your table to men only. Locking yourself in your hotel room and grazing on room-service chicken tenders isn't a great option either. Here's a better approach that some companies, like Airbnb, have adopted. Start by setting clear limits, and have an agreement with your board or in your code that the most senior leaders of any gender won't engage in any romantic relationships with other employees (and specifically define a romantic relationship to include anything sexual, one night or long-term). Have a specific conversation about it as an executive team, put it in writing, and make it part of the company policies, as Airbnb did. No misunderstandings.

Second, if you have dinners with work colleagues, make a point of including all your reports, either by meeting in groups or separate individual dinners with each person. During any dinner, take it upon yourself to set the right tone for the evening surrounding alcohol and appropriate conversation—that's a leader's responsibility.

Diversity supports respect. Another tool to combat harassment is to have diversity at all levels of a company, including leadership. Inappropriate behavior is less likely to go on, or be tolerated, in rooms where the power dynamic isn't tilted strongly toward one group. Underrepresented groups are more likely to be the target of bad behavior. Teams that are gender balanced are less likely to experience these sorts of issues.

Carefully manage situations where sexual harassment is most likely to occur—parties and out of town conferences. As Jillian said, calls to her SOS hotline spike during the holidays when people are drinking too much at company parties. Companies that throw huge, late-night holiday parties with unlimited alcohol are asking for trouble. You can have a good time by emphasizing events that align to the company's culture. For example, instead of a holiday party last year, Airbnb threw an "experiences" event in its lobby that highlighted hosts demonstrating their experiences . . . there was food and alcohol, but it wasn't the focus of the event, which ended early. I'd contrast that approach with companies that throw big holiday bashes where the booze flows until the wee hours of the morning, and there are even companies I've read about that hire professional models to walk around and mingle with the employees.

Don't rely solely on internal hotlines. Public companies must have hotlines for reporting harassment; many private companies do as well. Don't set one up, check the box, and consider your problem solved. Victims often avoid hotlines because they don't trust the process, and they understand full well that the lawyers and HR professionals who receive the complaints represent the company, not the victim. As we talked about in chapter 9, companies must constantly monitor all forms of relevant data about ethics and workplace safety, including reporting processes. Don't assume that your problem has gone away just because reports are declining. Do employees trust the process? Is there a different resource that might be more effective?

Consider, for example, a hotline that automatically forwards all allegations against management directly to a third party that independently investigates the allegations and reports the results directly to the board. Or appointing an independent ombudsperson, at the company's expense, to advise individuals who file a report. Such a process, if openly discussed with employees, sends a strong message that neither reports nor bad behavior will be ignored. This may be your only defense against Code Red scandals. In the FTI survey, 22 percent of senior-level women and 20 percent of senior-level men responded that they are concerned about an impending #MeToo incident at their organization. Wow. You have to periodically ask: Are we doing enough? What else can we do?

Focus on preventing the "first" improper act. Dan Ariely at Duke made an interesting point to me about sexual harassment. By the time someone is assaulting a coworker, threatening their job, or dangling a promotion for sex, you are at a crisis point and won't be able to easily correct that kind of monstrous behavior. Instead, he suggests, you should focus on preventing the first improper act—highlight the issues with simply touching another employee or the dangers associated with alcohol in the workplace. These areas are often the precursors for bad behavior and dealing with these smaller infractions is likely to be more effective. Ignore them, and the perpetrator becomes conditioned to rationalizing the bad behavior, to seeing the absence of consequences for the first small improper acts as permission to take the next unethical step. The ethical boundaries become unclear in their mind, and they may be emboldened to do things that could balloon into a disaster.

2. Changing times

Throughout my career in Silicon Valley, employment attorney Jackie Kalk at the Littler firm has been my go-to outside counsel to help me work through tough employment law issues. She recently told me that she's noticed several trends that I think are healthy.

First, in a number of jurisdictions around the country, victims of harassment can bring civil legal actions against bosses and other individuals who may control their ability to make a living. In the past, and in many parts of the country, victims might have been limited to bringing employment-related claims against the company employing the perpetrator. These new laws can play an important role in sending a strong message directly to the individuals in power whose behavior needs to change.

Second, lawmakers are cracking down on confidentiality provisions that prevent victims of harassment and discrimination from speaking out about their experience. These confidentiality provisions, which in the past have permitted perpetrators to continue to act without real consequence, are now banned in places like New York, California, and Oregon. Even the federal IRS has gotten into the act, ruling that settlement agreements containing these provisions must be treated as taxable to the employer.

Jackie also told me that she's seen a resurgence in companies requiring new executives to sign a "morals clause" in their employment agreements. This is huge, and I strongly support this. These clauses state that if the executive is let go by the company for an "integrity violation" such as discrimination, sexual harassment, bribery, or theft, the executive will forfeit any severance that they might otherwise be entitled to receive. Failing to include a carefully drafted morals clause can lead to an embarrassing parting gift to a fired leader who has behaved poorly while with the company, sending a terrible message to other employees.

3. Bystanders and cultural change

I think we need to identify and name a positive behavior that puts harassers on notice that their days are numbered. As a society and culture we need to deliberately develop more empathy and take action when people observe sexual harassment or inappropriate behavior anywhere, including in the workplace. As a culture we need to inspire and reward this behavior. It's the right thing to do as a human being, but it's also the right thing to do for the good of a company and to support future success.

My assumption is that many, maybe most, incidents of sexual harassment occur in relative privacy. I can't say that I've personally observed much beyond isolated inappropriate comments and jokes, since most people are smart enough to be on their best behavior in front of a company's lawyer. But after my conversation with Reid Hoffman, I've been intrigued with the concept of bystanders. I've been asking both men and women about what they've observed or been told about, or what they've experienced in front of other people. How have bystanders behaved? Have they tended to get involved, or do they look away?

A huge number admit they have looked away. Many men and women I've talked to about this can recall a time when they knew something wrong was happening, that a man with power was using it inappropriately to harass or bully a woman, and they did nothing. Even women who had been harassed themselves chose to stay at arm's length when it happened to someone else.

In the aftermath of the accusations against Harvey Weinstein, a screenwriter named Scott Rosenberg wrote a now infamous post on Facebook where he admitted he knew Weinstein was doing inappropriate things but had looked away. Rosenberg took aim at all the individuals around Weinstein who profited from their association with him and did nothing to intervene. "Everybody-fucking-knew," Rosenberg claimed in his post. "And do you know how I am sure this is true? Because I was there. And I saw you. And I talked about it with you. You, the big producers; you, the big directors; you, the big agents; you, the big financiers . . .

"If Harvey's behavior is the most reprehensible thing one can imagine, a not-so-distant second is the current flood of sanctimonious denial and condemnation that now crashes upon these shores of rectitude in gloppy tides of bullshit righteousness," Rosenberg wrote (his very long missive subsequently was taken down but was widely quoted after he posted it). "And this is as pathetic as it is true: what would you have had us do? Who were we to tell? The authorities? What authorities?"[5]

That's a legitimate question and a conversation we should all have. Inside a company, there should be a formal channel to report incidents of inappropriate behavior. But realize there are other sources of harassment than a boss or co-workers. As Reid has noted about venture capitalists, there is no centralized HR function to police VC behavior or that of investors more broadly, and investors do sometimes interact with employees of a company. An employee also might be harassed or propositioned by a customer or a consultant or a powerful partner who threatens retaliation if the employee objects or does not comply. What about concerns you can't prove, or gray-area interactions you witness where the perpetrator claims innocent intentions but you know they're not, or you can see the person is making someone uncomfortable? What are the levers you can push to formalize this behavior as unacceptable and create a deterrent?

The #MeToo movement has done a lot to increase awareness of inappropriate comments and overtures in a workplace. Victims are less likely to suffer in silence than they used to. But still, bystanders often look away. Even today, colleagues cannot be counted on to call out perpetrators or stand up for someone being harassed in their presence—and that's especially true in environments like sales or in creative fields, where employees may be competing with one another as much as with rival companies. In fact, a person may be much more likely to support a lower-level employee who is being harassed than a peer. In the FTI survey, 43 percent of the professional women surveyed who experienced or witnessed sexual harassment did not report the behavior; 31 percent of the professional men surveyed who experienced or witnessed it did not report.

✦

A senior executive at a software company, I'll call her "Sally," told me a story that happened years ago when she was a twentysomething graphic designer hired at a large ad agency's San Francisco office. The firm had been aggressively recruiting more women. Sally had been on the job six months and was getting a lot of positive feedback.

The account side of the firm invited its best clients to a dinner, and the CEO of the agency flew in from New York to meet and mingle with them. The agency team attending was encouraged to bring their spouses.

The account chief, Don, asked Sally's manager if both of them could attend the dinner so that there was some "creative energy" in the room. The manager agreed. Sally was engaged to be married, so she asked if she could invite her fiancé. Don said no, spouses only.

When Sally arrived at the event, Don made a beeline for her and began introducing her to the clients, making comments like, "Needless to say the office has brightened up quite a bit since Sally was hired," and "You want fresh, hip brands you have to hire fresh, hot talent." Sally clenched her jaw and tried to be pleasant. "I felt like a piece of meat being walked around."

By dinner Don had had several drinks; he got up and said a few words to the gathering of 40 or so folks. He ended by mentioning that the firm was going to be sponsoring a golf tournament at a prestigious course and they would all be invited. "And with any luck, we'll get Sally out there as well," he said, looking at her. "I'm sure I'm not alone in wanting to see her swing."

Sally says that all the men there—at least 20 of them—either laughed or were silent. She left as quickly as she could.

The next morning, the agency CEO's female assistant appeared in her cubicle. "Mr. X wanted me to tell you he was glad you could attend last night," she began. "Don was being Don and we hope he didn't make you too uncomfortable. You shouldn't have had to put up with that, so we're sorry about that." Then she left.

When Sally told her manager about the visit, he said, "Yeah, they asked me if you were OK. I told them not to worry, you could hold your own. But see, this is good that you did—and you're totally on their radar now. Good for you." As far as Sally knows, nobody ever talked to Don, and he never apologized. She tried to avoid him.

What an awkward mess. I can't find anything in this story that suggests leadership. Clearly, the harassment was premeditated: Don made sure that Sally would not have a date at the event to make it easier for him to parade her around like a trophy. The company executives in the room were all men (the only other women were their wives), and Sally says they just looked away. They might have taken a cue from the CEO if he'd seemed displeased, but he was more concerned with how the customers enjoyed the evening. Sally's manager essentially applauded her for "playing along" with harassment because it would be good for her career.

"I liked my job and I liked my manager," Sally recalls. "But at some level I felt like the men there from my office were jealous I was getting the attention, so they just figured OK, well, you're the teacher's pet, you figure it out."

Sometimes the path of integrity does not bring rewards, or even the right outcome. That doesn't mean it's not worth taking. We have to make supporting other people's basic human rights cool and automatic, and that's much more likely to happen if doing so is intentionally made part of a culture. Watching a colleague suffer harassment by a manager creates a code moment: *If I do nothing, I may get an advantage. If I intervene, it may not help and I could be a target as well.* Well, yes. Life isn't fair. But would you rather be proud of your actions or have to write emotional mea culpas on Facebook years later?

Jillian and I have talked about the importance of nurturing "empathetics" in our culture, or people who assertively support others who are put in difficult positions by those in power. Maybe it's about "humanstanding," putting yourself in someone else's shoes because it's the right thing to do, period. The only benefit to you may come in karma points—in an empathy-driven world, when you need support for a certain issue, someone you may not even know will lend you that support. It's time for men in a group witnessing something like Sally's discomfort at that dinner to find a way to stop it in real time, not just check in later with some lame show of sympathy.

At Airbnb I've gone to meetings of an internal group known as "able@," and I've been an advocate for improving our workplace for a better experience for those with physical handicaps. One thing you quickly learn is that there is far more to this commitment than providing special parking spaces and ramps; individuals have unique needs based on health and mobility. I've come to believe that the more sensitive we are to this as a company, the more inclusive our workplace will be, to the betterment of *everyone*. And, true to our values, we have a better chance to help make the outside world better.

From my perspective, there is something incredibly powerful in standing up for a group that isn't yours. It's an extension of the ethics goggles concept; you look through someone else's life-experience lenses; you consider their background, you listen to their perspective . . . and then you advocate for the importance of showing respect to everyone. It's about a straight couple standing up for gay marriage. It's about able-bodied people truly understanding what people with physical handicaps are going through.

As a corporate executive, am I getting out of my lane if I urge people to try to change human nature by sticking up for other people? Isn't that a conversation for social justice advocates or Sunday school teachers or maybe parents? Yes, those folks advocate for courage in the face of bullying and other harmful forms of abuse. But I hope it doesn't surprise you that I see fundamental brand and corporate liability issues as well. So let me also spell out the corporate-interest/bottom-line reasons to take serious and ongoing aim at sexual misconduct in the workplace and to encourage bystanders to speak up:

1. Sexual and other forms of harassment or discrimination are debilitating and distracting for victims, with the effects often lasting long after the behavior occurs.
2. This behavior can have significant effects on a company's results. A hostile work environment can reduce productivity. When you undermine a person's confidence, you reduce their ability to perform,

to trust colleagues, to contribute to a team. It can also make retaining high-performing employees difficult, as many people do not want to work at a company that allows this kind of thing to occur.

3. A culture that tolerates this behavior will eventually attract a lawsuit and/or media attention, and that is deeply damaging to a brand. It draws media attention to critics and disgruntled former employees, it can drive away customers, and it can make recruiting more difficult.

4. As an individual, when you stand up for a victim, you are standing up for yourself and your company or profession. You are saying that you value your own reputation and that you will not work in a place where people are treated badly because it will reflect badly on you as a human being. Jillian is not just standing up for women, she is standing up for venture capital, her industry, as a field that can have integrity and where people should be treated with respect.

5. To give negative feedback in the moment or to report a harasser at the first sign of troubling behavior, you may prevent escalation and further harm not only to the victim or other potential victims but even to the harasser. Perhaps a first warning, verbal or written, will make an impact and keep the harasser from escalating their behavior to something that ruins his or her career. Think of how you handle jokes that make you uncomfortable. You can laugh and go along, or you can frown and say, "OK, I don't think we need to be talking like this." That subtle but persistent feedback will shut those jokes down.

Changing cultural norms is not easy. Some people roll their eyes and say, "Well, you're a wide-eyed dreamer if you think you're going to get people to change." I don't agree with that. I think it's about being specific and intentional about your aspirations. It's easy to overlook that there have been many cultural practices that have become "uncool" in the last century.

When I was a child, throwing trash out the window of a moving car, believe it or not, was a common practice. So common, it helped spark the "Keep America Beautiful" campaign in the 1960s, which is best known for a moving television commercial showing a Native American man with a tear in his eye looking at roadside trash. Later, the state of Texas declared war on littering with a memorable campaign of roadside signs, television commercials featuring well-known Texans like Willie Nelson, and other messaging that warned "Don't mess with Texas." These efforts changed minds and sensibilities about littering. Today, if a stranger catches you tossing a recyclable in a garbage can, they might admonish you.

It's also true that people used to smoke anywhere and everywhere, oblivious to the discomfort of others such as fellow diners, fans seated nearby in a stadium, and passengers in the next airline seat. Today, doing so would be unthinkable, considered disgusting, rude, and in many situations illegal.

In the last 50 years we have gone from the *Mad Men* workplace culture of executives treating the women around them like a harem to a more respectful one. In the next frontier, harassers will need to see that they are out of step not only with the law but also with how civilized people behave.

I came across an intriguing story that tells me that this is beginning to happen—even among venture capitalists in Silicon Valley. A VC who resigned from his firm after multiple accusations of sexual misconduct with female entrepreneurs gave an interview to a newspaper. He talked about the accusations that had put him at odds with his partners and led him to leave his firm. According to the interviewer, the VC seemed to view his behavior as a sort of unfortunate result of not doing a good job at breaking up with the multiple women that he was dating (while married, by the way). The reporter distilled the argument that the VC was making: "I'm just bad at dating."

A number of VCs and other folks I know now refer to that phrase drily. When someone is accused of sexual misconduct or a serial harasser is mentioned as resigning suddenly, they say, "Hmmm, suppose he's 'bad at dating'?" I think that's a good sign. That's how cultures shift. We know from the playground that few things defang a bully better than a withering eye-roll by peers.

CODE MOMENT 15: SAM, SHE'S JUST NOT INTO YOU

Technical writer Sam has trouble making friends, and he's awkward around women in general. But he has been working on a product manual project for MediumCo with Ellen, a graphic designer. There is no reporting relationship, and both Sam and Ellen are single. One day, as they walk out of a meeting, Sam summons his courage and asks Ellen if she'd like to have drinks on Friday night. She smiles and says she has friends in from out of town Friday but "maybe another time." Ten days pass, Sam shoots Ellen the sixth version of an email he's been working on for an hour: "Trivia contest at Bayside Tavern Saturday. Want to be on my team?" One minute later she replies: "Darn it, I'm driving to my parents' house this weekend, leaving Friday night. Have fun—good luck!"

Is it OK for Sam to keep trying . . . or is this is a Code Moment?

For discussion, see appendix, page 268.

CODE MOMENT 16: "SURE, TOTALLY GET IT"

Luke has been assigned to offer technical support to Marco in marketing. They meet two or three times a week in Marco's cubicle. Marco is married to Greg, and they recently adopted twin sons. Luke is always touching Marco's arm or shoulder and over several weekends, Luke has swamped Marco with texts about the project. Annoyed, Marco finally changes their in-person meetings to phone calls. Luke drops by Marco's cubicle Friday afternoon of the fourth week. He suggests to Marco that they go get a beer; Marco replies, "Luke, I respect your skills, but I'm not interested in socializing. And let's try to handle questions in our meetings. I need to focus on my family when I'm home."

"Sure, totally get it," says Luke, smiling. As he walks away, Marco hears him say loudly, "You sick bastard." Marco walks into the hallway, where three other people are looking at him with concern.

Monday morning Marco gets a call from HR. Luke has filed a complaint saying that Marco has been demanding sexual favors in exchange for recommending him for a bonus for this project. Another colleague tells Marco that Luke has posted a statement on Facebook saying, "It ain't right my tormenter acts like Mr. Family Man when I'm supposed to shut up and do my job."

HR investigates. Marco's officemates heard Luke call out Marco, but there is no evidence to back up Luke's claims—or exonerate Marco. Then, HR gets an anonymous voicemail on the ethics hotline. "I worked with Luke X at another company. I just heard he accused someone of demanding sex. He's done this twice before."

Yikes! What would a high-integrity HR team do?

For discussion, see appendix, page 270.

11

Who you do business with defines you: Extending the integrity message to a community

Businesses with a significant Internet-centered customer base confront a unique challenge: taking the path of Intentional Integrity requires them to look not only at their employees but also at their own user community for signs of inappropriate behavior. They must weigh difficult trade-offs between values such as freedom of speech, tolerance, and inclusiveness on a platform. But the stakes keep getting higher: individuals who have committed extraordinary acts of violence or espouse hate often use Internet communities to advocate for their extreme views. High-integrity, courageous Internet platform leadership can promote and model positive behavior in society more broadly.

In the early days of online platforms, pioneers like America Online (AOL), eBay, and Yahoo! understood that they were not just creating new kinds of businesses, they were creating and managing communities. People went to these sites to connect, to share and consume information, even to offer support to one another. Pez collectors went on eBay to buy but also to meet other Pez collectors.

The trend has continued in a new generation of platform companies such as Facebook, Uber, Lyft, YouTube, Poshmark, Pinterest, and Airbnb. Fishing guides, car mechanics, and investment advisors post free instructional videos on YouTube to get "followers" and build their brands. People go on Airbnb not just to reserve a room for the night but also to see listings and plan trips—guest reviews and the availability of different accommodation options, for example, can shape an entire family vacation.

Platforms exploded in popularity in part because they created an unprecedented opportunity to allow users to connect with other people who care about what they care about. Ultimately, commerce platforms profited by charging fees, and social media platforms benefited from selling advertising, paid placements, and, yes, data about community members.

As we've seen, online sites that started out as hubs for new insights, camaraderie, and more efficient points of connection developed a dark side as well. Some companies hosting and nurturing these digital ecosystems have exploited relationships on their platforms and pursued revenue in unethical ways. For example, Facebook was fined a record-setting $5 billion for abusing the privacy rights of its users when it failed to adequately monitor and police researchers who collected data on 87 million Facebook users and passed it to Cambridge Analytica. Among other things, Cambridge Analytica used the information to design subversive campaigns to influence the 2016 presidential election.[1]

The "community" issue I want to zero in on has become acute for platform companies, although the larger issue also impacts more traditional companies of every size and industry. The bulk of this book has focused on how organizations promote an ethical work environment. But internet companies also must think about customers and users who don't conform to the company's values. It's in the same vein as Patagonia refusing to let its fleece be embroidered with the logo of companies that don't protect the planet. It's about Dick's Sporting Goods deciding that, despite its deep commitment to hunters and its general support of the Second Amendment, it was no longer going to sell weapons to individuals under age 21 or semiautomatic weapons that are becoming the tools of mass murder across the country.

At some point, Intentional Integrity demands that companies must make judgments about certain users or customers' behavior and sever their relationship with those whose values are inconsistent with their own.

I watched Internet platform community rules evolve as an early Internet user on America Online, and I was directly involved in creating such rules at eBay two decades ago. The topic has only grown in importance since then. It's increasingly clear that Internet platform companies can't just sidestep questions about what their customers and community members are actually *doing* on their platform versus the platform's own values. If companies don't embrace and display integrity in how they manage their community, a tiny fringe faction of their customer base can do lasting damage to their brands.

The literal frame

A company's web page, complete with its name and logo and other branding, creates a literal "frame" around the content on its site. Hate speech or images and videos containing offensive content are obvious things that platform companies may ban on their sites. But it's not just about what users post that is relevant to what is "in your frame."

I'll start with a serious but relatively contained hypothetical. Let's say I welcome you as a service provider on my dog-walker platform. You pass my background check and agree to follow my rules. Dog owners sign up online and use the platform to request a qualified walker, who then goes to their home and gains access through a hidden key or keypad. It's a model that requires real trust.

You accept an assignment, go to a client's home, and take Fido to the park. But you ask friends to pick you up at the client's house. You let them inside to wait in the kitchen while you put Fido back in his crate. They help themselves to a couple of beers from the fridge. You didn't realize this until later—but the owner's security camera captures it all in high def.

Even though my website is "just a platform" and you the dog walker are not my employee, my brand brought you and the client together. Your friends violated the law, but your poor judgment in letting them in the house impacts my brand. If I want to develop and grow a trusted platform, I can't just shrug and act like a few bad apples are going to slip through the vetting. I need to proactively educate service providers on how to behave, reinforce this message clearly and repeatedly, and create serious consequences such as banning rule-breakers from the platform when they fail to comply with my policies.

If Fido's owner posts the security video online and leaves a bad review on Yelp, potential customers who might not even have thought of something like this happening will be turned off. I might bend over backward to make it up to the client with free walks, apologies, and some plan to better educate dog walkers so this doesn't happen again, but I could still lose customers even though I'm "just the middleman."

Navigating a "cesspool"

The issues in the dog-walking example are pretty straightforward. Now, let's turn to a platform that in August 2019 became a flashpoint for what some claimed was overtly encouraging violence. America was reeling from back-to-back horrific mass killings in El Paso, Texas, and Dayton, Ohio. In the space of two days, 30 people were killed and several dozen injured. The Dayton gunman was killed at the scene by police; the El Paso shooter was apprehended and is in custody.

The perpetrator of the El Paso incident[2] was a user of the 8chan Internet community, an anonymous discussion platform started in 2013 as a home for unrestricted free speech. According to media accounts, it soon became dominated by discussions around a variety of ugly and extreme behaviors, including pedophilia, violence, racism, and domestic terrorism. In fact its original founder, who had left the organization by the time the El Paso shootings occurred, called for it to be shut down.[3]

Before traveling from Allen, Texas, to El Paso to open fire in a Walmart, the shooter posted a manifesto on 8chan and urged others to share it. It describes his plans for mass murder of Hispanics "invading" the United States. This followed two other recent mass shooting incidents in New Zealand and California where the perpetrators also posted material on 8chan before committing horrendous murders. When these events occurred, "Embrace infamy" was the slogan on 8chan's home page.

No one expected much ethical soul-searching from 8chan's leaders. However, after the El Paso shooting, attention shifted to web infrastructure and security companies that provided 8chan with technology—most notably a San Francisco company called Cloudflare. Cloudflare is a large web services and infrastructure company that claims to work with over 20 million websites and for 10 percent of the companies in the Fortune 1000. It counted 8chan as a customer, and had sold 8chan services to protect it from hackers and denial-of-service attacks. Cloudflare purports to be neutral, against censorship—just a utility for the web. It had been criticized in the past for working with other groups with antisocial values, including a neo-Nazi site that it eventually stopped supporting after the lethal white supremacist rally in Charlottesville, Virginia, in 2017.

After the El Paso shooting, Cloudflare's general counsel told the *Washington Post* that it did not intend to stop working for 8chan, insisting that "inserting ourselves as the judge and jury on these things is very problematic. . . . It's easy for folks to approach us with one website, but for us, we need to come up with a rule that we can apply to over 20 million different web properties."[4] Separately, the CEO of Cloudflare, Matthew Prince, told *New York Times* columnist Kevin Roose that he was disgusted with 8chan but torn about the trade-offs in severing ties to them. Banning 8chan "would make our lives a lot easier," Prince told Roose, "but it would make the job of law enforcement and controlling hate groups online harder." The *Times* story said there was disagreement among the Cloudflare staff about taking on the role of a censor.[5]

Not long after the CEO was quoted, Cloudflare reversed its position and said it would no longer sell 8chan its services. In a blog post, Prince said that he made his decision in part because 8chan had "repeatedly proven itself to be a cesspool of hate."[6]

Then, there followed a chain reaction of other companies grappling with fallout regarding 8chan, which has since rebranded itself as 8kun. According to GeekWire, Amazon confirmed that it was looking into a situation with a Seattle company called Epik, which uses Amazon Web Services to host some of its backup sites.[7] Epik briefly helped revive 8chan after Cloudflare ceased protecting it (and hackers bombarded it with denial-of-service attacks), although Epik later reversed that decision. Amazon said it wanted to make sure that AWS was not indirectly enabling 8chan through Epik. Geek-Wire shared the content of an email it said an Amazon spokesperson had sent: "8chan's content is hate speech and is unacceptable according to our Acceptable Use Policy. Although 8chan is not hosted on AWS, we are working with their direct provider (Epik) to ensure that 8chan is not indirectly using AWS resources through any of our customers." Epik, meanwhile, was using servers from a company called Voxility; Voxility immediately shut off access to those servers when it realized they were carrying 8chan traffic. Complicated? Yes, and no wonder the Internet is also called the "Web."

I don't know the teams at Cloudflare, Epik, or Voxility, but this example strikes me as a good demonstration that every company needs to understand what it stands for and what its mission is *before* a crisis erupts. *Like it or not, who you do business with, and who you take money from, defines you.* I don't underestimate the policy challenge that the Cloudflare general counsel focused on initially. No company likes the idea of censoring content. I've been in those shoes. But appearing to dither over whether you want your company's brand associated with three horrific mass murders is something that rises well above the mechanics or details of policy. I'm glad Cloudflare ultimately made the right ethical decision.

You can't look away

Fast-growing companies grapple with a variety of integrity moments when trying to get market traction. For example, Uber faced one that speaks to a platform's indirect impacts on users that can't be ignored. *New York Times* reporter Mike Isaac has written a book called *Super Pumped: The Battle for Uber,* in which he talks about Uber's 2015 effort to quickly scale drivers and riders in São Paulo and Rio de Janeiro. To grow the business, Uber removed friction in the sign-up process—all someone needed to do to sign up and use Uber was an email address or a phone number. "A person could access Uber with a bogus email, then play a version of 'Uber roulette': They'd hail a car, then cause mayhem. Vehicles were stolen and burned; drivers were assaulted, robbed, and occasionally murdered. The company stuck with the low-friction sign-up system, even as violence increased."[8]

As in the dog-walking example, Uber didn't commit those crimes or deliberately put drivers in danger, but it was unquestionably a factor in those negative consequences. Isaac says, "Uber executives were not totally indifferent to the dangers drivers faced in emerging markets. But they had major blind spots because of their fixation on growth, their belief in technological solutions, and a casual application of financial incentives that often inflamed existing cultural problems."[9] The consequence, according to Isaac, was the murders of sixteen Brazilian Uber drivers.

The other side

It's not difficult to find examples of companies that have turned a blind eye (or are tempted to turn a blind eye) to the second- and third-level consequences of what their platforms or companies have created. Tech company leaders and investors are typically obsessed with "first-mover advantage" in the early days of a platform start-up's life, when gaining market share before copycats jump in becomes a fixation. If leaders waited to ponder the potential social and ethical implications of every decision, they might be out of business before the answers even matter.

It's also only fair to point out that policing a global online platform is a very difficult and expensive challenge, and companies often invest considerable "behind-the-scenes" efforts that its users may not be aware of. For example, Facebook has extensive "Community Standards" rules, including descriptions of what criteria the site uses to remove posts and how decisions can be appealed. Clearly, the company has thought about and struggled with how to approach incredibly complex, bizarre, even chilling content. For example, under "Violence and Graphic Content," Facebook warns, "Do not post: Imagery of violence committed against real people or animals with comments or captions by the poster that contain: Enjoyment of suffering; Enjoyment of humiliation; Erotic response to suffering; Remarks that speak positively of the violence; Or remarks indicating that the poster is sharing footage for sensational viewing pleasure." It goes on: "Do not post: Videos of dying, wounded or dead people if they contain: Dismemberment unless in a medical setting; visible internal organs; charred or burning people unless in the context of cremation or self-immolation when that action is a form of political speech or newsworthy; victims of cannibalism."[10]

When I worked at eBay, we wrote one of the first comprehensive sets of community standards on the Internet. And our team had to look at plenty of offensive, violent, and graphic listings, but at least that universe was limited to items for sale. I don't envy Facebook and YouTube trying to be specific about the limitless variety of photos, videos, and commentary its community members might post. In fact, a number of my colleagues from the early eBay Trust and Safety days are on those Facebook and YouTube teams, still struggling with these tough issues.

It's one thing to have a rule and another to enforce it. I doubt most people realize that these extensive Facebook standards exist. I imagine they assume there is some kind of security team that is in place to investigate offensive items when they're reported. There was a fascinating story that appeared in *Vanity Fair* in early 2019 that discussed the difficulty Facebook has had in creating automated systems for finding and taking down hate speech or other offensive language. The presumption that human beings are making decisions about individual posts generally is not correct; Facebook and other popular platforms today are policed mainly by software rules designed to catch prohibited speech and images before they are posted. As the story explains, however, these platforms are once again limited by all the variations they tell the system to look for, and they won't be able to catch posts by creative users who will go to extraordinary lengths to reverse engineer and evade that software. At one point on Facebook, attacks or insults aimed at "white men" were disallowed, while insults or threats to "Latino theologians," for example, were not, simply because such a specific threat had not been imagined and prioritized in the software.[11]

YouTube has struggled with offensive content as well. Defining legal and illegal activity is much easier than defining good and bad taste, or the point where humor crosses a line and becomes crass exploitation or cruelty. In August 2019, the *Washington Post* interviewed YouTube moderators charged with enforcing standards and recommending videos for removal. Because YouTube is essentially in partnership with some of its "stars" or channel leaders, it stands to lose considerable advertising revenue if it removes sensational content that attracts enormous numbers of viewers. The story described situations where critics say the company made decisions that went against its own standards because it wanted to maintain its connection to sometimes outrageous but undeniably revenue-generating channels.[12]

For example, YouTube's popular channel leader Logan Paul, whose brand image is that of a funny millennial dude, posted a video of himself appearing to mock a Japanese corpse, a suicide victim who had hanged himself from a tree in a forest near Mount Fuji and whose body had not yet been taken down. Was temporarily suspending Paul from YouTube's "preferred advertiser" program a sufficient punishment for this and other videos of dubious taste he had made? Is it ethically acceptable for platforms to be more lenient with their most popular contributors? I would say no, but ultimately, these are tests of leadership that need to be addressed head-on, consistent with the values of each platform. If this is how YouTube's leadership manages their platform, they should admit that, and then users can choose to embrace or reject that point of view. I think the best leaders explain their position on these types of tough calls without clinging to talking points, but rather in a human and authentic manner, openly recognizing the challenges of "getting it right."

There is an organization called Chief Executives for Corporate Purpose (CECP) that represents leaders of companies with more than $6.6 trillion in revenues, who meet periodically to talk about "critical success factors in building businesses for the long term." At its 2019 meeting, the key takeaways the organization reported involved cultivating and sustaining a dynamic workforce by building trust; supporting diversity and being accountable; listening to voices from key stakeholders (employees, communities, consumers, and investors); taking a long view; and, apropos of the subject of this chapter, acting on company values and being prepared for the blowback—but also support. It is fully aligned with the goals of Business Roundtable in trying to broaden CEOs' views of their stakeholders and their concerns.[13]

A great example of long-term thinking about broader community issues came at the meeting from Dick's Sporting Goods' CEO Edward W. Stack, who told the CECP gathering, "I'm a firm believer that our nation's most precious natural resource is our kids. We knew there would be a lot of blowback when we made our decision to take assault-style rifles and high-capacity ammunition off the shelves, and there was. But what we weren't ready for was the outpouring of support for what we did."[14]

Dick's isn't an Internet platform company, but Stack had the courage to admit that a tiny minority of potential customers' behavior represented such an affront to his company's concern about the health and safety of kids that he wasn't going to sit back—he was going to act. Some hunters were angry and stopped shopping at Dick's in the wake of its decisions, but other customers began shopping there in part to support the company's new gun policy. I have friends who now go out of their way to try to buy gear from Dick's when they need cleats for their kids or tennis balls or just about anything sports related, and they write emails and tell store managers that they appreciate their stand on sensible gun policies. In May 2019, the company reported that revenues were growing again, and its decision to lower its emphasis on hunting and diversify into categories that had more year-round appeal appeared to be on track.

Clearly, you'll have to set your ethics goggles to a "wide angle" when you fix them on the issues of a platform community or your customer base. However, the first step still begins with you: What are your values?

What is your purpose? How do you want people to behave who associate themselves with your brand or buy your products? Are there lines you can't let them cross without consequences?

Déjà vu

These days, there seems to be a resurgence of white supremacy organizations and hate speech. What's causing their reemergence, why are they gaining new acolytes? I've personally been involved with two companies that faced questions about their enabling of white supremacy messages on the Internet—and they occurred nearly two decades apart. In both cases, the CEOs chose a course of integrity in making decisions that put them at odds with some of their own customers.

Early in eBay's life, Starbucks founder Howard Schultz was a director there. He returned from a trip to Auschwitz, the site of a World War II concentration camp. He was deeply affected by his visit, and he was concerned about the rise of white supremacist rhetoric and propaganda items like T-shirts, posters, and Nazi-related items appearing in the United States. Some of these things were being listed on eBay. In a board meeting, he advocated for banning all Nazi-related items immediately.

Our CEO Meg Whitman asked me to investigate this. I was surprised to find that we were actually talking about two distinct kinds of merchandise. The first was authentic Nazi-related memorabilia. Many American service members picked up various souvenirs before they left the European theater during World War II: Nazi helmets, medals, caps, uniforms, bayonets, various propaganda posters and books, and other items. As far as we could tell, most of the sellers of authentic items were NOT promoting Nazism, and there were plenty of collectors of these items who were not Nazi sympathizers.

In some cases, the original owners or their heirs needed money, and being able to sell these assets was their right, just as selling assets like a stamp or coin collection might be. And the buyers might be people like Susanna Bolten Connaughton, an author and historian I know whose father spent two years in a Polish POW camp run by the Nazis during World War II. She is part of an international group that is working to create a museum about that camp, and she often searches eBay for photographs and memorabilia of the period that include references to or photographs of Nazis. In fact, museum curators in general are big users of eBay, as are researchers who need references for movie and television show costumes and sets.

The second group of items were *replica* items and pro-Nazi propaganda on T-shirts, posters, banners, or flags, or replica uniforms created and traded among white supremacist, Nazi-sympathizing groups. These items were materially different, and their market was different—they actively sought white supremacist buyers.

Deciding what to do with replicas was easy—we immediately established a rule banning their sale on eBay. The historical items were more challenging. Initially, the eBay team was reluctant to ban those items. Where would we ever stop if we began picking sides involving items related to various historical conflicts? From Ireland to Israel to Uganda to Vietnam, items connected to one or another set of combatants or factions ended up on eBay. Certain items triggered intense emotions within the eBay community, but while I was comfortable recommending that we remove items attacking ethnic or religious groups or advancing other white supremacy agendas, we had concerns about banning authentic items. I tend to agree that when you start "banning" historical items, you run the risk of burying and forgetting history.

But as Meg conveyed in her book *The Power of Many*, Howard did not buy that argument.[15] He reminded the board that even though it's really tough to draw a line, that's what leaders do—they draw lines. He said the bottom line was that we were profiting by allowing people with sinister and even violent motives and messages to trade items on our platform. He kept asking Meg, "What do you want the character of your company to be?"

Eventually, following orders from the board, we banned all white supremacist propaganda and almost all Nazi-related items, except for those with very specific historical significance, such as authentic photographs.

Over time, we became comfortable with drawing lines to ban items that Americans were free to talk about or own but that did not reflect what we wanted our platform to represent. We banned entire categories of "murderabilia," for example—items like the refrigerator a serial killer stored severed body parts in. We banned Ku Klux Klan white sheet hoods. Meg decided, and subsequent CEOs have agreed (although eBay is constantly revising and updating its rules), that you must consider the connection of your brand to the messages and impact of what appears on your website.

That said, most people aren't going to consult some lengthy list of rules before they try to post an item to sell or search for something they're interested in. In the very early days of eBay, all we could do was make the rule and assign employees to routinely search for keywords in listings or respond to reports of violations from the community. Eventually we created software (fondly known internally as eLVIS, for "eBay Listing Violation Inspection System") to find recalled and dangerous items like jarts, pelts or products derived from endangered animals (like cheetah or tigers), prescription drugs, weapons, alcohol, or explosives; the software would flag the listing for review before or as it went up, and the team would review it.

So despite what the Cloudflare GC said, the challenge of creating a policy that applies broadly and fairly is not new, but the difficulty in doing so should not be allowed to obscure the question: What do you want your company to stand for? It's not easy to tackle these threats to a company's image or brand, but you can't put it off indefinitely either, pleading complexity. If you do, you lack integrity—and you risk a brand disaster.

The "moment you embrace adventure"

My second brush with white supremacy as a work issue was more recent.

At Airbnb, we use our community standards code to address a number of user-behavior issues related to privacy, safety, fairness, security, authenticity, and reliability. In terms of privacy, for example, we expressly prohibit hosts from using video cameras in sleeping or bathroom areas of listings, and we insist that hosts fully reveal the existence and placement of any other cameras on the property. Meanwhile, we ask guests not to take or share photos or video of the private areas of a home or the owners without their express permission.

We didn't just make up our community standard rules to use as legal shields, we did so to actively promote certain values and behaviors on our platform and beyond it.

Here's a situation that was one of my proudest moments at Airbnb. In 2017, organizers of a white supremacist rally in Charlottesville, Virginia, told visitors to their website to check Airbnb to find a place to stay while attending the rally. We say in our community standards that users—hosts and guests—must agree to "accept people regardless of their race, religion, national origin, ethnicity, disability, sex, gender identity, sexual orientation, or age." By definition, the purpose of this rally was to promote bigotry and racist views.

Brian Chesky, our CEO, had no trouble making the decision—Airbnb was not going to profit from this. It went against our values. We checked the names of prominent white supremacists who had been speaking out and announcing their intention to attend the rally, and we searched to see if they had reservations booked on Airbnb. We canceled the reservations, alerting them and the hosts that by advocating hate speech against racial groups they had violated the terms of using Airbnb. Protest organizers vowed retribution, boycotts, etc. I couldn't tell you if any of that happened, but we didn't lose sleep over being boycotted by white supremacists. Forfeiting short-term revenues to stay true to our values was in the best long-term interest of our stakeholders.

For platform companies, software tools and analytics are evolving that can head off problems before they occur. But software alone won't solve these dilemmas. Values and integrity are needed so that you can do the right thing even when it's hard. The behavior of your community members on your Internet platform becomes your brand, just as much as a logo sewn to a shirt you manufacture or the quality of the fries in your fast-food restaurant does. In the early days of the Internet, it was fashionable to say that you stood for the First Amendment and freedom of speech, openness, accepting all participants, all items or videos or pictures without judgment. Those days are past.

Conclusion

A superpower for our times

I've now covered the Six Cs—the who, what, when, why, how, and how-often basics of nurturing integrity in the workplace.

But at Airbnb we also look at integrity as a superpower and as a vital component of what our CEO Brian Chesky calls creating a twenty-first-century company. As I'll explain in this final chapter, a twenty-first-century company reaches beyond the next quarter's financial results; it can't be successful unless it balances the needs of all its stakeholders and contributes to creating a better world for everyone. And so, in hopes of getting everyone—business people, communities, policy makers—fired up about why this matters, let's unpack the notion in more detail. Think of this final chapter as being about what's possible when choosing a path of integrity becomes automatic.

My work over the last twenty years has convinced me that integrity pays back much more than it costs in time and resources. But in researching this book, I've also tried to reality-check my ideas with a diverse set of leaders in a number of different kinds of organizations and companies: traditional global corporations, venture capital, academia, politics, media, tech, retailing, start-ups, family-owned businesses, and others. I've also spoken with individuals in unique roles at different levels of organizations. You've read some of their comments, and their help and support have shaped the messages of this book.

Airbnb CEO Brian Chesky shared his own personal Code Moment

when one of our host's apartments was vandalized by a user of our platform. Another real-life integrity moment I'd like to share comes from Adam Silver, the commissioner of the NBA. On a Friday in April 2014, the online celebrity tabloid site TMZ went live with a jaw-dropping audio clip: A woman who had been dating Donald Sterling, the owner of the Los Angeles Clippers, gave TMZ an audio recording of him chastising her for posing with professional athletes and posting the photographs on social media. Among the comments Sterling made was this one: "It bothers me a lot that you want to broadcast that you're associating with black people."[1]

For the Clippers and for the NBA, this was a Code Double Red. From a basic human perspective, Sterling's racist comments were appalling. And from a business perspective, the thought of a team owner saying something that would clearly be deeply offensive to two of his main stakeholders—his players and fans—was sheer idiocy.

As an avid sports fan, I know professional sports is an arena where the best and worst of human nature can be found. Come-from-behind victories, a player overcoming injury or adversity, great displays of teamwork—all are the stuff of inspiring, iconic moments. But there are also astonishing examples of the opposite of integrity, such as athletes using illegal performance-enhancing drugs or taunting opponents with offensive slurs. Or when athletes turn the same aggression they use against opponents their own size on their spouses or partners.

At the time the Sterling tape surfaced, the NBA was still recovering from another scandal in which a veteran referee admitted he had bet on dozens of games he officiated, and some around the league claimed he had called more fouls on opponents of the team he picked to win. Adam Silver had only been the commissioner for a few months, and handling the cantankerous billionaire owner Sterling fell on his shoulders.

Talk about a complex slate of stakeholders to consider: players, fans, sponsors, other NBA team owners, the media, civil rights activists, Clippers team employees, and head coach Doc Rivers (himself an African American) were all impacted in a variety of ways, and all reacted differently. For his part, Silver listened to the recording within 24 hours of TMZ's posts; he says he was dismayed and frustrated. First question he says he asked his team: *Are we sure this is actually Sterling?*

As social media exploded with negative posts, Silver was determined to investigate and base his decisions on facts, not rumors. Meanwhile, the Clippers were in the playoffs, and many questions flew around the NBA ecosystem: Will the players boycott the next game in protest? Would Clippers coach Doc Rivers quit?

As he waited for his team to analyze the audio clip, Silver says he thought about the NBA's legacy of brave individuals fighting for equality. One of the most legendary was Boston Celtics center Bill Russell, who played during a period of open and aggressive racism in the United States. Once, on a team road trip in Kentucky, a restaurant refused to serve black members of the Celtics, and Russell led his teammates in refusing to play a scheduled game. He later opened an integrated basketball camp in Mississippi in the early 1960s despite the Ku Klux Klan menacing him, and he famously went to Washington, DC, to sit in the front row when Dr. Martin Luther King delivered what became known as the "I Have a Dream" speech.

Over time, the NBA came to embrace equality as a core value. Silver says he realized that Sterling's comments struck at the heart of the league's commitment to equality and respect for all athletes regardless of race, religion, national origin, or other fundamental qualities unrelated to their basketball skills.

By Tuesday morning Silver was satisfied that it was Sterling on the recording, and he announced the NBA would fine Sterling $2.5 million and ban him from the NBA for life. He also said he would work with the NBA's ownership group to force Sterling to sell the team. It was the harshest penalty ever levied against an owner. Privately, some raised the question whether the league had the right to weigh in on a recording of a private conversation made by a person (Sterling's girlfriend at the time) who appeared bent on revenge. However, many had no such misgivings. LeBron James tweeted: "Commissioner Silver thank you for protecting our beautiful and powerful league!! Great leader!!" Dallas Mavericks owner Mark Cuban added: "I agree 100% with commissioner Silvers findings and the actions taken against Donald Sterling."[2] One by one, stakeholders gave Silver thumbs up for taking a hard stand. Doc Rivers did not quit, Clippers players did not boycott the playoffs, and planned public protests were canceled.

Over the next several months, the combative Sterling made sure the conflict didn't go away quickly or quietly, but Steve Ballmer, the former

CEO of Microsoft, bought the team for $2 billion by the fall of 2014. Donald Sterling made an appearance on CNN where he claimed he had been "baited" by his former girlfriend to make the comments on the recording, and then he went on to make more offensive and inappropriate comments. Sterling is now gone from basketball. When I met Adam Silver, he was in his fifth year running the NBA.

✦

Without consequences, the commitment an organization makes to its values rings hollow. Figuring out consequences for ugly behavior is a stressful experience; nonetheless, ethical leaders don't shrink from these situations. Values-based decision-making in the NBA case sent an important and powerful signal not just to the basketball world but to the entire country. When respected and popular players such as LeBron James applauded Silver's leadership, it broadcast to the world that courage in the face of a scourge like racism matters. Courage reaches across divisions between stakeholders. Integrity in the face of turmoil allowed a broad slate of stakeholders to move on with confidence that the NBA had strong leadership. Clippers players, coaches, and team employees could be proud of their team again and stand apart from one man's ill-tempered racist rants. Sponsors and fans stayed loyal.

Silver is an example of a leader who has shown that, by making multiple tough decisions, a commitment to integrity can create a powerful and positive energy for an organization. He often advocates for hiring more women into not only the NBA office itself but also specific teams, including as coaches. He was instrumental in deciding to move the NBA All-Star Game out of Charlotte, North Carolina, when the state passed a controversial law about transgender bathrooms that seemed, again, to flout the league's commitment to equality. "Even if people disagree, I think they will respect you if you tie your decision to your company's values. Equality is part of the DNA of our league," Silver told me.

He also shared with me some mistakes he's made. In 2019, he did not act on rumors that teams were negotiating with players before the supposedly hard and fast free agent period began. *Sports Illustrated* took the NBA to task when a slew of leaks and announcements showed half a dozen teams had violated the rule. He says today, "I should have realized it was corrosive to have a rule on the books and not enforce it." So at the next owners' meeting, he focused on important questions: Do we want to have this rule? If we have it, how far should we go to enforce it? Check emails? Phone logs? "I think it's OK to openly talk about how complex it is to face these dilemmas and how difficult decisions can be. I'm not smarter than anybody else, and these situations are not clear-cut. But it is up to me to be authentic and transparent." Silver says he sees his job, and that of any leader, as being willing to "lean into complexity."

✦

At Airbnb, embracing integrity also energizes us and inspires us to run our company in alignment with that value. One reason Airbnb encourages me to speak about Intentional Integrity to other companies, organizations, and leaders is that we believe that elevating integrity as a value can unleash a virtuous cycle, encouraging other organizations to contribute in a more positive way to issues that impact everyone. Issues like climate change, promoting diversity and equality, supporting healthy oceans, working to diminish violence in society, and helping those struggling with basic life challenges, such as affordable housing, healthcare, and better access for the disabled. Maybe even how we view and treat one another in our civil discourse.

When companies are engaged as ethical participants in a community, whether online or in the "real world," they represent a powerful force. I had a conversation with Brian Chesky about how he came to embrace the point of view that involves both a long-term view of corporate success and a broad perspective in terms of paying attention to all stakeholders. He pointed out that his personal background is different from that of many tech CEOs.

Brian's parents were social workers, and he began his career as an industrial designer, studying at the Rhode Island School of Design (RISD). "Artists don't want power, they want influence. Power is compelling people to do things, influence is inspiring people to do things. I never tried to have a lot of power, or I wouldn't have aspired to create a website renting air mattresses for the night." But more specifically, "At RISD there was a trend around ethical design, making products good for the environment. If you made something that wasn't inherently good for society, if its essence didn't shine through, it wasn't a good design. The idea was we should be responsible for things we make; it was ingrained in me at

RISD." After he and friends Joe Gebbia (who also attended RISD) and Nathan Blecharczyk launched Airbnb, Brian says that it was natural for them to have a different point of view than technologists or leaders who came from financial backgrounds. "We had a wider lens about what we were doing," Brian says. "We wanted to be a force for good in the world."

When strong leaders see themselves as having that power, which prepares them to exercise it within their own sphere of influence inside their company, great things can happen. Jonah Goldberg of the American Enterprise Institute recently wrote a piece on the political polarization plaguing America, arguing that both the left and the right are stressing the wrong antidotes. He writes that most of the issues ripping us apart involve centralized government and partisan efforts to use media to "nationalize" points of view, to suggest the "other side" is not behaving like true Americans. Instead, "What we need is communities, and the idea of national community is a myth. Conversation is done face-to-face and person-to-person, and so is community."[3]

Strong communities are built and held together by people who live and work side by side, and the work dynamic is important and sometimes overlooked. Unlike governments, companies are united by one leader, one board, one mission, and employees working toward shared goals. Companies generally are civil places where decorum is expected; they aren't prone to ideological lurches in messaging or policy. Large companies have the power of money and global orientation, with employees in offices around the world. They must rise above divisions of country. When a company's employees feel valued, trusted, and inspired by the company's higher purpose, they think beyond paychecks and bonuses and do their best out of pride and in the spirit of building something good and important.

At Airbnb, our mission is to help create a world where everyone can belong anywhere. It impacts everything we do, and yet we also know that we can't do it alone. The nature of our business means we need to think about living, breathing places. Places where our hosts live. Places our guests travel to for interesting and fun experiences. Global issues like pollution, climate change, discrimination, and privacy are threats to the entire human community, but they play out in unique ways in millions of places where stakeholders need to lean into the complexity and work together. It follows that we believe all companies are stakeholders in the future of our planet and the conditions that our fellow human beings confront. Bound by a commitment to integrity, we can make the world better.

A fundamental shift in thinking

New York Times columnist David Brooks points out, "In a healthy society, people try to balance a whole bunch of different priorities: economic, social, moral, familial. Somehow over the past 40 years economic priorities took the top spot and obliterated everything else. As a matter of policy, we privileged economics and then eventually no longer could even see that there could be other priorities." Brooks says it's become way too common for investors to "demand that every company ruthlessly cut the cost of its employees and ruthlessly screw its hometown if it will raise the short-term stock price." He adds, "We turned off the moral lens."[4]

Not every company put away its ethics goggles. I look around today and see companies who are acting in ways that rebalance the priorities Brooks cites. My prior company Chegg has a devoted cadre of employees who support Second Harvest Food Bank in their communities, and the company has donated a quarter of a million dollars to fight hunger. The company chose that cause for a very important—and I would say nonobvious—reason directly linked to its mission and purpose. "Our objective is developing employees who do everything they can to serve the student. Well, 36 percent of students in this country are hungry," CEO Dan Rosensweig explained to me. The company even learned that 50 percent of students at a university in its own backyard, San Jose State, report that they skip meals due to cost. Imagine the issues we could tackle if more companies thought about their customers not just as a revenue source, but in a holistic way. What do they need, how can we help them achieve their goals?

The idea of returning to a better balance of corporate priorities is gaining many advocates, even among some investors. JPMorgan Chase CEO Jamie Dimon and Warren Buffett of Berkshire Hathaway jointly wrote a 2018 op-ed in the *Wall Street Journal*, noting, "The financial markets have become too focused on the short term. Quarterly earnings-per-share guidance is a major driver of this trend and contributes to a shift away from long-term investments. Companies frequently hold back on technology spending, hiring, and research and development to meet quarterly earnings forecasts that may be affected by factors outside the company's control, such as commodity-price fluctuations, stock-market volatility and even the weather." Ultimately, they continued, this fixation is "depriving the economy of innovation and opportunity."[5] In other words, "short-termism" is bad for these companies, and it's bad for all of us.

We've already mentioned the movement on one of the iconic procapitalist, pro-business organizations—Business Roundtable—on this issue. If we want this movement to continue, I believe it will begin with the conversations described in this book. It demands that we set specific policies intentionally based on higher values and reflecting diverse input. Everyone in a company must hold one another accountable. Authentic cherry-tree moments when individuals admit a mistake and take responsibility should become a national aspiration again, one that avoids the spin and lies that sap our spirits.

Being a leader around integrity means constantly evaluating processes and strategies for impact and making changes when necessary. For example, one of those integrity traps we've talked about is how compensation incentives can distort a company's ethical calculus. When employees are evaluated and rewarded on throughput but not quality, quality slips. As long as shareholder return is high, some leaders may ignore cornercutting that escalates to fraud, bribery, and general dishonesty. When compensation plans and bonuses are based on meeting narrow financial and stock price targets, even employees well below the C-suite may ignore serious harm to certain stakeholders if the behavior offers them immediate benefits.

At eBay, when we realized our feedback system by itself wasn't enough to police behavior on the platform, Meg Whitman made sure that we pivoted. Satisfying buyers became a larger factor in computing compensation metrics. As a result, our folks changed their attitudes toward sellers who failed to deliver a high-quality buyer experience. The point: you will not get everything right on the first try, but if you find that actions aren't living up to your values and standards, you must assess, adjust, fix, and move forward.

Airbnb and other progressive companies are rallying around ideas like Simon Sinek's, an author who coined the term "infinite time horizon," to suggest that while a modern company must set and work to meet growth targets, its real goal should be to lead its industry indefinitely. To accomplish this goal, the company must constantly acknowledge and balance the interests of all stakeholders and assess its long-term or broader impact. "One-dimensional, pessimistic, stick-to-your-guns people are not going to thrive in the new world. People are looking for leaders who are purpose-driven. Employees expect their leaders to be an embodiment of their values," Brian Chesky believes. "What a twentieth-century leader looks like is different from what a twenty-first-century leader looks like. A twentieth-century leader was white, male, straight. Today a leader can come from anywhere and look like anything. There isn't a look of a leader. What matters is how they behave. They have to have a much longer time horizon."

Wachtell, Lipton, Rosen & Katz partner Marty Lipton in 2019 wrote a white paper he sent to his firm's clients in which he specifically addressed the responsibilities of boards today.[6] Lipton, prompted by some recent court cases, identified more than two dozen duties of modern boards, and I was struck by how many—including the very first he named—addressed ethics and the issue of being open to stakeholder concerns. He said, first and foremost, that boards are expected to "recognize the heightened focus of investors on 'purpose' and 'culture' and an expanded notion of stakeholder interests that includes employees, customers, communities, the economy and society as a whole and work with management to develop metrics to enable the corporation to demonstrate their value."

It would have been unheard-of ten years ago to see a corporate law firm prioritize these issues.

When you respond to values-related issues, you will always hear from those who say, "OK, today it's white supremacy; what will it be tomorrow? Any big event raises issues some people object to. Are the motives of why our guests visit a place really our business?" At Airbnb our answer is yes—if our customers or partners express views antithetical to our mission and values and attach them to our brand, we feel obliged to act. It would be hypocritical of us to expect our employees to follow our rules based on those values but then profit from transactions that betray them.

Now, realize that the more an organization emphasizes ethics and values in front of its employees, the more likely employees are to hold up a mirror to the company's broad array of business practices. The scope of those questions may be unpredictable. Is the company fundamentally an ethical one if it profits by secretly polluting the skies or seas or if it turns a blind eye to other companies using its platforms for unethical purposes?

This might feel a little scary. You think, we're a company, not an advocacy organization. Every single employee might have a unique political or advocacy agenda they would like to see us support. Why would we start down this path and encourage our employees to prioritize ethics when that could backfire and empower them to question our behavior and motives and demand our response to every imaginable issue? Is this unleashing a genie that could be tough to stuff back in the bottle?

The bottle is broken. The increased transparency created by the Internet, the increasing power of social media platforms, and the increased power of the individual employee and globalization in general have all combined to change the world. The risk of being exposed for unethical behavior or practices is higher than it has ever been. Mark Weinberger, former CEO of the global consulting firm EY Global, has observed, "CEOs speak on behalf of more people than ever, and we're held accountable in more public ways . . . in a divisive political climate, our people, our clients and our customers increasingly expect us to speak out publicly when issues arise that conflict with the stated values of our companies. In the last few years, we've all seen the pressure businesses have faced when they've been perceived to stand on the wrong side of one issue or another. It all impacts an organization's brand, which is an increasingly important currency."[7]

◆

More than ever, all of a company or small business's stakeholders have a voice and a way to connect with one another. Just think how easy it is today to imagine these scenarios:

- A hair salon employee anonymously posts a complaint on a neighborhood social media site about their shop's use of banned, toxic products. Without saying a word, customers read it and find a new salon, and the state health board opens an investigation.
- A tire shop puts in fine print the caveat that the super low prices it emphasizes in its advertising are for retreads, not new tires. After arriving at the shop planning to buy tires and realizing that they will

be charged three times the advertised price, customers flood Yelp with complaints about the shop's "bait and switch."

- Students traveling in a developing country discover that an organic food chain is exploiting overseas labor there to keep costs low, so they record video on their phones that they then post on YouTube. The video goes viral; consumers launch a boycott.
- Customers who feel they've been systematically cheated by a bank tweet their frustration and ask for others who feel the same way to contact them. They assemble a class to file suit faster than you can say, "Can I tell you about some of our savings account options?"
- Neighbors realize a manufacturing facility has ignored environmental regulations, and they announce a rally in an email blast. Hundreds of people show up, and elected officials call for the company to cease production until its practices conform to rules.

As a company's leader, you either embrace integrity or wait for the day when the world will force you there. You may not be able to respond to every concern, but you better find a way to listen to concerns and be prepared to act on those that are core to your mission. Keep aligning your actions to your purpose and make sure no single stakeholder's concerns are consistently being prioritized over the needs and input of other stakeholders whose support you are going to need on your infinite journey. Ultimately, profits are essential; but a company built to last knows that forming trusting and solid partnerships with employees and others is the only path to long-term success.

Balance

I have been very specific in many parts of this book about how to approach certain legal and ethical issues. But I'll be honest: I have no template or process to avoid angering or disadvantaging at least one set of stakeholders in any one decision you make. You are never going to make every stakeholder happy with every decision, and you will undoubtedly harm some stakeholders with decisions from time to time, as eBay did when it banned teacher textbook sales on its platform. This is the challenge of leadership. The best you can do is consider the issues raised and try to find a way to acknowledge their importance over time; if you are authentic and transparent in your dealings, you open the door to finding common ground in the future.

So as you reflect on the Six C process, don't just think about it as a set of rules for employees to follow or guidelines to punish the scofflaws who violate them. One reason the process begins with determining a company's mission and fundamental values is that it helps illuminate that what you're really doing is removing obstacles, unlocking your company's potential, and tapping into your employees' best skills and energy to drive your business with purpose and values.

I want to finish up with a few thoughts on the even greater energy you can unlock by combining Intentional Integrity with its close cousin, Intentional Inclusion.

What does inclusion look like?

It's easy for teams, and whole companies, to fall into the trap of homogeneity. It can begin subtly, with a hiring manager emphasizing that new hires must be a "good culture fit." It's human nature—we tend to like people who are similar to ourselves. We might subconsciously browse LinkedIn like a catalog and land on those folks who look familiar. Maybe they went to the same college we did, or we share a former employer. In fact, it's easy to spend 15 minutes looking over your own LinkedIn connections through the lens of homogeneity. You might consider: How much does your network look like you?

The idea of a cohesive, tight-knit team can be appealing . . . but it's also problematic as time goes on. When it's based on discrimination, it's illegal. When it's propelled by cliques or favoritism, it leads to trouble.

When the boss is close friends with a direct report and there is a disagreement among their spouses or children, it can bleed into the workplace. When two friends are up for the same promotion and one gets it, there may be intense jealousy that disrupts morale and performance for the whole team. Or there may be a sense that the promoted manager owes his college-buddy direct report favors because, after all, the other guy knows a few secrets the manager would prefer to keep secret.

Or for whatever reason, someone who doesn't fit the mold joins the team. An excellent contributor who is a recovering alcoholic declines to attend the team's now standard Friday post-work pub gathering, but they don't want to give up the ritual, and now the new employee feels excluded. A gifted programmer from Belarus has a thick accent; she hears colleagues who were all born in the United States mock her behind her back. The "different ones" become the "out group," an easy target for ridicule and abuse. Where the "different ones" are women, an "in group" boys club may egg each other on to make inappropriate remarks, or advances, or deny them advancement.

Diversity and inclusion in the workplace are not interchangeable concepts. Diversity reflects deliberate and targeted hiring and assignments. Inclusion is intentional and assertive energy committed to making diverse teams work.

Our recruiter Lilian Tham has worked at a number of prominent high-tech companies in the United States, and she's told me that many companies say they want diversity but aren't willing to do what it takes to get there. At Airbnb, we require that candidate slates for open positions be diverse, and as Lilian notes, "We make it hard to ask for an exception." Companies also sometimes neglect to consider the kind of support candidates representing diverse groups need to prosper on the job. Even when they recruit strong, diverse talent, she says, appropriate bridges are not always built that help these employees get integrated and excel in their roles. But she believes that Airbnb's emphasis on integrity, which begins at orientation, sets an important tone for new employees. "We want people to bring their whole self to the table and having a culture that encourages trust and vulnerability creates an environment where people feel like they can do their best work. A company whose foundation is built on integrity supports that culture."

In my ethics presentation, I not only talk about the rules but also about challenging situations where we've made mistakes. "Having someone on the executive team talk about inclusion this way gives people permission to be vulnerable," Lilian believes. For example, if one of our managers makes a remark or tolerates a conversation that is offensive or off-putting to another employee, then we can clearly point out that this is not OK because of our explicit commitment to a spirit of inclusion. We encourage the offended person to speak up and be heard—instead of internalizing the experience as a rejection and becoming angry or sullen, or maybe even leaving.

Since Airbnb's mission is to make everyone feel like they belong everywhere, we probably think more about the concept of belonging than other companies do. We physically connect people in a world full of unique and complex cultures and practices. For our guests, a sense of "belonging" can derive from many different things: the ability to visit a destination that, thanks to our platform, no longer is financially out of reach; enthusiastic accommodation of a guest's service animal; a host who also offers an experience designed around a guest's interest in jazz or stargazing.

Or, sometimes it's simply about being treated as a human being.

Much has been written about the fact that black guests have reported having a tougher time getting accepted in some hosts' Airbnbs. It's a sad truth that racism exists on the Airbnb platform, as it does all over the world. Despite the fact that every user on Airbnb is required to pledge that they will accept all, regardless of their race, sex, gender, etc., not everyone lives up to that pledge. We believe that failure is often the result of "unconscious bias," the fact that some hosts are more comfortable with guests that are "like themselves." Whether the bias is intentional or unconscious, it's wrong, and stories about cases of unacceptable treatment have surfaced in the media.

Inside the company, some of our employees were shocked to read about discrimination occurring on the platform. For many of them, living in a city like San Francisco that is generally very accepting of different cultures and lifestyles, discrimination was something they had only read about in history books. But if they spoke with some of our African American employees, they'd learn about how discrimination is ongoing in their lives—including at home in San Francisco. One African American employee told me about the many times he had been pulled over by police for petty infractions or no reason at all just driving around in San Francisco. I've never been stopped in the city. It's clear that my black colleagues experience the world differently than I do, and as an executive I feel it's vital for Airbnb to have that experience reflected inside the company. When the subject of racial discrimination comes up, I want these voices around our table to make sure the assumptions of those who have never experienced it don't dominate the discussion. You don't know what you don't know.

If we ignore the feelings and dignity of our employees and fail to tap the richness of experience and perspective diversity brings, we'll probably fail over time to best serve our hosts and guests. We won't see our diverse customers in a realistic way. We won't maximize the value of our human capital. Eventually we won't attract or retain the top talent.

Once you get past those steps . . .

Earlier, I introduced you to Srin Madipalli, who is an inspiration to me in proving the value of intentional inclusion.

Srin was born in London. He began his career as a genetics researcher before becoming a corporate lawyer. Later, he realized what he really enjoyed was business, and so he enrolled in Oxford to get an MBA. After that, he taught himself to code and launched a start-up.

As his résumé would suggest, Srin is a high-energy person with a bias for action, even though he was born with spinal muscular atrophy and has been in a powered wheelchair since childhood. His family never had the resources to travel with him when he was growing up, so before he went to Oxford, he and another wheelchair-bound friend decided to take a four-month trip around the world. And what they discovered was that for individuals in wheelchairs, to say travel can be difficult is a profound understatement. The overall supply of accessible accommodations is low, and there are few resources to help people find them.

So Srin started his own company called Accomable to both gather data on wheelchair-accessible travel options and encourage hoteliers and others to outfit their accommodations to be reliable choices for disabled travelers. He wrote software tools that made it easier for the hospitality industry to specifically describe and display photographs of their physical grounds and features so travelers with special needs could make good decisions. Imagine navigating a world where you have taken a long flight, arrive in the middle of the night, pick up your key, and then realize that there are two significant steps between you and your motel room—and no ramp. You call the innkeeper for help and say, "This room is supposed to be ADA compliant," and then you hear, as Srin once did, "Well, once you get past the steps, it is."

In the beginning, the Airbnb platform treated wheelchair accessibility as a yes/no question. The host might check yes, not realizing that the question is not just about stairs and ramps. Wheelchairs often require extra-wide doorways, especially in bathrooms. A guest who needs assistance from a person or a special sling for getting in and out of bed needs extra room around the bed.

When Brian realized there was a gap between what some of our listings promised and the experience of people with disabilities, he challenged us to address that gap. In 2017 we acquired Accomable, and Srin and his team joined us to work on shrinking that gap. Today, Srin is a product manager helping to create products that provide hosts and guests with much more specific information about accessibility in our reservation system. Employees like Srin are critical to giving us the insights to understand some of our customers and do a better job. He can help us make the world better for disabled travelers.

I was thinking about our intentional efforts to address needs of physically disabled travelers when I read Apple CEO Tim Cook's 2019 commencement speech at Stanford. Cook noted that too many tech companies invent innovative technologies but then shrug and throw their hands up when there are complications or consequences for society that they didn't anticipate. "It feels a bit crazy that anyone should have to say this. But if you've built a chaos factory, you can't dodge responsibility for the chaos. Taking responsibility means having the courage to think things through."[8]

Aiming at infinity

A big part of thinking things through is realizing that a mostly homogenous workplace can't anticipate the many issues of not only employees who may not fit the dominant profile, but also of potential customers and many kinds of partners a company may need to be successful. Janet Hill is a principal with Hill Family Advisors in Fairfax, Virginia. She grew up in segregated New Orleans and says she never knew a white person until she enrolled at Wellesley, where one of her classmates and friends was Hillary Rodham Clinton. Hill began her career as a research mathematician and became an expert in corporate responsibility and human resource planning, and she has served on the boards of many large companies, including Dean Foods, Progressive Insurance, and the Carlyle Group, and on the board of trustees of Duke University. A staunch advocate for diversity in corporate America, Hill and I have discussed the importance of both diversity and inclusive thinking by companies. She notes, "We are about 335 million people. Black, Hispanic, Asian, mixed-race people are half of our population. How can you build an effective company in any industry without tapping into the talent of half the country? Diversity improves the opportunities for good behavior in a company. As soon as I limit my pool, I limit my opportunities for effectiveness, and I increase the chances that bad, 'clubby' bad, behavior will occur."

Once leaders make a habit of looking around a room and paying attention to who is there and what their issues might be, they start to change a culture. For example, Srin told me with a smile that a member of his team was recently planning an off-site team meeting and announced the possibility of a cycling excursion. Srin thought: *Hmm, doesn't seem like that would work for me.* But the planner immediately turned to Srin and explained that he'd found a cycling group in the Bay Area that works with individuals who are in wheelchairs, and they have special cycles to allow them to fully participate alongside those with standard bikes. That's intentional inclusion. Everybody wins when everybody feels included and their talents are nurtured.

We've talked about the transparency challenges of the Internet. Remember that good news can spread far and fast as well. A few examples:

Many buyers of Toms shoes, where the company donates a pair of shoes to the developing world for every pair purchased, have become fervent evangelists for those shoes because of the "one-for-one" concept.

Yes, Dick's lost some customers when it banned assault rifles, but it gained new ones from those who respected its courage for taking a business risk in a core category. Many of those shoppers post messages on social media encouraging others to buy everything from kids' soccer cleats to yoga mats from Dick's.

When the discrepancies in the pay for the U.S. Men's and Women's National Soccer Teams became an issue during the 2019 Women's World Cup, various lawsuits and organizational posturing began. But the LUNA nutrition bar brand didn't wait for the wheels to turn, it stepped up and committed over $700,000 to the team, about $31,000 per player, to bring the women's pay in line with the men's.[9] Those are not lottery winning–sized numbers, but player after player was quoted as saying it meant a lot to get that kind of support, not just financial but moral, for equality— from a company. It set an example for other companies that sometimes you can just step up and, well, "do it."

Start the fire

When I was young, I remember once walking out of the grocery store with my mother, Kitty Chesnut. In the middle of the parking lot, she stopped, looking at the money in her hand that she had gotten from the cashier. "We've got to go back inside," she said. "The clerk gave us the wrong change." We walked back in, and I recall waiting impatiently as my mom got the attention of the cashier and began to talk. I remember the surprise and gratitude from the clerk, the effusive thank-yous. The clerk had not "shortchanged" my mom; she had given my mom too much money, and my mom was returning it. There would have been a dozen "good" reasons for my mom to just keep the few extra dollars that day, and I've heard those reasons from other people—the store makes a lot of money, their prices are ridiculously high, we spend a lot of money in that store, I'm sure they've shortchanged me in the past when I didn't notice it, I don't have time to go back in and deal with it, it's their mistake and their problem. But my mom's explanation that day taught me a critical lesson about integrity. "It doesn't belong to us," she explained. She repeated that lesson to me many times in many different contexts, always driving home a point that stuck with me. That's what I would call leadership from the CEO. And as my kids will tell you, we've marched back into a couple of stores to return excess change or pay for an item that accidentally didn't get charged. They roll their eyes and complain a bit. But I look at it as a learning opportunity, not an inconvenience. And I still enjoy the stunned expression on the cashier's face.

It can be discouraging to read the news. Every day, it seems, there's another integrity scandal. Cheating to get into schools. Sexual predators. Corporate financial scandals. Corporate cover-ups. Fake news. And as we take in the bad, I think we all approach an ethical fork in the road on how to respond. The low road is, "Everyone else is getting theirs, I need to get mine." The high road is, "I've had enough of all this . . . and somehow, in my own way, I need to do something about it."

Dishonesty is contagious. But so is integrity. And a great place to start is at work. The workplace provides the sort of close human interaction where the contagion of integrity can spread, fueled in each company by a shared mission and vision, and ideally supported by a leader who understands the responsibility of the position. We can bring out the best in each other.

But it won't happen automatically. Intentionality is the match that starts the fire. I hope this book starts a conversation about how integrity can become the dominant value in your workplace. We have a unique and important opportunity to be a powerful force for good—if we act intentionally and with integrity.

Appendix:
Discussion of Code Moments

Table of Contents

For 11 years, Regina has worked as an executive assistant to Mike and two years ago he became the CEO. She's been to Mike's home for staff holiday parties, and she's friendly with his wife, Sally.

One day Sally calls and tells Regina, "Mike left his iPad home; I just read a flirty text from a number in Illinois. Regina, is Mike having an affair?"

Regina's heart sinks. Mike has been distant lately, and he has asked Regina several times to coordinate his schedule with that of a vendor's female executive who lives in Chicago.

"Sally, I don't know anything about that," Regina tells her. "Might it be a wrong number text?" Sally just hangs up.

Minutes later, Mike calls Regina and yells: "What the hell is wrong with you? Why didn't you cover for me with Sally?"

"Mike, I didn't know what to say."

"MIGHT be a wrong number," he again yells. "That's all she heard. Why didn't you tell her you were SURE it was a mistake? Regina, you're supposed to have my back. I need an assistant I can trust." He hangs up.

Regina, the ball's in your court. What do you do?

1. Say nothing to anyone. This is Mike's private business. Regina should ask Mike to tell her exactly how he expects her to handle calls from Sally going forward and any other specific instructions.
2. Report Mike to HR for insulting and berating her. It's not her job to patch over his personal indiscretions, and she does not want to have to lie for him.
3. Watch and wait. Regina's knowledge is her best defense against his retaliation; Mike will soon realize he needs to tread carefully around Regina.

DISCUSSION OF "REGINA AND THE TELLTALE TEXT"

If a leader engages in deception and selectively ignores the code of conduct, the situation often inspires others to behave unethically, and can even lead to tacit or overt blackmail. As soon as secrecy about one or more code violations exists, the violations tend to multiply like rabbits. That is why it is so critical for the leadership of a company, especially the CEO, to commit to a high-integrity path.

Now, the three options. First, isn't Mike's affair a private matter? Not at all. By engaging in a relationship with a vendor's executive, Mike is setting up a classic conflict of interest. How can he objectively evaluate whether the vendor is doing a good job, and whether they should be awarded new work, if he's having an affair with a leader at that company? If a competitor emerges with a better product, how will Mike resolve the conflict between doing the right thing for his romantic relationship and the right thing for his company?

Mike is also bringing the relationship into the workplace by using his assistant's energy to enable this affair. Perhaps Mike really does need to be taking all those business trips to Chicago. But he might also be using company resources to pay for flights and hotels to enable the affair. Berating Regina for not lying to his wife raises personal integrity issues.

Another important question is whether Mike's board should be concerned about Mike's infidelity. Arguably, what Mike does on his own time, and at his own expense, is none of the company's business. But if Mike's wife files for divorce alleging infidelity, will it end up in the media? And even without the vendor connection, will employees trust their CEO if they read about the allegations? While personal romantic relationships, children, home life, and hobbies are private matters, lying and using company resources to create a false narrative that could compromise the company's reputation is an integrity code violation.

◆

It's tempting to say that the second choice is the right one and that Regina should report Mike. But to whom? If she reports it through the company's anonymous hotline, Mike will know that she is the reporter. To the general counsel or head of HR? That's the best answer, though it still leaves her vulnerable to retaliation from Mike. While I would want employees to report a situation like this, the truth is that such a report here would place Regina in an extremely difficult position. There's no denying the imbalance of power here that could impact her livelihood and future. It's not fair to ignore how intimidated and vulnerable she may feel. That's what makes Mike's behavior and threats to her particularly odious.

Most likely, they will have an uneasy truce for a while. But then the code dilemma shifts to Regina, as expressed in option 3: Will she seek an unfair point of leverage against him? Lobby for a raise or a promotion or more vacation? Will she become a co-conspirator—covering for Mike's travel or lying on his behalf? Then she would be committing code violations. Loyalty is not an excuse for dishonesty.

Going forward, Regina has lost respect for Mike. He's put her in a terrible spot. Regina has choices to make, and we hope she'll look at the big picture and not follow Mike's example down a treacherous course. Meanwhile, Mike's future is now clouded by this inappropriate relationship in ways that do not involve Regina. What if he tries to break off the relationship and his mistress threatens to expose him? Issues around sex and attraction in the workplace are some of the most difficult and potentially explosive threats to a brand that companies face.

Intentional Integrity is powerful, but it can also be fragile if a company's leaders don't fully embrace it. And it's hard for a leader to separate integrity at work from integrity in their personal affairs.

Charlie is the CEO of ISP-Co, a Midwestern telecom provider that has experienced a number of regulatory setbacks. His government affairs chief, Larry, calls to tell Charlie that one of the telecom commission members told Larry she is having a problem with her email account, hosted by ISP-Co. Her password is no longer working. But here's the thing: her estranged husband is the account holder, and customer service has told her they can only talk to or investigate issues for account owners. She's worried he is reading her email. Larry told her he might be able to help.

Larry tells Charlie this is a chance to help her and the company and improve their relationship. He wants Charlie to relax the rules.

Although it's not one of his own making,
this is a Code Moment for Charlie. Should he:

1. Overrule the privacy protocol and investigate the situation for a potential friend of ISP-Co? He should not commit fraud or tamper with the estranged husband's account, but Charlie has the right to access that data, and if he can give her more information, he could win her support for the company in the future.
2. Tell Larry to reiterate the privacy policy and suggest that her call makes it look like she is unfairly using her position for personal gain?
3. Call the commission member and be sympathetic? He should explain why he cannot help her but offer ideas and support for what she's going through.

DISCUSSION OF "WHO'S YOUR CUSTOMER, CHARLIE?"

Obviously, Charlie should not bend the account privacy rules. If he does, many bad consequences could result . . .

Larry will know and may ask for more favors like this in the future.

Customer service will realize something weird is going on when the CEO orders unusual research and access into the account.

The commission member may say something to her estranged husband based on improperly obtained information, and he could publicly accuse the company of violating his privacy.

This is the sort of situation that ends up in the rumor mill (and maybe on Glassdoor or Blind). And if the CEO can do it, then why can't everyone do it? It could give license to reps to peek at the emails of their boyfriends and girlfriends.

As CEO, Charlie has a duty to protect the company's interests, and he could use a friend on the commission. But rationalizing an abuse of the privacy rule for a "greater good" is an integrity trap.

My advice is to follow number 3. Charlie should call the commission member and listen to her concerns but explain his ISP's policies about data privacy in clear terms: the legal owner of the account controls the account, and the ISP can't go in and give access to others.

However, Charlie can suggest that the commission member call her ex and be straightforward. Explain that she just realized he controls access to her email, and her account appears to be frozen so she'd like to arrange for all contents to be forwarded to her and then for the account to be closed. Alternatively, she might ask her personal attorney to make the call.

Be sympathetic to Charlie, but you have to hold the line.

Inappropriate personal favors rationalized for the greater good are remarkably common—and the Achilles' heel of many otherwise ethical people.

LightCo's marketing manager, Serena, enters engineer Paul's cubicle and sits down to discuss a product rollout. As Paul explains the schedule, Serena sees the top of a flyer poking out of his briefcase that says "NRA Member, You're invited to a march for gun rights." She also notices that Paul has a coffee mug on his desk that shows him wearing camo and holding up a dead duck.

Serena's niece was killed in a school shooting. She gets teary, stands up, and says, "I can't help you." She goes back to her desk and drafts an email to HR. "The gun lobby is the most unethical, immoral organization in America and one of its members works for our company. I cannot perform my job if I am forced to work with a collaborator in my niece's murder. Our ethics code bans weapons at work, why do we allow people to promote gun ownership in our workplace?"

HR pays a visit to Paul and asks him about his interaction with Serena. Paul explains that the flyer was in his bag because he grabbed his mail on the way to work, not because he was advocating for the NRA. He says he never said—or planned to say—a word about guns to Serena or any other employee. Then he gets angry. "There is a First Amendment in this country and I have the right to my opinion," he says. "She wears a crucifix, so why does she get to advocate for Christianity?"

Whose Code Moment is this?

1. The NRA is a controversial organization. Its name elicits strong feelings, and Paul needs to be warned to stop doing anything that appears to promote its interests.
2. Serena may have a good reason to be upset, but that's not Paul's fault. HR can't force him to do anything and is not obligated to accommodate her.
3. HR needs to intervene and assign Serena to a different project. Her right to work in a trigger-free environment trumps other considerations.

DISCUSSION OF "PAUL, SERENA, AND A DEAD DUCK"

Wow. This example raises several important issues and shows how messy and difficult certain kinds of ethical conflicts can be.

If this were a sporting goods company selling hunting equipment and guns, employees who belong to the NRA might be the rule, not the exception. Its stated values might even explicitly include supporting the Second Amendment. Serena likely never would have applied to work there. But this is a lighting company. For our purposes, we'll assume LightCo has no specific policies or stated values related to guns. But let's say it does explicitly state that its values include creating a respectful and tolerant working environment for all employees and eradicating discrimination against protected classes. So in this workplace conflict, whose interests are paramount?

First, let's address some relevant larger concepts: one is that all individuals have the right to their own beliefs, but there is no overarching "right to free speech" in the workplace. The First Amendment prevents the government from limiting speech and dissent. It does not apply to private employers. An employer can ban discussion or advocacy about anything it wants to—politics, guns, eating meat, red shoes, anything. It can ban employees from discussing "controversial subjects" in general in the workplace (bad idea to be so vague, but some companies do that). It can even ban nonwork discussion, period (obviously not a recruiting advantage, but it's legal as long as it's enforced fairly). I'm told that workplace conflicts around the 2016 presidential election became so heated and distracting in parts of the country that some companies banned any discussion of the election at work.

Second, your cubicle is not your castle. There is no "personal space" inside the walls of a workplace where the rules don't apply. It matters a lot that Paul had the flyer in his bag, not pinned to his wall, and that he said he did not intend to share the NRA march invitation with others. Publicly displaying a flyer arguably would be advocacy even if he doesn't mention the subject to other employees.

Third, although it is legal to specifically prohibit discussion of any subject (except labor organizing), it also violates federal law to discriminate against certain protected classes, including by race, gender, national origin, and religion. This is relevant because you might ban talking about or advocating for controversial subjects in your workplace, but there are symbols or clothing that may have a controversial component and are related to a protected class. A Black Lives Matter T-shirt, for example. A tattoo that insults women.

Religion is one of the most complex classes. An employer generally cannot ban religious symbols from the workplace in part because they may be an element of belonging to a religion (for example, some Muslim women keep their heads covered at all times in public, and many Catholics wear ashes on their foreheads on Ash Wednesday). Federal law says that an employer must make reasonable accommodation to a person's religious beliefs and rituals—and yet you could imagine a similar "triggering" scenario to Paul and Serena's erupting when a person who might have been molested by a member of the clergy has to collaborate with a Catholic wearing ashes on his forehead.

But back to Paul and Serena. The company should carefully investigate exactly what happened and not make a knee-jerk decision. Clearly, Paul is entitled to his personal beliefs, and it seems fair to say that a piece of paper sitting in his briefcase is not advocacy. However, Serena's reaction should not be brushed aside. Companies with integrity want to create a workplace where people feel safe and welcome. Her niece's death triggered an understandable emotional response to the subject of guns, and suddenly Paul became the face of that.

None of the three specific options I offered represents the clear and appropriate path. As it stands, there is no code violation here. But human resources should talk to each employee individually with the goal of resolving the matter by establishing a welcoming and respectful workplace. They might suggest, after explaining the depth of Serena's issue, that Paul leave NRA materials at home in the future and switch mugs as a gesture of good faith. Not because he doesn't have the right to his opinions, but in the interest of moving forward. In a session with Serena where management and HR does some authentic listening, they might ask if she is willing to again attempt to work with Paul. If not, what is her vision of a transfer that properly uses her skills and experience? The tone of these conversations should be: we care about you, and how can we make this work? But let's be honest: there are other relevant factors, such as whether this is a small, family-owned business with nowhere to transfer Serena or a company with 600 employees and four divisions that might be able to accommodate her easily.

Depending on how it goes, the company may pursue other options as well. Going forward, it may explicitly prohibit any form of advocacy in the workplace that is extraneous to the company's core mission. So, yes, wear a T-shirt promoting energy-saving LEDs, but leave other messages or symbolic products to your weekend wear. From now on, only blank, no-message mugs or mugs with the company logo may be used in the office.

I'm seeing more and more references in lawsuits and news stories to values in the workplace colliding with those that may be expressed by jewelry, tattoos, head scarves, and T-shirts carrying advocacy language (or with messages that offend some employees). It is very difficult to come up with highly specific rules for all the potential variations, and setting a standard is even more difficult if some employees work in customer-facing roles and others tend to work independently. For example, banks may decide to ban any and all visible tattoos for tellers, for example, but they may not feel the need to do that for back-office data processors or graphic artists who design flyers and posters.

Some expression dilemmas are not about deeply held religious beliefs, politics, or personal expression so much as they are business decisions. Imagine, for example, a car dealership in a town where passions about rival high school football teams run hot. The week of the big game, management might say, "We are going to be agnostic. Please do not wear any fan gear at work, because we don't want to drive off potential customers who think we're biased to one of the teams." Or, they might encourage their employees to wear their school colors with pride, hoping the clothing creates a welcoming spirit of fun and community-building. Either path might be fine; the dealership gets to figure that out for itself.

Intentional Integrity sometimes means imagining how you will handle issues that in fact are not core to your values and beliefs.

NaturalCo sells clothing made from organically harvested cotton. Its advertising promotes its carefully sourced and certified green fabrics by contrasting it with environmentally damaging processes used for other fabrics. NaturalCo has never bothered with a code of ethics because obviously the company is all about integrity. Its corporate slogan: "Gentle on your body, gentle to the earth."

Samantha sources raw materials for NaturalCo and travels to remote areas around the world. In Southeast Asia, she negotiates a deal to buy organic cotton for 15 percent less than the company had been paying. The CEO sends a congratulatory email. A high bonus later reflects her work on this contract.

A year later, a national magazine runs an investigative feature on child labor practices in the region where Samantha closed this deal. NaturalCo is listed as a buyer of cotton that has been picked by children as young as seven years old from a local orphanage. The owner of the cotton farm has been arrested.

The CEO summons Samantha to his office. "This could ruin us! This is obviously why the price was so low. Why didn't you ask more questions?"

Samantha replies: "I don't remember you caring why the price was low. You sent me to get a good deal on certified organic, and that's what I did."

"Yeah, well, your judgment sucks and you're fired. And we'll be putting out a press release saying we had no idea our cotton was being picked by children."

"That's simply not true—I knew and you didn't care," Samantha says. "Fire me and I'll see you in court."

Houston, we have a Code Moment. What should the CEO do next?

1. The CEO's duty to shareholders is to protect his brand by firing Samantha and negotiating a severance that includes a nondisclosure agreement. He can then publicly plead ignorance and launch a campaign for higher labor accountability by cotton growers.

2. Samantha knew this deal was shady and that the grower violated labor laws. The CEO should fire Samantha and refuse to pay the severance, which is essentially blackmail. He should hold her personally accountable for this lapse of judgment both internally and externally.

3. The CEO should admit publicly that he personally should have done more research on the labor element of its sourcing operations and pledge to do better going forward. He should lead an internal overhaul of the company's values that results in a code of ethics. He should back off his kneejerk reaction of firing Samantha because she was not solely to blame.

DISCUSSION OF "A NOT-SO-GENTLE ETHICAL DILEMMA"

NaturalCo created a classic integrity trap: We believe we are good people, and therefore everything we do is going to be good and reflect admirable values and integrity. No need to spell it all out in a code.

Except values sometimes come into conflict, and some are sacrificed for others. Many companies have faced situations like NaturalCo's. The Body Shop was launched many years ago as an eco-friendly company. It was among the first to offer refillable bottles, and it promoted its desire to source ingredients from indigenous farmers. It also became the target of activists with many different related agendas, and it faced a real mess when one of its suppliers in Colombia was accused of forcibly evicting peasant families to develop a new plantation.[1]

I suspect many CEOs would gravitate to option 1. Firing Samantha may create a clean slate and an appearance of decisive action; the NDA creates a smokescreen for who was actually at fault. Did Samantha know and not tell leadership? Did leadership know and not care? With Samantha signing an NDA we'll never know. Choose that option and write a big check.

Option 2 might seem like a tempting show of integrity, but it's not. Scapegoating an employee while you're trying to rebuild your brand is a bad idea.

The best approach is option 3. It's not unlike the dilemma Starbucks faced at the store in Philadelphia where the manager made a bad decision, but the company realized it had been vague in its policies and confronted the situation. NaturalCo is facing a significant Code Moment, and there is no sure path to success here. Leadership made several mistakes: It should have thought about the broader ethical dimensions of holding itself up as a "green" company and put in place processes to help ensure that it walked the talk. It failed to establish clear ethical sourcing principles up front and to encourage Samantha to communicate the reason the raw materials were cheaper. The company put a cost target on the wall and defined success too narrowly. A contract that saves 15 percent today and destroys your brand reputation tomorrow is the definition of a bad deal.

Consumers will forgive a company that admits it screwed up much faster than a company that hides behind NDAs and hypocrisy.

Your CEO encourages employee team backpacking trips and outings to promote communication and teamwork. Most employees enjoy these activities, and they seem to be good for morale. Trip highlights become the basis of lots of inside jokes, weird nicknames, and friendships.

You're an operations executive and you get an email from an employee two levels below you: "Last weekend I finally signed up for my team's backpacking trip to Yosemite. I avoided the last several, but it's all everybody talks about for two weeks. Ten of us had a nice hike. But around the campfire after a few glasses of wine, one guy said let's do 'the game.' He said we should go around the circle and talk about our first sexual experience and what it taught us. I was freaked out. I don't feel I need to share something that personal with colleagues. I said I was not comfortable. Our manager said, 'We can start with other folks, and then you can decide if you want to play. It's actually fun.' I went to my tent and heard them snickering. The next morning, I felt isolated and humiliated. Since when is something like this part of our job description? I would like to discuss a transfer to another team."

Is this an overly sensitive employee—or a Code Moment?

1. This is something to take seriously at two levels: It sounds like the manager and team were disrespectful to this employee; she deserves an apology. More than that, it's time to rethink your team-building activities.

2. Fire the manager immediately. This looks like a hostile workplace environment lawsuit ready to explode. What's this "game" thing, which clearly has happened before?

3. This is political correctness run amok. The employee went on the trip freely, and she's an adult. She doesn't sound like a good fit for the company. Call the manager and ask what kind of performer she is. If she's a strong performer, she may need coaching and encouragement to be a team player; if she's not, it may be time to move her out.

DISCUSSION OF "THE GAME IS ON, THE VIBE IS OFF"

Based on these facts, I think number 1 is the way to go. After investigating, you'll need to at least sit down with the person who suggested the game, and the manager, to talk about what went wrong and that person's role in it. You may decide there should be stronger consequences for the manager, but I think you'll need to know more. Did he originally suggest the game, or did someone else? Did he perceive this employee's discomfort? Did he seek to reassure her in any way? Was he snickering?

The larger point is, team building is great, but it has to be well considered and organized in a thoughtful and respectful way. Work teams love off-sites. The legal department, not so much. It's not unusual for off-site weekends to blow up and create legal issues, personal resentments, and other problems. The strength of something like a backpacking weekend is also its weakness: you get a fuller picture of who your colleagues are. Maybe they're braver or funnier than you realized, or maybe they have feelings about nature that endear them to you and the rest of the group. You return to work with more trust and collegiality. But when you blur the lines between "work life" and "personal life," people let down their professional guard, and their professional judgment can go down with it. The "game" might be appropriate among friends or couples on a personal camping trip—it's not appropriate on a work outing. And these sorts of outings can also reveal someone who drinks too much, or has political beliefs that offend you. You may end this type of weekend with less respect and affection for your colleagues than you had at the beginning of it, just like this employee did.

Off-site meetings are notorious minefields of sexual harassment. You have folks under stress away from their families, drinking alcohol, sleeping in close quarters. Introducing an overtly sexual subject like the "game" is an invitation for trouble, and the manager needs to remember he's the team's manager, not their therapist.

As an executive, you should thank this employee for alerting you to these issues and reinforce that you can understand her discomfort. Depending on what else this woman has experienced in this group, you could be looking at a legitimate complaint about her work environment, and you should take her request to transfer seriously. Talk frankly to the manager in this case, but also advocate for a larger discussion about off-sites. Encourage other leaders to take a step back from the details and think about what you want off-sites to accomplish. Are they being run in a way consistent with your values and goals? Are the activities unduly dominated by strong-willed managers or thrill-seekers?

Off-site bonding events need to be well considered. Are they uniting your team or dividing it?

Work has been really tough, so on behalf of your team you ask if you can build a fun themed bar area in the corner of your workspace. The team manager, Meredith, loves the idea and personally donates her neon Jose Cuervo lights. She also approves spending $500 on margarita ingredients and plastic glasses with the company logo. Meredith makes it clear, however, that this is your project and you need to manage it. Everyone on the team agrees that they won't actually use it before 4:00 p.m., unless it's a special occasion.

Is this a Code Moment?

1. No, your code of ethics allows responsible drinking by adults. How people interpret that is their responsibility.
2. Yes, because you've taken the lead here and you should prepare an email reminding everyone that this is intended as a celebration, not a resource for getting hammered. If you're going to serve alcohol, you also need to monitor each person's drinking and not let anyone drive who has had too much.
3. Yes—it's your manager's Code Moment, and she failed it. There is no way a work group needs a full-time bar on site, and it's likely to create problems.

DISCUSSION OF "JUST ANOTHER TEQUILA COFFEE BREAK"

This situation is a blinking yellow light of caution: it might turn out fine or it might trigger a Code Red. We aren't talking about a one-time party but an ongoing alcohol resource for this team. I'd urge the manager to think through this idea and own it herself if she goes ahead with it.

I actually had my Airbnb staff do a video about party and alcohol usage before the holidays so work groups could keep some specific thoughts in mind during team outings and parties. However, why does a work team need a bar that's potentially "open" every day? Will other teams be invited to join the fun, or does this become an exclusive perk of working for this team? Perhaps most ominously, unless every member of the team loves margaritas, the potential exists for this to create division. Some folks may want to end each day with a margarita, but maybe others would like to use that extra half hour before they go home to work instead of drink; maybe they'd prefer a stretching class or a group walk as a team-building exercise instead. Now you get the "Oh come on, loosen up" comments, which can get tiresome and breed resentment.

This is the difficulty of alcohol-related issues in the workplace: they can turn on a dime. You can have 100 perfectly fun, sane, incident-free gatherings, and then one person drinks too much or mixes medication with alcohol, or someone decides after two margaritas that it's the perfect moment to rip into the manager he thinks is out of earshot. The partners of employees who now have tequila on their breath when they arrive home late for dinner a couple of times a week are not amused, and a strained family life can become a distraction.

Again, blinking yellow light.

Alcohol abuse can lead to significant violations of the code of ethics. Make sure you are not organizing events around drinking for its own sake.

Marty worked for five years at BigCo, a large, well-known public company that makes skateboards, bikes, and other recreational equipment. He was recruited to NewCo. He left BigCo on good terms and he signed an exit agreement with BigCo saying he would not compete or share secrets for two years.

The day after he arrived at NewCo, which has a code of ethics that says all media inquiries must be cleared through the communications team, a reporter that Marty knows from a business magazine sends Marty a message through LinkedIn: "Hey, congrats on the new job—how about coffee, would love to catch up." Marty respects the reporter's work. It's flattering to hear from him. They meet, and Marty realizes that the reporter wants to talk about the rumor that BigCo's motorized skateboards are being returned in droves by unhappy customers. The reporter says that some of the skateboards have malfunctioned and caused serious injuries. "I know you had nothing to do with that division, but what's the scuttlebutt on how this happened? I've heard a teenager is in a coma after an accident on the new Xmodel, and there may be a lawsuit."

When the reporter mentions the injury, Marty groans out loud. He'd heard rumblings internally that the BigCo engineering team had issues with components used in the skateboards but that management overruled them to hit a shipping target. Clearly, he knows something.

Can Marty tell the reporter what he knows and still maintain his integrity?

1. No. He should not be talking to the reporter. He is violating his new employer's policy on giving interviews without clearing them with the communications team. He should explain that he doesn't want to speculate and end the meeting.
2. He should insist that the reporter agree to not use his name in print or in writing—then he can say whatever he wants.
3. If Marty's conscience is bothering him, he should tell the reporter he will call some former colleagues and encourage them to talk to him off the record.

DISCUSSION OF "MARTY AND THE MEDIA QUANDARY"

Marty's caught in an ethical dilemma, and any one of the three options might be "unethical" depending on your perspective.

A free press is an important component of any democracy, and over my lifetime, reporters have played a critical role in exposing wrongs and changing the world with investigative reporting. I have a tremendous respect for the press, and in this case, this reporter's work could promote public safety. But that doesn't mean that, as a company, you want your employees to talk openly with any reporter who calls. Companies, particularly publicly traded ones, should speak with one voice, and a failure to control rogue communications can have serious legal and brand implications.

Companies often instruct employees not to speak directly with reporters about the company or to give any interviews without clearing them with the communications team. One reason for this is that individuals who are not used to speaking with reporters may be inclined to say more than they really know or to share information that is confidential or inaccurate. Reporters are good at flattering and drawing out the people they interview, but speculating out loud with a reporter can expose an individual and a company to embarrassing and brand-damaging publicity. Marty doesn't know all the facts about the potential skateboard design issues, and what little he does know is based on secondhand office gossip.

In hindsight, perhaps Marty should not have agreed to this meeting, and now he can't win. If he refuses to talk to the reporter, he's living up to his obligations to BigCo, protecting the company's confidential information as part of his exit agreement. And he's fulfilling his promise to his new employer by following its policy. But he has to live with the knowledge that his silence might be helping to perpetuate harm to consumers—he's protecting a secret that places young people in harm's way. Is it his place . . . his legal or moral obligation . . . to blow the lid off this situation? And if so, does that ethical obligation outweigh his other obligations?

Marty may think that cooperating with the press is an ethical choice, and that might be the right course here. But even that isn't so clear. The obvious questions include: If this is such a matter of conscience, why didn't Marty try to remedy this problem when he worked there? Is this just sour grapes? Did Marty sell all of his stock in BigCo when he left, and would NewCo benefit from a story that hurts BigCo? Will this appear as an effort by NewCo to deliberately leak bad news about a competitor through a back channel? It's a classic case where the appearance may be at odds with reality, but it's still damaging.

This example also serves as a reminder that the agreements a person signs when they join or leave a company should be read and considered carefully. A departing employee's severance agreement may address pay for unused vacation, the disposition of the employee's stock or options, or continued insurance benefits. Partly in exchange for those considerations, the employee may agree to not discuss any material information he or she acquired while working at the company, including knowledge of trade secrets, designs, product release schedules, or other competitive information. Violating those agreements could leave that person vulnerable to a lawsuit from the previous employer.

Marty can choose option one, and then on his own he can encourage his former colleagues to address whatever the issue is that led to unsafe products. Under some whistleblower laws, he might enjoy certain rights even as a former employee. But circumventing his new company's policies and getting involved with the media to pursue a positive outcome here might be a code violation and a perilous course.

Interacting with the media is best left to a company's communications team, for a number of reasons, though potential whistleblower activity and public safety put a different ethical frame on this seemingly straightforward policy.

You are a marketing executive for a global restaurant chain that is making a big push in Asia. You hear through the food grapevine that at a local university, a group of hospitality school professors have done insightful research about the differences of marketing food to different Asian cultures. You reach out to the professors and ask for a meeting to discuss marketing in Thailand, but also their work in the larger region. You also say you would consider creating a consulting relationship between them and your company.

They respond that they are open to the idea and anxious to meet, and that it happens that they have been trying to raise money for a research trip to Japan, where they plan to meet with regulators to discuss the hurdles foreign companies sometimes face when trying to open restaurants there.

You have plenty of funds in your budgets to send them to Tokyo for a few days. Consulting relationships are usually straightforward, right?

DISCUSSION OF "DEFINE 'ACADEMIC'"

I didn't offer three scenarios to choose from because this seems like such an easy, straightforward case. What could the possible ethical dilemma be?

I want to reinforce how important it is for any company operating or establishing formal relationships in a foreign country to understand the rules and laws of that country. There is no evil intent here. But the problem is that in some countries, university professors are government officials. To sponsor any government official on any kind of trip risks triggering provisions of the U.S. Foreign Corrupt Practices Act (or in the United Kingdom, the UK Bribery Act), in addition to local anti-bribery laws.

On one hand, the trip could be construed as a legal arrangement to hire these individuals to perform specific services. The question is, do the laws of Thailand allow government officials to be hired as consultants to foreign companies, or hired at all without some kind of process designed to approve such a request? Moreover, if the trip is construed in any way as lavish or luxurious, you could risk being accused of bribing government officials for other purposes. Who would accuse you of that? Rival academics jealous of you supporting these professors, perhaps. It might be positive for a Thai government auditor's career to uncover and report an illegal relationship. An Asian competitor trying to make it hard for you to win hotel restaurant contracts might be looking for your company to slip up.

As a company expands operations to new countries, it must collect relevant data about existing laws and practices to avoid doing something that would be perfectly fine in the United States but could create a scandal in a different country. A company needs to explicitly educate employees to get clearance for any kind of financial underwriting or payment, including just paying expenses, to any government official, and must take pains to determine what constitutes a government official.

Tory works in data analytics for SportsCo, an e-commerce company that puts sports team logos on items like backpacks and coffee mugs. She loves her job. She gets high marks from her manager. Tory just finished an analysis of winter clothing purchasing patterns from the SportsCo customer database, including a spreadsheet of the top 1,000 buyers by spend in cold-weather states, along with their addresses and emails. Marketing plans an email campaign selling team logo parkas, gloves, and hats.

Tory's sister Katy has started a home business knitting beautiful, bulky sweaters with an unofficial version of football team logos. Katy is struggling to make ends meet.

After she sends her report to marketing, Tory prints out a copy, and three days later an envelope arrives at Katy's house in Minneapolis. Tory has written on the cover: "Thought this would be helpful, and you could even target these folks with an email to get sweater orders." Katy calls Tory. "This is awesome—you won't get in trouble for sending this, will you?"

"Of course not. I had to do this report anyway and nobody cares about ten sheets of copy paper. I saw my boss's poker party invitations on the copy machine last week."

Is there a flag on the field for Tory?

1. Tory's sister is not a competitor of SportsCo. Everybody wins. There is no ethical problem here.
2. Tory has every right to use company equipment for personal use, just like her boss does. There was no additional cost to the company by her copying this report, so it's OK.
3. This represents a conflict of interest and improper sharing of confidential information, as well as a violation of customer privacy.

DISCUSSION OF "TORY AND THE TEN SHEETS OF COPY PAPER"

Tory's actions were completely inappropriate, and the answer is number 3. The problem here is that she focused on the trivial (the cost of copy paper) and ignored the fact that she had essentially stolen and distributed her company's intellectual property—the buying patterns and identity of customers. Her motivations were not evil, but this act is no different than a foreign hacker getting into SportsCo's database, stealing data, and selling it to competitors. A customer of SportsCo who ends up communicating with Tory's sister and learning how she got the customer's information may be very angry at SportsCo.

I cited this example in the communication category because I believe SportsCo has failed to communicate the practical implications of data privacy and intellectual property. How big a competitor Tory's sister represents is irrelevant. Tory's rationalization seems based in a misunderstanding and poor judgment, not malicious intent. But at some companies in this environment where privacy of customer data is so critical to customer trust, her mistake could result in severe consequences, even termination. There's a bigger issue—the company has not invested in clarifying the importance of customer data privacy and must do so immediately. This is a teaching moment for everyone.

A secondary issue in this example is that companies do need to establish a clear policy on when, and how, employees can use company assets for their personal use. A failure to do so leads to rationalizations and misunderstandings like this one. Why not simply ban all personal use of company property? Again, with the blending of personal and professional lives, that's easier said than done. If an employee sends a personal email using a company laptop, at some level that wears down the keyboard and uses company Wi-Fi bandwidth . . . is that an integrity violation? If I take a pen from work and leave it at home, have I stolen company property? Be very explicit, without being ridiculous. You need a plan that provides for flexibility—by all means ban any personal use of company confidential information, but permit personal use of equipment or resources with a "minimal" (a couple of dollars or less) financial impact to the company. Or develop a stricter approach . . . but the key is to be clear and intentional about what's allowed and what's not.

Customer information and data privacy abuses are a common prelude to a Code Red. A company must have a data-privacy strategy, and it must invest heavily in making sure that employees understand how data privacy failures can impact their brand.

You are the president of a midsized bank and active in your community. Your friend and neighbor wants to get his house set up with new A/V equipment and Internet. The neighbor asks if you know anyone good. "I know exactly who you need," you tell him. "I've got a really terrific IT support person on my team and I'll check with her about when she might be able to do it."

"Fantastic!" your neighbor says. "I'm happy to pay her, I just want someone competent."

"No charge, happy to help you out," you say, although you intend to pay the IT tech yourself.

Is this arrangement OK?

1. If the job will be done on the employee's own time with the customer's equipment, then there is no problem.
2. As a manager, you cannot personally pay this person for work outside the office. It's unethical.
3. You are putting an employee on the spot. Do you really want to be an A/V services broker?

DISCUSSION OF "WIN-WIN-WIN, OR NO GOOD DEED GOES UNPUNISHED?"
Every issue in the three options is worth thinking about, but it's also possible that this scenario could work out just fine. I would call this a "yellow light," a proceed-with-caution scenario. It's a good example of promoting internal resources like ethics advisors to help folks think through potential problems and solutions before they act.

Especially in smaller communities, it's not uncommon for employees at various levels to engage one another's networks (and family members and friends) in transactions like contracting side jobs, buying a car, or house-sitting. Although the motives may not be nefarious in any way, you will see, if you put on your ethics goggles, that complications and conflicts of interest do arise.

Let's assume the facts of this situation are completely aboveboard—there is no ulterior motive to you asking this particular IT person to do this work, she's just very competent. You are fully able and prepared to pay the going rate, and you are simply doing a favor to your neighbor and hoping the employee will appreciate the chance to make some extra money. You see it as a win-win-win. But if you move ahead, what expectations or relationship does this project create that could be problematic later?

1. If you ask the IT pro directly about this specific job, she may feel pressure to agree, or she may even feel pressure to not charge much or at all. If, down the road, you do not give her a promotion or assignment she desires, how will it look if she says you pressured her to do this favor?

2. Do you manage her team? How many IT folks are on it? How will others react to hearing that you picked her over one of them?

3. What happens if there is some issue with the job—let's say she cancels appointments three times and the system isn't ready for your neighbor's big Super Bowl party. Your neighbor is angry, and so are you. Can you be sure you won't extend this irritation to judging her performance at work going forward? If you don't give her a sufficient raise or an assignment she wants, will she bring this up and claim it's retribution for this moonlighting problem?

One option that may allow you to avoid some of these land mines is to post a note on the bulletin board or other internal communication channel saying that you know someone who needs a few hours of set-up help and will pay the going rate—is anyone interested in some extra weekend or evening work? Another advantage of posting the job openly is that it removes secrecy—which is always inoculation against accusations of favoritism or suspicious motives.

Creating a financial relationship between an executive and a lower-level employee outside the office can raise many ethical issues. Proceed carefully.

You manage the ethics advisors at your company. First thing on a Monday morning, an advisor comes in and shuts the door. She says that she overheard a conversation between two women she could not identify while she was in a bathroom stall. One said, "I went to make a photocopy today, and on the glass was an agreement between Trevor Jones [a high-level executive] and Louise Crawford [his administrative assistant]. He is loaning her $100,000 with repayment to be 'mutually agreed upon over the next five years.'" Then the other said, "Are you kidding me? Louise is late every morning and he never seems to care, but when anyone on the team is late, he always makes a comment. Trevor is such a jerk. I'll bet you 20 bucks he is sleeping with her."

Well, that sounds messy. What should you do?

1. This was not reported to the company through official reporting channels. It's hearsay, and the evidence was gathered in violation of Trevor and Louise's Fourth Amendment rights—you need to ignore it.
2. A loan between a boss and an employee is not explicitly prohibited, but this relationship should be investigated.
3. You can't do much in this case, but you can suggest that the team working on the new version of the code of ethics address transactions between employees. Something of significant value such as a loan or a gift could be a conflict of interest and should be reported to the ethics team.

DISCUSSION OF "ON THE GLASS"

First let's talk about the wrong option, number 1. People who have watched a lot of *Law & Order* and other crime shows pick up the criminal justice lingo and assume things like Miranda rights ("You have the right to remain silent") or laws regarding the collection of hearsay evidence (secondhand recounting) somehow apply universally. Over the years I have heard employees try to argue that things they say or do after hours are "inadmissible."

So let's be clear: As a private employer, I'm not limited by the rules that might apply to prosecutors or government action. I don't have to worry about criminal rules of evidence. This "overheard" conversation is enough to put a company on notice of potential issues, and the company needs to act. If I hear that someone's left a document about a personal loan to a direct report on a copy machine, and when I ask them about it they invoke their right to remain silent, well, OK, pack up your stuff, you're out. If you say somebody is framing you and that loan does not exist, that's a different story. That's why we investigate.

Back to Trevor's loan. The right course is some combination of numbers two and three. And this is exactly the kind of scenario I want all employees to be thinking about.

Sure, loan a colleague or direct report a few dollars for a sandwich or donate $20 to a food bank fund-raiser during the holidays. But $100K? A substantial financial arrangement like this between a manager and a direct report is unusual and a bright red flag. I have seen such loans become an inappropriate way to buy the silence of an employee about other matters, including sexual favors or improper expense accounting. What's more, the discord their relationship clearly is causing on the work team needs to be addressed.

After some preliminary investigation that might involve reviewing emails on company equipment, Trevor needs to be told that an employee saw the loan note on the copier. If he admits he left it there and explains it, his answer will suggest the next course of action. If he denies that such a loan exists and someone is trying to frame him, this answer may suggest another. Trevor needs to think about his relationship with his assistant and how others are perceiving it.

The investigation should be conducted with an open mind, and colleagues of both employees should be asked about whether anything about Trevor and Louise's relationship is causing issues in the workplace. My gut and experience say it would be highly unusual for a boss to loan an employee that much money unless they have a relationship that is inappropriate enough to create tension and discord on the work team. Louise's loyalty should be to the company first, not to her boss. A transaction of this size makes that very difficult. At minimum, if he loaned her the money, even for some kind and noble purpose like medical bills for a child, Trevor has displayed poor judgment.

Managers must maintain some professional distance between themselves and direct reports. Be cordial, be kind, and be caring. But loaning significant amounts of money or involving oneself in a direct report's life as if they were a family member is not appropriate.

Elliott runs international operations for a pharmaceutical firm based in Miami and has always traveled extensively. It turns out that Elliott has two families: a wife and twin daughters who live in Miami, and a companion and a son in Brazil. Brazil companion knows about Miami wife. Miami wife does not know about Brazil companion.

Elliott has legitimate business reasons to travel to Brazil, but lately he has been advocating that his company expand its operations there even more. He's said he wants to spend half his time there. He's made a good business case to do that, and the plant there has been productive and efficient.

Elliott's longtime rival Stewart gets a tip that Elliott has a second family in Brazil, and that Elliott's U.S. family is in the dark. Stewart has also learned that a small group of Elliott's direct reports know about his two families and are covering for him. Stewart arranges a meeting with the general counsel, to whom he suggests that Elliott's first priority is having a business excuse to fly to Brazil and support his second family on the company's tab, and that there are better expansion opportunities elsewhere.

Carnaval is much more fun than sorting this out. Now what?

1. Elliott's personal relationships are his business. The GC should discuss the matter with the CEO, and if Elliott's performance is good and it appears he is operating in the best interest of the company, nothing further should be done.

2. The GC must confront Elliott. The potential conflict of interest here creates, at a minimum, the impression that his judgment about business in Brazil is impaired by his personal relationship there, not to mention that the company is being used to finance and enable his deceit. Further, the burden of secrecy Elliott has created around these two families creates a potential for scandal or blackmail going forward.

3. Knowing that Elliott maintains this level of deceit in his personal life suggests he lacks integrity and character, and that is reason enough to fire him.

DISCUSSION OF "BLAME IT ON RIO"

Situations like this are not as rare as many people might think. Over my career, I've learned about at least half a dozen men who tend to travel a lot and who have chosen a complicated life path by creating and supporting a second family in another city or country—typically a woman and one or more children that his first wife and children do not know about. In each case, the situation went on for years before it came to light.

It's not the job of a workplace code of ethics to address the complexity of an employee's marriage. Practices like bigamy, polyamory, affairs, and other lifestyle choices are typically beyond the concerns of a workplace. But we all know it's not that simple. Lines between "personal life" and "work life" are increasingly blurred, and employees who engage in certain secretive or abusive behaviors outside the office can embarrass their company and damage their company's brand if that behavior becomes widely known. For example, the NFL has had to grapple with multiple incidents of spousal abuse by its players. This sort of off-field conduct has nothing to do with football performance—but high-profile employee misdeeds can reflect so poorly on the employer that a failure to suspend or discipline the employee is seen as the company condoning the bad behavior. The proper course is number 2, and, depending on what an investigation unearths, termination might well be in order.

The world is changing. Consumers want more from companies, and customers want to trust the leaders of the companies they do business with. If the CEO of a family-oriented brand is exposed for leading a "secret life," trust in the brand may be undermined and might force a board to take action.

There's another level to this example. The fact that Elliott's Brazilian companion is not an employee, a vendor, a customer, or any other kind of business partner removes one level of conflict of interest from this equation. But Elliott regularly flies on the company's tab to Brazil, and now he wants to spend even more time there. Elliott has set himself up to be accused of having a conflict of interest. The fact that Brazil might be a promising market for the company isn't the point—Elliott probably can't make a clear judgment on the case for expansion because he has a personal interest in spending more time there. But even if he could somehow assess the situation impartially, news of his affair is now in the workplace, and his work colleagues will never completely trust that his views are impartial. He's lost the trust that leaders need to be effective, as jealous coworkers will always question his motives.

The GC has to interview Elliott and take a very hard look at his expenses. If the evidence shows that Elliott has been traveling excessively to Brazil or supporting his second family with company money, he's finished. But even if Elliott has managed to navigate the affair without leaving an evidentiary trail of expense fraud, he can't credibly advocate for expansion in Brazil. His actions will likely undermine the company's trust in his judgment and hurt his career. That may finish his career at this company as well.

There are other variations on this theme. At different companies, I've been involved in investigations where two employees, married to other people, use their work travel to meet for trysts away from home. Colleagues may find out, and sometimes they feel bad for the spouses. A colleague may send an anonymous tip to one or both of the spouses, who may even show up at the office, furious. Sometimes a tip goes to a manager or the general counsel suggesting the company check into the two parties' travel records because they're inventing reasons to travel that aren't material to getting their jobs done. Often, it's clear that even when the two people may not be traveling together or even work in the same department, they repeatedly, sometimes over a period of many years, have managed to both be in Boston or Atlanta or Seattle over the same two or three days at the same hotel. An investigation needs to take place and check into whether either party has a control relationship with the other. More questions: Was a manager allowing unnecessary travel by either party? Did they use company resources inappropriately? And finally, did those who knew about any of these otherwise "secret" relationships constitute an "in group" that received benefits or other consideration as a consequence?

Hiding a possible conflict of interest from your work is ultimately a self-defeating strategy.

Terry's a new hire to the security team at ProCo. One afternoon, Tina, the company's chief technology officer, invites Terry to join her in a conference room. Tina hands Terry a wallet card with a list of a ProCo competitor's customer database server addresses, as well as a username and password written on it.

Tina smiles grimly: "We have seen some posts on Blind that suggest these guys have been hacking us. One of our sales guys found this card. He did not steal it or buy it or ask anyone for it. That makes it fair game." She pushes a laptop toward Terry. "I want you to find some diner or coffee place on the other side of town with Wi-Fi. Use this laptop, and see if you can get in these databases and let me know what you find. Download anything that might be related to us, and also copy any directory you can find. Don't use it for anything else, and bring it back to me."

Terry stammers, "Have we called the FBI?"

"We will, but we need evidence. And we need to get it before they go in and seize everything." Tina stands up: "Don't let me down, Terry, you have a bright future. And don't talk about this with anyone; this is a highly confidential assignment. Not even your manager—you got that?"

Nobody said protecting the company's data was going to be easy . . . but how should Terry handle this mission?

1. Terry should go straight to the general counsel's office and ask for a meeting. He should dust off his résumé and be prepared to quit if the GC tells him to follow Tina's order.
2. Terry should go to his manager and discuss this conversation. He will want corroboration from his manager that he is just following Tina's orders. If the manager also tells him to do this, then that is another order, so he won't be blamed. But he should keep a real-time journal of everything that happens so he can defend himself.
3. If the company sees evidence on Blind that it is being hacked, it's likely true; this rival company started the war and deserves what they get.

DISCUSSION OF "PASSWORD PIRACY"

Tina is proposing a scenario in which Terry would commit corporate espionage, a criminal act. Knowingly logging in to a private database with a username that is not yours is like noticing car keys on the ground next to a Porsche and then driving off with the car. Does it matter if you think the Porsche owner stole your Honda Civic two weeks ago? It does not. It's a crime to rummage around a database you know you're not supposed to have access to—you're deliberately using false credentials, and the crime charged is generally wire fraud; in this case it might also be theft of trade secrets.

The information posted on Blind could be an internal leak, or it might just be made up. Because it's anonymous, material posted on Blind is not evidence of anything. It can't excuse this sort of behavior.

This is a very difficult and stressful dilemma for Terry. To demonstrate integrity, Terry has to play a long game here, one that will define his career. Terry signed an agreement when he joined the company saying that he will obey the law. That promise is the starting point of any code of ethics. Any request at any time in any place that clearly violates the law, even if it comes from the CTO, demands a cherry-tree moment from the employee asked to perform it: "No, I know this is illegal, and if you want me to do illegal things I do not want to work here."

Loyalty does not excuse this behavior. Tit for tat for the other company stealing secrets is no excuse. Just following orders is no excuse. Do we think that a person with the strength of character to say no to this behavior is going to find another job more in line with his values? I, for one, do . . . the answer is number 1.

Committing to follow the law is fundamental for any legitimate code of ethics.

Rick hates conflict. But he has strong views about many subjects, so he goes to the anonymous website Blind and lets it rip. Two examples:

"Our recycling fixation is BS—we spend all this time separating paper from cans, blah blah blah and I've seen our maintenance folks just dump it all into the trash. More phony lib-speak that means nothing from our PC execs."

"Sure have been a lot of 'high'-level meetings in Building 4 after hours this month. I hear the new GM of the Orion project grows his own premium weed and will share. And by share I mean sell."

You're the general counsel of Rick's company, and you've received an anonymous tip on your ethics hotline that Rick is the employee who posts harsh, sometimes inappropriate comments under one of three different usernames. The tipster claims to be a colleague of another employee in IT who created the fake emails for Rick so he could register different names to use on Blind.

Do you rip the mask off the poster?

1. Ignore the tip and the posts. Once you start following up on information posted on anonymous sites, where will your liability end?
2. Take a deep breath and monitor the posts. Some of the information in these posts suggests some ethical issues at your company. Focus on investigating those, not on shooting the messenger. Assign an investigator to look into the recycling and drug sale allegations posted online.
3. Assign an investigator to look into the emails and network use of both the IT employee and Rick. If what the anonymous tipster says is true, they have both violated company rules by conspiring to abuse the company's email address for nonwork purposes and should be terminated.

DISCUSSION OF "THREE BLIND MICE"

It might be tempting to bury your head in the sand and hope this mess just goes away, but you can't do that. Like it or not, you're on notice about a potential problem, and you need to follow up on it. (And by the way,

I'm not a fan of the "what you don't know won't hurt you" school of thinking—you're better off knowing about problems and dealing with them.)

First, you must look into the allegations of marijuana distribution— whether marijuana is legal in your state or not, it's not likely that this distribution channel is licensed (or collecting the appropriate taxes). That's potentially a criminal violation. Even worse, as of this writing, distribution of marijuana is still a federal offense, and using company property as a distribution point means that your company property could be subject to federal forfeiture if Rick is arrested. That's a tough thing to explain to a board, particularly if you had knowledge and did nothing about it. You have various options here—you can install a video camera in Building 4, investigate Rick's badging records, or make a surprise late-night visit, thereby confirming the rumor.

Second, I'd follow up on the recycling issue. There's probably no criminal offense here (unless your local law requires recycling). Still, if this sort of thing is going on, it undermines the credibility of your "green" initiative and, more broadly, trust in leadership. A quick check of the trash could confirm this rumor.

Third, you have a problem in the IT department if in fact employees are permitting the creation of fake email accounts. You might be able to reach back to the tipster for a name of the perpetrator, or you can at least instigate an independent audit to go in and look at your email records to determine whether there are false accounts. Those same records might also help you figure out who is using those accounts and who is behind the anonymous posts.

If the drug-selling rumors turn out to be false, you need to quickly deal with the person spreading the malicious rumors. If the rumors are true, it's quite possible that the poster has some level of whistleblower protection . . . but at a minimum you'd like to talk to the employee and encourage them to use an official reporting channel.

The age of transparency creates issues that are hard to deal with— that doesn't mean you can ignore them.

Technical writer Sam has trouble making friends, and he's awkward around women in general. But he has been working on a product manual project for MediumCo with Ellen, a graphic designer. There is no reporting relationship, and both Sam and Ellen are single. One day, as they walk out of a meeting, Sam summons his courage and asks Ellen if she'd like to have drinks on Friday night. She smiles and says she has friends in from out of town Friday but "maybe another time." Ten days pass, Sam shoots Ellen the sixth version of an email he's been working on for an hour: "Trivia contest at Bayside Tavern Saturday. Want to be on my team?" One minute later she replies: "Darn it, I'm driving to my parents' house this weekend, leaving Friday night. Have fun—good luck!"

Is it OK for Sam to keep trying . . . or is this is a Code Moment?

1. Ellen hasn't given him a hard no, so until she does, he can pick his moments and keep trying.
2. Sam, try a different approach. Ask one of her colleagues to see if she likes you or whether you should back off.
3. Sam, yellow light. Leave Ellen alone if she doesn't make the next move. If you keep asking, it starts to become inappropriate pressure.

DISCUSSION OF "SAM, SHE'S JUST NOT INTO YOU"

If Sam worked at Airbnb, he would have already violated our policy: one and done. He's got the classic human dilemma of having a crush on somebody who may or may not be interested. That's a shame, it really is. Perhaps, outside the office, you can be a little more persistent. But at work, you must move on.

The heart of this dilemma is: the company's values include the right to feel safe and free of harassment in the workplace. That means Sam is not free to just keep asking and trying to wear Ellen down to get a date. Going to work should not mean having to navigate all the imaginative scheming of a rom-com movie. Yes, Ellen initially said "maybe another time," but when Sam asked again, she did not reinforce that she was interested in going out with him. After two attempts, Sam absolutely must take a step back. Enlisting a colleague in this scheme could pile on more issues, ultimately creating an unpleasant environment for Ellen.

I suspect some of you are thinking: she didn't say no. When she said "maybe another time" it sounded to you like "please ask me again!" Others are thinking: "Sam, wake up! Anyone who uses their parents as an excuse is just not into you." This is the misery of unrequited love, as old as humanity. There is no specific code language that can address human yearning, and I don't blame Sam for his feelings . . . but there is a point where invitations begin to feel like stalking, and enlisting others to plead your case as you might have in junior high is unprofessional and unacceptable.

A fair and reasonable company policy about asking a colleague for a date is one and done.

Luke has been assigned to offer technical support to Marco in marketing. They meet two or three times a week in Marco's cubicle. Marco is married to Greg, and they recently adopted twin sons. Luke is always touching Marco's arm or shoulder and over several weekends, Luke has swamped Marco with texts about the project. Annoyed, Marco finally changes their in-person meetings to phone calls. Luke drops by Marco's cubicle Friday afternoon of the fourth week. He suggests to Marco that they go get a beer; Marco replies, "Luke, I respect your skills, but I'm not interested in socializing. And let's try to handle questions in our meetings. I need to focus on my family when I'm home."

"Sure, totally get it," says Luke, smiling. As he walks away, Marco hears him say loudly, "You sick bastard." Marco walks into the hallway, where three other people are looking at him with concern.

Monday morning Marco gets a call from HR. Luke has filed a complaint saying that Marco has been demanding sexual favors in exchange for recommending him for a bonus for this project. Another colleague tells Marco that Luke has posted a statement on Facebook saying, "It ain't right my tormenter acts like Mr. Family Man when I'm supposed to shut up and do my job."

HR investigates. Marco's officemates heard Luke call out Marco, but there is no evidence to back up Luke's claims—or exonerate Marco. Then, HR gets an anonymous voicemail on the ethics hotline. "I worked with Luke X at another company. I just heard he accused someone of demanding sex. He's done this twice before."

Yikes! What would a high-integrity HR team do?

1. After checking both parties' text and email records, HR cannot resolve the situation. It's one person's word against another's, and what happened at another company is irrelevant. The company can't discipline either person, it can only reassign Luke so he's not working with Marco.
2. It's a better statistical risk to believe the victim who reports a crime. Since officemates heard Luke curse when he left Marco's cubicle, that tips the scales toward Luke's side of the story.

3. The company should investigate Luke's history, based on the anonymous tip. But that presents its own set of challenges, since calls to references and his past employers are unlikely to surface answers and (if the anonymous tip is false) will unfairly cast aspersions on Luke. It may be hard to confirm, but it's wrong to ignore a pattern of behavior—having a hotline that enables a company to reach out to the anonymous party with follow-up questions would definitely help in a situation like this.

DISCUSSION OF "SURE, TOTALLY GET IT"

What a mess. I recently read a story about an alleged sexual harasser who, in response to allegations of misconduct that several victims had leveled against him, said, "There's no need for investigation. It's all true." That sort of honesty, while refreshing, is unusual. These cases are often complex, gray webs that present companies with two entirely different stories, and they challenge you to find the truth.

Option 2 is clearly the wrong course. You can't rely on (unsubstantiated) statistical beliefs about whether the first reporter of an incident is the truth teller. Luke's curse doesn't really prove anything. You need facts. That means you need to do an investigation. Assuming you've properly given employees notice that you have the right to review their work computers and emails (and assuming that's legal in your area), you'll want to conduct a full and fair investigation that includes looking at available email and text records. You can interview employees near Marco's cubicle to see if anyone noticed or overheard anything. The text records may show that Luke repeatedly initiated weekend text exchanges, which could support Marco. You can also try to follow up on the anonymous tip—if it came through a hotline that enables two-way communication with an anonymous reporter, you can ask for more details (name of former employer or the possibility of other victims) that will assist the investigation. You can even try to contact Luke's past employers to corroborate the anonymous tip, but realistically, former employers are not likely to comment.

These are frustrating situations: there is a real victim, but who is it? Both people cannot be telling the truth. In our example we know that Marco is innocent, but when I'm the person handling the investigation, I don't know that. I call these 50-50 cases.

But something has changed in relation to 50-50 cases. The #MeToo movement is usually associated with women's empowerment and speaking out against harassment, but there is a legal consequence to other victims of harassment who also come forward. Predators tend to follow patterns. And prosecutors and judges have started to accept repeated patterns of all kinds as legitimate and relevant evidence. Cases like this one, where someone has made a similar claim multiple times and is accusing someone who has never been accused of anything inappropriate, are being seen in a new light.

I don't relish taking on a more involved investigatory role in a case like this. Once again, that is why I am so determined to PREVENT as many difficult workplace incidents and inappropriate behavior as possible. I encourage any employee who is feeling uncomfortable pressure from a colleague to seek guidance from an ethics advisor, a manager, or from human resources.

When any employee is the victim of a potentially career-ending accusation, that person deserves your best effort to get to the truth.

Postscript

Integrity in a crisis

As I was making the final edits on this book in January 2020, storm clouds in the form of COVID-19 were gathering in China. I sent emails to my Airbnb colleagues in our Beijing office, inquiring about their health. At the time, I recall thinking about how scary it must be "for them." It wasn't sinking in that the United States was also on the brink of a pandemic. I turned to other matters; the book galleys were printed and mailed to reviewers and others involved in the project in anticipation of a May launch.

I was in the car listening to the radio on March 11, 2020, when I learned that Adam Silver had made the decision to suspend the NBA season after one of its players, Rudy Gobert, tested positive for COVID-19. Faced with a big integrity decision on a short time deadline, Adam got it right. His decision would give critical support to public health officials, political leaders, and others watching the infection rates grow, that despite all the serious consequences for the economy and schools and life in general, they needed to take immediate action.

In the middle of this swirling change, a friend who knew I had a book coming out asked, "Do you think anyone will care about integrity when businesses are worried about survival?" Without hesitation, I responded, "I think this is going to force everyone to think about integrity more than ever." And I realized I needed to write this final chapter.

✦

Tough times reveal character. For a company, a crisis is a pressure test for your integrity. Lead with it, and you will win the admiration and appreciation of your stakeholders and the benefits that come with it. Fail it, and the fallout will haunt you long after the crisis is over—assuming your company is still around.

I've been fortunate to work alongside executives who showed both integrity and character during crises. In 1999, eBay hit the limit of its system architecture, and there were frequent platform outages, ultimately triggering a catastrophic failure that lasted 21 hours. Our CEO Meg Whitman created a war room where executives and engineers lived nonstop for several days, taking naps on cots, until the engineering team got our system back up and running and stable.

Then, we sent out an email to customers: Meg acknowledged that we had failed them and promised to go beyond our contractual obligations and refund all their fees during the period when we were down—even for auctions that weren't supposed to end until well after the outage. She promised we would invest in a more robust architecture to prevent future outages. In other words, she focused first on regaining trust, even though it created a significant hit to our earnings. Some worried Wall Street would punish us for taking that path. Instead, the opposite happened: buyers and sellers stayed engaged, investors remained supportive of our platform, and eBay survived this near-death experience.

Just two years later, on September 11, 2001, another crisis would again test the character of the company. The first 9/11 integrity dilemma was simple to resolve: we discovered that, within hours of the planes hitting the World Trade Towers in New York City, people had listed rubble from the scene to sell on eBay. Our Trust and Safety team already had a policy that prohibited listings that involved a seller profiting from a disaster, and we quickly removed the listings.

That same day, we got a call from New York governor George Pataki, who told us that celebrities and others wanted to auction personal items as a fundraiser to benefit the families of victims of 9/11. The entire company quickly embraced the idea, and within 72 hours we launched Auction for America. Ultimately, 230,000 items changed hands and raised $10 million for survivors. We took no fees for the transactions. We would act similarly during other crises. During Hurricane Katrina, our systems managers could see that our sellers and buyers from New Orleans had disappeared from eBay after they had to abandon their homes. We responded by depositing $1,000 in their individual PayPal accounts.

I saw in these experiences that leaders with integrity who operate with accountability to a broad slate of stakeholders can survive crises and emerge stronger.

And it's true too that establishing a culture of integrity stands to help you immensely when crises hit, by establishing an environment of trust and a reflexive wish to do the right thing. Employees will tend to trust their leaders; suppliers are open to working through short-term challenges together; customers, even when inconvenienced, are inclined to give the company the benefit of the doubt. When a company falls into patterns of short-term thinking, cover-ups, and shooting the messenger, on the other hand, the mistakes compound and ultimately lead to chaos and failure.

◆

I spoke to a number of groups about integrity in the immediate aftermath of COVID-19. Its impacts had hit all of us either directly or indirectly, and there was quickly a lot of discussion about companies and executives who had or had not handled it well, or even appropriately. Make no mistake, these are difficult times. Even companies who have done everything right, who have invested time and energy in creating a strong, positive, healthy culture based on values and respect, have had to wrestle with difficult trade-offs, some involving layoffs, mandatory personal time off, pay cuts, business unit shutdowns, and other actions impacting hardworking people who had done nothing wrong. So I set out to develop a framework that would help guide them in making tough decisions.

Before I get into that framework, I want to make some broad observations about the kind of behavior that I believe reflects integrity and the kind that rings hollow or cynical. Like me, you probably received assurances from companies that they are "there" for you. "We are all in this together," say others. And then, the pitch: buy a new car and we'll delay your first payments for a couple of months! A friend of mine actually got a "We are here for you" email from a yacht broker. Just what you need in the middle of a pandemic!

Other companies are taking meaningful and concrete actions that will leave a lasting positive impression. Some auto insurers, for example, refunded a percentage of premiums during shelter-in-place since the rates of car accidents dropped. That refund was an unexpected surprise for customers who had been laid off or seen their incomes decrease. Internet companies lifted data limits and suspended certain fees to support people stuck at home watching movies and trying to keep their children amused.

Other companies sought to help directly with the medical crises. A team at Bloom Energy volunteered to refurbish nonworking ventilators, helping to save lives. A number of clothing companies, including Brooks Brothers, LVMH, the sports gear company Fanatics, and Eddie Bauer, shifted production to make masks and safety gowns for hospital workers.[1] The book publisher Scholastic announced it would support free lunch programs for children whose schools were closed. It also partnered with actors to read books to children at home over Instagram and Facebook and encourage donations to local food drives.[2]

Assessing how you can and should contribute as a constructive member of the larger community struggling with a challenge leads me into the first element in the framework I have created.

Step one: Do a rigorous stakeholder assessment

At the dawn of any crisis, you need a 360-degree assessment of the impact on your stakeholders. For obvious reasons, the nature of the crisis tends to set your priorities in doing this. In a situation like COVID-19, companies with employees working in close proximity had an immediate and serious safety issue. The concerns of an assembly-line workforce would be quite different from the dilemmas of an advertising company that caters to the travel industry and uses a lot of independent contract writers and designers.

There was a wonderful story in the *Los Angeles Times* about a CEO that demonstrated a principled response to dealing with COVID-19 by focusing first on his employee stakeholders.[3] Kevin Kelly, the CEO of Emerald Packaging, a family-owned plastic bag company located in Union City, California, was driving to work when he heard an FDA official talking about the importance of implementing social distancing and sanitation procedures inside workplaces. This was the same day the NBA made its crucial decision to halt play, and before most companies had moved.

Kelly arrived at work and called an all-company meeting—by tele-conference—and announced new procedures designed to keep everyone safe. In the ensuing days he added two weeks of sick leave for all employees and cautioned anyone who was unwell to stay home. When asked at the meeting what a person should do if he or she was the only person who could do their job or operate a specific piece of machinery, Kevin repeated that regardless of the consequence to the business, they should stay home—and made the employee repeat that important message. Everyone laughed but got the message. I like how Kevin handled this: he prioritized the safety of his stakeholder employees over other longer-term factors, and did not assign these conversations to human resources or bury the message in an email. He realized the message had to come from the top, live, with feeling, for it to have credibility.

His leadership team also banned meetings of more than five people and staggered break and lunch periods, insisting that employees avoid mingling and socializing. He had his staff fill spray bottles throughout his plant with alcohol and encouraged constant disinfecting of workstations, door handles, banisters, and other places where employees might be touching surfaces. Considered an essential business (Emerald makes the plastic bags that carry lettuce and fresh vegetables, among other things), Emerald even looked around its community to see how it could support neighbors. Kelly decided to order 270 burritos for a free lunch every week to help keep a local lunch spot in business.

As CEO, Kevin Kelly might have focused on the business and his market share and left the facility decisions to various lieutenants. However, what he realized on that drive to the office was that protecting his employees' health and safety was a "moral obligation" and had to be his Job One. And as the weeks passed, despite his own concerns about his family's health, he made a point of being in the office every day. A leader can't ask his team to do something that he or she wouldn't do themselves.

On the other hand, I've been concerned by the experience of many grocery store and drugstore employees. In mid-April 2020, the United Food and Commercial Workers International Union issued a press release saying that 30 supermarket workers had died of COVID-19 and several thousand had reported respiratory symptoms.[4] The union complained that some stores were slow to protect workers by limiting the number of customers allowed in a store at one time. Many retail operations trumpet ideas like "customer obsession," and it was essential that people were able to buy groceries and get their prescriptions. But in some cases, big retailers failed to see that the mixed message of talking about customer stakeholders' health but not protecting the health of their employees with the same apparent vigor would lead to a backlash.

I also believe when you ask employees to work in potentially dangerous situations, the company's leaders should not sequester themselves in the filtered air of the executive suite. Spending some time at a cash register or stocking shelves may give insights that inspire a leader to recommend further precautions, and employees will appreciate and respect your willingness to see the situation from the front lines. It also sends the message that you wouldn't ask them to do anything you wouldn't do yourself.

Of course, employees are just one of the stakeholders a company's leaders must consider. Among the others:

Shareholders. Your investors will want to know, are you conserving cash? Should you delay certain investments until the situation stabilizes? Have you prioritized what projects may need to be cut if the situation becomes prolonged? Do you need to downsize? There is nothing unethical about attending to these issues, but their importance should not be so elevated above others that safety or business strategy is neglected.

Partners, suppliers, and landlords. Does your success depend on a partner supplying a key ingredient or material? Do you know what their pressing issues are? Do you need to support their business in order to support your own? And can they help you? If you're struggling with cash, have an honest conversation with them about your challenges, and get a sense of how much flexibility they can offer you on payment terms—with good partnerships, everyone is invested in each other's success.

Customers. Are you reaching out to make sure you understand what customer needs are? Are they strapped for cash? Should you consider extending a payment plan before they simply default? Do they need products they're having trouble finding that you can help procure? Are there segments with special needs? With COVID-19, it sent a positive message when many stores created special hours for vulnerable elderly people to shop and try to further limit their exposure to the virus.

Your community. What is happening to your neighbors? Do they have specific challenges you can help with? Do you have facilities you can lend to volunteer groups who need to meet or assemble relief supplies? Can you donate food or items to community members who are suffering or struggling? Even helping in little ways can make a big difference. For example, when San Francisco Bay Area family shelter Life Moves was struggling to find food for its families, over 20 Bay Area companies volunteered to donate the snacks that were left behind when employees began sheltering and working at home.

◆

As we discussed earlier in the book, all smart companies are moving to a more stakeholder-focused orientation rather than one focused on shareholders. The modern realities of business and the increased transparency of social media have forced companies to take the concerns of their employees and customers even more seriously. If you're perceived as opportunistic or exploitive in a crisis, criticism can quickly spiral into customer boycotts or issues with partners. If you lend a helping hand, the benefits to your reputation going forward could be significant.

Amazon, for example, is fighting a number of fires on the integrity front as I write this. On one hand, the company's extensive distribution network is allowing millions of people to shelter more safely in place thanks to food and essential product deliveries. Amazon is making a positive contribution to our country by moving vital goods around the world and into the hands of consumers. On the other hand, protests by some warehouse workers that Amazon is not adequately protecting their safety have led to isolated walkouts and criticism of Amazon's management. It didn't help when a memo was leaked that cited comments made by the company's general counsel attacking a worker leading a protest as "not smart or articulate," and outlining a strategy to deflect criticism to the worker's behavior rather than Amazon's.[5]

Amazon is in an unenviable position. However much good Amazon is doing for people by delivering goods, it's also perceived as a behemoth that is profiting from the huge increase in business. That makes it much more important for the company to continuously evaluate its treatment of all of its stakeholders.

Step two: Use empathetic, honest communication

In a crisis, regardless of what information they're communicating, the best leaders are direct, authentic, and empathetic. They acknowledge that fear and uncertainty exist, making employees feel better that they're not alone in their concerns. They are honest about the challenges faced; paying lip service to "we'll all get through this together" when you already know a third of the company will have to be laid off are approaches that are disrespectful and can backfire.

Employees always perceive and notice more than leaders think they do. They have seen their leaders' body language when they are confident, and from nonverbal clues alone they will sense something is wrong or that they are not hearing the full story. If you tell them their health and safety is your number-one priority, and then you tell them they need to sacrifice and not overreact to warnings from government officials or health experts and come to work even if they don't feel well, do not be surprised when they start to question everything you tell them. If your communication is inconsistent, evasive, or robotic—as if a lawyer wrote every word and warned you not to stray from the script—you may unintentionally feed fears.

So what do you say in a crisis? Try to imagine what your employees are worried about and prioritize those issues. In a financial crisis like the recession of 2008, the overarching fear of many employees was layoffs; during COVID-19, initial worries included physical risk of exposure to a pathogen from other workers or customers and balancing obligations to work and children during widespread school closures. Smart executives specifically addressed that the company needed to be flexible instead of maintaining rigid expectations. I was impressed in early April 2020 when Microsoft announced it would offer special 12-week parental leave to employees dealing with school closures due to the pandemic. Most companies did not have the resources to offer a benefit that generous, but the efforts of leaders who shift meetings, schedules, and deliverables around to free up employees as needed during the day does not go unnoticed by employees and builds loyalty.

During other natural disasters or crises, an entirely different set of issues may be more prominent. What if everything is fine at work, but a large number of employees have lost access to their homes in a flood?

What if there has been contamination of a company's major food product and the company's efforts need to shift from producing and shipping it to tracing and recalling it? What if there is a broad disruption in the power grid? Again, it's impossible to imagine all the scenarios that could create a significant threat to a company's business or long-term viability. Whatever the issue, your employees are looking to the c-suite for information, a realistic assessment of where things stand, and, if possible, reassurance that their concerns are being addressed.

Especially when you suspect you will have to lay people off or make radical changes to your strategy or near-term operations, don't put on a false show of optimism. It's not possible or wise to communicate everything you know at all times, and there may be dependencies you are trying to work out before you can plot your next steps. If you're seeking additional funding, for example, or have applied for some kind of special program that can help retain workers, there may be a period of time when you simply don't have answers to some questions. It's okay to say you are investigating every option to continue operations, and you will update as soon as you know more.

Step three: Be alert for new opportunities

When the business climate shifts and your resources suddenly aren't aligned with customer demand, be creative. Talk to your stakeholders, listen to their insights, and be open to new opportunities and ways of doing business.

During COVID-19, the emergence of easy-to-use online selling platforms created new opportunities for companies whose retail stores were forced to close or whose usual supply chains were disrupted. Many restaurants shifted to a take-out or delivery model much more rapidly than they could have in the past. In the COVID-19 context, even as travel sites and home-sharing services experienced low demand, companies like Grubhub and Uber Eats surged with unprecedented volumes of food delivery orders. Airbnb launched an online version of its Experiences business. I heard of companies in decidedly nonessential businesses, like custom T-shirts, shifting their online marketing presence to promoting essential items such as paper products. My workout trainer began training me and other clients over Zoom.

It takes courage and a lot of hard to work to change course, but following the old adage of "find a need and fill it" is never bad advice in a crisis. These pivots can also lead to new business lines and relationships that can create long-term benefits.

Step four: Making hard decisions with integrity

In any kind of crisis that significantly impacts revenues, companies may have to conserve cash by cutting nonessential projects and investments, and in some cases laying off workers. Layoffs aren't necessarily unethical; unfortunately, they were necessary at Airbnb. Some CEOs may rightly conclude that if they don't cut a certain percentage of the staff, the company will be severely handicapped financially. Cutting employees offers a chance for those remaining to keep the company afloat until a recovery is underway.

I know there are some executives who, in crisis, move swiftly to cut expenses to the bone. I've even heard them say it is the "least disruptive, least cruel" approach, because while it is hard on those who are laid off, leadership can then reassure the remaining employees that there is enough business and cash reserves to keep them employed for a specific period of time. I've heard it said this approach "removes fear" for remaining employees and allows those let go to get a jump on finding a new job at the start of a crisis before many other companies also resort to layoffs.

I tend to think that an overnight, radical slashing of costs is not the best way to go. But whether fast or measured, any cost cutting must start at the top—leaders may need to "eat last," as author Simon Sinek counsels, but in a crisis they need to sacrifice first. A CEO cannot credibly implement layoffs or cut benefits without beginning at the leadership team, the group that is presumably compensated well and can weather the financial storm more easily than line employees. Not surprising, then, that Adam Silver and Brian Chesky—who lead companies hit hard in the crisis—started cost-cutting measures at the top, with their own salaries and the salaries of their leadership team.

For some companies, there may be incremental options that stop short of layoffs.

Some companies, as a first step, may ask employees to take all their vacation and accrued sick pay to save cash obligations in hopes that conditions will improve and they won't have to be laid off.

Another option is a furlough—typically a proposal to an employee that they will not receive a salary for the foreseeable future, but their healthcare and other benefits will continue and their stock options will vest to a certain date, at which point their situation will be reevaluated. This sends a signal that even though it must conserve cash, management is hopeful that the employee can and will return and wants to make that process easier and more appealing. Obviously this gives the employee an opportunity to look for another job, but it also keeps open a door that both parties appreciate. And you can continue to show appreciation to furloughed employees. One pizza chain in Atlanta had to furlough a number of employees, but the chain decided to regularly deliver free pizzas to their furloughed staff in an effort to provide food to and stay in touch with their teammates.

In announcing any cost-cutting options—especially layoffs—I recommend making sure to emphasize the details of the "why." For example, when Marriott announced it was going to furlough tens of thousands of employees in the wake of COVID-19, the CEO Arne Sorensen explained to employees that its worldwide occupancy rates were at just 25 percent, down from 70 percent the previous year, and its occupancy rate in China was just 5–6 percent. He said Marriott had been impacted by COVID-19 far more than it had been by 9/11. It was no secret that global travel had almost ground to a halt, but informing employees about the dimensions and scale of the challenge with specific references reinforced the need to act. If you don't give specifics, employees may attribute the moves to general indifference to them, or speculate about executives who won or lost turf battles, or repeat theories like, "They've been wanting to shut down this unit for a long time, this just gives them an easy out." By the way, Sorensen also announced he would be taking no salary for the remainder of the year, and the rest of the executive team's pay would be cut 50 percent.[6]

Secondly, even though it represents an expense, a company laying off employees in a crisis should, if feasible financially, provide transitional assistance, which can include a financial severance package or extended healthcare benefits. This is a good thing to do for valued and respected employees you've had to let go, and it also has a psychological benefit for existing employees to see that the company has a heart and intends to act in as generous a way as is reasonable. The financial impact to Airbnb's business has been substantial, as it has been for the entire travel industry, and it has been painful, personally and professionally, for Airbnb leaders to let go a number of Airbnb employees.

◆

The COVID-19 crisis has not only severely impacted Airbnb employees but also its host and guest community. In most cases, Airbnb allows hosts to set their own policies about canceled reservations. For hosts who had come to depend on renting out space as a significant part of their income and explicitly set strict reservation standards, Airbnb requiring that they give refunds while the world is locked down could impose significant hardships. On the other hand, with millions of would-be travelers literally prohibited from leaving their homes for anything short of buying food and basics or an emergency, charging them for vacation travel they might legally be prohibited from taking was also troubling.

Ultimately, Airbnb permitted many guests to cancel their reservations. But true to Airbnb's multiple stakeholder philosophy, the company also put aside $250 million dollars to help compensate hosts whose reservation policies were impacted. What was inspiring to me was when Airbnb employees also jumped in to help individually. Every Airbnb employee gets a travel credit each quarter to travel on Airbnb's tab. A number of employees surfaced the idea of donating their credits to hosts, and on their own, unprompted by management, over 2,000 employees donated over $1 million to hosts in need.

◆

One day, the pandemic will end and life will return to some sense of "normal." When it does, no matter your role—family member, parent, friend, employee, manager, CEO—people always remember how you behaved and how you made them feel during a crisis. In some sense there is no better test of integrity, and no time at which integrity is more valuable.

Acknowledgments

"When you live by the code of your own light, that's impeccable integrity. Impeccable integrity has its own symmetry, its own sound of elegance, excellence, and brilliance. When someone with impeccable integrity walks into a room, people feel it. They think, I want that."

—Carlos Santana, September 2019

When I began working on this book, I wanted to focus on the nuts and bolts of helping businesspeople sort through specific dilemmas and scenarios by being intentionally ethical. I also wanted to make the larger argument that doing so could make the world better. But as the book evolved, I found myself having a fascinating set of conversations with people from so many different vantage points, life paths, and ethical and moral frameworks. By the time I finished, I was challenging and expanding my own definitions and frameworks that I'd assembled over two decades trying to help companies chart an ethical course. I realized that people connect with the concept of integrity in many different ways, from the entirely practical and legal implications to the spiritual, almost mystical dimensions that musician Carlos Santana talked about with me one morning.

But as Carlos said, when you meet someone who is on an ethical path, you perceive an undeniable sense of good energy; you may even experience a powerful inspiration to be a better person.

My thank-yous have to start with Jillian, the love of my life, without whom this could never have happened. From her "You should write a book" through connecting me to Tim, my editor, and reconnecting me with Joan, my writing partner, and coaching me through the entire process as my agent and partner, to being tucked in my heart every day, this book is filled with her wisdom and light and love. I'm extraordinarily lucky to have you by my side every day. Tim Bartlett and the St. Martin's team have been wonderful partners for me. Thank you for your guidance and believing not just in the book, but in what it stands for. I'm so grateful for my writing partner, Joan O'C. Hamilton, who wanted me to write a book from our first conversation in 2010, and who signed on to help in 2018. She did far more than just write my ideas down, she was a true collaborative partner who brought her own stories and strong sense of integrity to this project, and I couldn't ask for a better colleague in writing this book.

This book is a memoir of a life's journey, and I've been taught by some world-class leaders and colleagues and friends along the way, starting at the top with my best man, Jerry Erickson, and treasured friends Wilbur Vitols, Nash Schott, Joyce Vance, Kevin Etheridge, and Jimmy DiNardo. From my days as a federal prosecutor, thank you to the federal judges in the Rocket Docket who shaped me as a young lawyer—Judge Bryan, Judge Cacheris, Judge Hilton, Judge Brinkema, Judge Ellis, Judge Hudson, Judge O'Grady, Judge Sewell, and of course, Judge Williams. Thank you to the entire EDVA U.S. Attorney's Office family, especially Helen Fahey, Richard Cullen, Chuck Rosenberg, Tom Connolly, Peter White, James Comey, Roscoe Howard, Jim Trump, Randy Bellows, John Nassikas, Tim Shea, John Rowley, Neil Hammerstrom, Jay Apperson, Andrew McBride, Gordon Kromberg, John Davis, Rosie Haney, Jan Purvis, Larry Leiser, General Rich, Justin Williams, and Mark Hulkower, and our colleagues across the river John Martin, John Dion, and Robert Mueller.

At eBay I was lucky to be taught by some of the finest leaders I've ever come across—Mike Jacobson and Maynard Webb—who each unselfishly continue to pour so much of their life wisdom into teaching me law and business and integrity; I'm deeply grateful to both of you. To Meg Whitman, for giving a federal prosecutor a chance in Silicon Valley and supporting and believing in me. To Marty Abbott, who simply would not let me fail. To Brian Swette, John Donahoe, Josh Kopelman, Wendy Jones, Michael Dearing, Bill Cobb, Jamie Iannone, Rajiv Dutta, Bob Swan, Kristin Yetto, Jeff Housenbold, Maggie Dinno, Lynn Reedy, Andre Haddad, Lorrie Norrington, Gary Briggs, Mark Rubash, Jay Lee, Joe Sullivan, Steve Westly, Lorna Borenstein, Alex Kazim, Kip Knight, and so many other eBay leaders for life lessons in leadership. To the incredible eBay legal team, folks like Brad Handler and Jay Monahan, Geoff Brigham, Kent

Walker, Mike Richter, Lance Lanciault, Allyson Willoughby, Tod Cohen, Allison Mull, Jay Clemens, Kyung Koh, John Muller, Scott Shipman, Jack Christin, and Alex Benn. And to everyone in the eBay Trust and Safety family who gave so much to create a trusted marketplace—Jeff Taylor and Lulu Laursen and Eric Salvatierra and Matt Halprin and Carolyn Patterson and Dinesh Lathi and Ken Calhoon, Vikram Subramaniam, Tong Li, Xin Ge, Sameer Chopra, Mariana Klumpp, Mike Eynon, Laura Mather, Martine Niejadlik, Hseuh Tsang, Grace Molnar, Amjad Hanif, Lynda Talgo, Brian Burke, John McDonald, Colin Rule, Randy Ching, Tim Kunihiro, Sophie Bromberg, the King brothers Jeff and Jeremy, Larry Friedberg and Dave Steer, and Ellen Silver, Sarah McDonald, Chet Ricketts, Kai Curtis, Sean Chaffin, Kathy Free, Gary Fullmer, Bryan Richards, John Canfield and Kevin Embree, eLVIS, Lissa Minkin, and Paul Oldham, Amanda Earhart, Amidha Shyamsukha, Tim Paine and Monica Paluso, Zach Pino, Susan Dutton, and the whole incredible team in Draper, Utah, and John Kothanek, Alastair MacGibbon, Mat Henley, Andy Brown, Oliver Weyergraf, Michael Pak, Garreth Griffith, Christian Perella, Angela Chesnut, Stony Burke, Dave Carlson, Jeff Parent and Kevin Kamimoto, and so many others who were part of that journey as the pioneers of Internet platform trust and safety.

At Chegg, what a team. Huge thanks to my mentor and good friend Dan Rosensweig, and to Heather Hatlo Porter, Chuck Geiger, Nathan Schultz and Andy Brown, Esther Lem and Jenny Brandemeuhl, Robert Park, Mitch Spolen, Elizabeth Harz, Anne Dwane, Tina McNulty, Mike Osier, Heather Tatroff Morris, John Fillmore, and my good friend Dave Borders! You all stuck together and built something great. Students first!

And the Airbnb team, it starts at the top and the integrity starts with Brian, Nate, and Joe. Thank you for building a different kind of company with an inspiring mission that we can all be proud of. Thanks to Belinda Johnson, Beth Axelrod, Greg Greeley, Jonathan Mildenhall, Chris Lehane, Joebot, Alex Schleifer, Dave Stephenson, Fred Reid, Margaret Richardson, Aisling Hassell, and Melissa Thomas-Hunt and the whole executive team for leading in the Intentional Integrity journey. To the finest collection of in-house legal talent in the world—the 150-plus lawyers around the world led by Renee Lawson, Garth Bossow, Fiona Dormandy, Rafik Bawa, Sharda Caro, Darrell Chan, Kum Hong Siew, Ruben Toquero, Claire Ucovich, and Shanna Torrey, who work as partners with the business to spread belonging, and who believe in practicing law with integrity and a smile, my deepest thanks to you all for giving me the incredible life experience of working with you as a true team. Special thanks to Kate Shaw, Peter Urias, Sarah Robson, Samantha Becker, Jordan Blackthorne, Julie Wenah, Jen Rice, and all of the Ethics Advisors, for teaching me so much about diversity, inclusion, and ethics. Special thanks to Karen White at the AG Alliance, Jackie Stone at McGuire Woods, and Geoff Eisenberg for all their support, wisdom, and friendship through the years.

My thanks to everyone who gave their time and thoughts so generously to this book—Reid Hoffman, Ben Horowitz, Josh Bolten, Srin Madipalli, and Lilian Than, superlawyer Jackie Kalk, General Eric Holder, Priya Singh and David Entwistle from Stanford Health, David Westin, Thomas Friedman, Dan Ariely, Yael Melamede, President Jim Ryan, Kim Scott, Jeff Jordan, Paul Sallaberry, Janet Hill, Chai Feldblum and Sharon Masling, Jim Morgan, Donald Heider, Jim Sinegal, Commissioner Adam Silver, and Carlos Santana.

Most importantly, thank you to my family. To my children, Bianca and Cliff, with love, who each in their way helped me figure out ways to evolve and communicate integrity through doing my toughest job, being a parent. They are the two most wonderful children a parent could want; I am extraordinarily lucky to have them at the center of my life. To Justin Manus, Mandy, Blake, Nick, Brock, and Mariana Salzman, Mark and Mara DuBois, Elizabeth Manus, Jom and Lisa Bloch, Alexis and Jordan and Caroline, and Babyus, for so fully making me part of your wonderful family. With love and gratitude to my uncle, Cliff Waddell, who put me through college and law school and, more importantly, has been there for me as my mentor and father figure and friend for the entire journey; none of this could have happened without you. To my dad, I hope your "pal" did you proud. To my grandmother, a steady source of pure love and support in my life. And of course, my first teacher and model for integrity, my mom, Kitty Chesnut. This one's for you and all the love you poured into me— Mom, just wish you were still around to go to the local bookstore to buy the first copy and read it in your favorite rocking chair.

And last, to anyone who's ever been inspired by Intentional Integrity, and wants to bring it into your own workplace, I'll leave you with the same message Carlos Santana sent me off with—"Go to the cleaners, get out your cape, and soar."

Notes

Introduction: Show of hands?

1 2019 Edelman Trust Barometer, January 2019. https://www.edelman.com/trust-barometer [accessed November 6, 2019].

2 Richard Edelman, "Trust at Work," Edelman, January 21, 2019, https://www.edelman.com/insights/trust-at-work [accessed October 19, 2019].

3 Jessica Long, "The Bottom Line on Trust," Accenture, October 30, 2018, https://www.accenture.com/us-en/insights/strategy/trust-in-business [accessed October 19, 2019].

4 Ryan Suppe, "Salesforce Employees Ask CEO to Reconsider Contract with Border Protection Agency," *USA Today*, June 26, 2018, https://www.usatoday.com/story/tech/2018/06/26/salesforce-employees-petition-ceo-reconsider-government-contract/734907002/ [accessed October 19, 2019].

5 Kate Trafecante and Nathaniel Meyersohn, "Wayfair Workers Plan Walkout in Protest of Company's Bed Sales to Migrant Camps," CNN Business, June 26, 2019, https://www.cnn.com/2019/06/25/business/wayfair-walkout-detention-camps-trnd/index.html [accessed October 19, 2019].

6 Daisuke Wakabayashi, Erin Griffith, Amie Tsang, and Kate Conger, "Google Walkout: Employees Stage Protest over Handling of Sexual Harassment," *New York Times*, November 1, 2018, https://www.nytimes.com/2018/11/01/technology/google-walkout-sexual-harassment.html [accessed October 19, 2019].

7 "On the Other side of Prime Day, Amazon Workers Brace for 'Two Months of Hell'—NBC News," Kazal.hu, July 16, 2019, https://kazal.hu/2019/07/16/on-the-other-side-of-prime-day-amazon-workers-brace-for-two-months-of-hell-nbc-news/ [accessed October 19, 2019].

8 Akane Otani, "Patagonia Triggers a Market Panic over New Rules on Its Power Vests," *Wall Street Journal*, November 4, 2019, https://www.wsj.com/articles/patagonia-triggers-a-market-panic-over-new-rules-on-its-power-vests-11554736920 [accessed October 19, 2019].

9 "Business Roundtable Redefines the Purpose of a Corporation to Promote 'An Economy That Serves All Americans,'" Business Roundtable, August 19, 2019, https://www.businessroundtable.org/business-roundtable-redefines-the-purpose-of-a-corporation-to-promote-an-economy-that-serves-all-americans [accessed October 19, 2019].

Chapter 1: Spies, jarts, and racism

1 "An Assessment of the Aldrich H. Ames Espionage Case and Its Implications for U.S. Intelligence," Senate Select Committee on Intelligence, November 1, 1994, https://fas.org/irp/congress/1994_rpt/ssci_ames.htm [accessed October 19, 2019].

2 Jarts are a good example of how relentless some sellers can be when they smell opportunity—and how banned items can gain an outlaw cachet that makes them even more prized by some buyers. When I was at eBay and sellers learned that we were banning jarts, they tried a new tack: listing "Jarts box only!" where they would sell you the box and then, guess what, throw in the jarts for free. We banned this practice as well, but I've noticed that "box only" listings have recently reemerged.

3 In August 2019, there was a remarkable investigation by the *Wall Street Journal* titled "Amazon Has Ceded Control of Its Site. The Result: Thousands of Banned, Unsafe or Mislabeled Products." Just like tech companies that have struggled to tackle misinformation on their platforms, Amazon has proven unable or unwilling to effectively police third-party sellers on its site. The *Journal* found over 4,000 products for sale "that have been declared unsafe by federal agencies, are deceptively labeled or are banned by federal regulators." I confess I felt some sympathy to the challenge of policing this issue on such a broad platform, but it is imperative to act in support of customer safety, not just demonstrate an intention of it; https://www.wsj.com/articles/amazon-has-ceded-control-of-its-site-the-result-thousands-of-banned-unsafe-or-mislabeled-products-11566564990 [accessed November 9, 2019].

4 Brian Chesky as quoted in *Time*, September 8, 2016, "Airbnb CEO: 'Bias and Discrimination Have No Place' Here," https://time.com/4484113/airbnb-ceo-brian-chesky-anti-discrimination-racism/ [accessed November 9, 2019].

Chapter 3: C is for Chief

1 EJ, "Violated: A Traveler's Lost Faith, a Difficult Lesson Learned," Around the World and Back Again, June 29, 2011, http://ejroundtheworld.blogspot.com/2011/06/violated-travelers-lost-faith-difficult.html [accessed October 19, 2019].

2 Lyneka Little, "San Francisco Burglary Inspires Changes at Airbnb," ABC News, August 2, 2011, https://abcnews.go.com/Business/airbnb-user-horrified-home-burglarized-vandalized-trashed/story?id=14183840 [accessed October 19, 2019].

3 Leigh Gallagher, "The Education of Airbnb's Brian Chesky," *Fortune,* June 26, 2015, https://fortune.com/longform/brian-chesky-airbnb/ [accessed November 10, 2019].

4 Kevin Short, "11 Reasons to Love Costco That Have Nothing to Do with Shopping," *Huffington Post*, December 6, 2017, https://www.huffpost.com/entry/reasons-love-costco_n_4275774 [accessed October 19, 2019].

5 Kara Swisher, "Who Will Teach Silicon Valley to Be Ethical?," *New York Times*, October 21, 2018, https://www.nytimes.com/2018/10/21/opinion/who-will-teach-silicon-valley-to-be-ethical.html [accessed October 19, 2019].

6 Danny Hakim, Aaron M. Kessler, and Jack Ewing, "As Volkswagen Pushed to Be No. 1, Ambitions Fueled a Scandal," *New York Times*, September 27, 2015, https://www.nytimes.com/2015/09/27/business/as-vw-pushed-to-be-no-1-ambitions-fueled-a-scandal.html [accessed October 19, 2019].

7 Jasper Jolly, "Former Head of Volkswagen Could Face 10 Years in Prison," *The Guardian*, April 15, 2019, https://www.theguardian.com/business/2019/apr/15/former-head-of-volkswagen-could-face-10-years-in-prison [accessed October 19, 2019].

8 Lydia Dishman, "How Volkswagen's Company Culture Could Have Led Employees to Cheat," *Fast Company*, December 15, 2015, https://www.fastcompany.com/3054692/how-volkswagens-company-culture-could-have-led-employees-to-cheat [accessed October 19, 2019].

9 James C. Morgan with Joan O'C. Hamilton, *Applied Wisdom: Bad News Is Good News and Other Insights That Can Help Anyone Be a Better Manager* (Los Altos, CA: Chandler Jordan Publishing, 2016).

10 Matt Stevens, "Starbucks C.E.O. Apologizes After the Arrest of Two Black Men," *New York Times*, April 15, 2018, https://www.nytimes.com/2018/04/15/us/starbucks-philadelphia-black-men-arrest.html [accessed October 19, 2019].

11 Kim Bellware, "Uber Settles Investigation into Creepy 'God View' Tracking Program," *Huffington Post*, January 6, 2016, https://www.huffpost.com/entry/uber-settlement-god-view_n_568da2a6e4b0c8beacf5a46a [accessed October 19, 2019].

12 Amy Conway-Hatcher and Sheila Hooda, "The Rearview Mirror and the Road Ahead on #MeToo: Action Items for Corporate Boards," Law.com, January 10, 2019, https://www.law.com/corpcounsel/2019/01/10/the-rearview-mirror-and-the-road-ahead-on-metoo-action-items-for-corporate-boards/ [accessed October 19, 2019].

13 Sarah McBride, "WeWork IPO Turns Contentious at SoftBank's Vision Fund," *Los Angeles Times*, September 6, 2019, https://www.latimes.com/business/story/2019-09-06/wework-ipo-turns-contentious-softbank-vision-fund [accessed November 2, 2019].

14 Stephen Bertoni, "WeWork's $20 Billion Office Party: The Crazy Bet That Could Change How the World Does Business," *Forbes*, October 24, 2017, https://www.forbes.com/sites/stevenbertoni/2017/10/02/the-way-we-work/#71dd3cef1b18 [accessed October 19, 2019].

15 Daisuke Wakabayashi and Katie Benner, "How Google Protected Andy Rubin, the 'Father of Android,'" *New York Times*, October 25, 2018, https://www.nytimes.com/2018/10/25/technology/google-sexual-harassment-andy-rubin.html [accessed October 19, 2019].

16 Jennifer Blakely, "My Time at Google and After," *Medium*, August 28, 2019, https://medium.com/@jennifer.blakely/my-time-at-google-and-after-b0af688ec3ab [accessed October 19, 2019].

17 Connie Loizos, "Google Lets Drummond Do the Talking," *TechCrunch*, August 29, 2019, https://techcrunch.com/2019/08/29/google-lets-david-drummond-do-the-talking/ [accessed November 10, 2019].

18 Phillip Bantz, "Ex-Google Employee's Account of Sexual Misconduct, Mistreatment Is Familiar Tale of 'High Talent' Privilege," Law.com, August 29, 2019, https://www.law.com/corpcounsel/2019/08/29/ex-google-employees-account-of-sexual-misconduct-mistreatment-is-familiar-tale-of-high-talent-privilege/ [accessed October 19, 2019].

19 Shona Ghosh, "Google's Latest Explosive #MeToo Claims Are Yet Another Sign of a Destructively Permissive Culture Built Up over Years," *Business Insider*, August 29, 2019, https://www.businessinsider.com/google-rocked-by-david-drummond-claims-2019-8 [accessed October 19, 2019].

20 Connie Loizos, "Alphabet's Controversial Chief Legal Officer David Drummond Is Leaving, Saying He Has Decided to Retire," *TechCrunch*, January 10, 2020, https://techcrunch.com/2020/01/10/alphabets-controversial-chief-legal-officer-david-drummond-is-leaving-saying-he-has-decided-to-retire/ [accessed January 14, 2020].

21 Reuters, "Alphabet Legal Head Drummond Exits, Giving Its New CEO Chance to Shake Up Team," *New York Times*, January 10, 2020, https://www.nytimes.com/reuters/2020/01/10/business/10reuters-alphabet-executive.html [accessed January 14, 2020].

Chapter 4: Who are we?

1 Reed Abelson, "Enron's Collapse: The Directors; Eyebrows Raised in Hindsight About Outside Ties of Some on the Board," *New York Times*, November 30, 2001; Nicholas Stein, "The World's Most Admired Companies: How Do You Make the Most Admired List? Innovate, Innovate, Innovate," *Fortune*, October 2, 2000, https://archive.fortune.com/magazines/fortune/fortune_archive/2000/10/02/288448/index.htm [accessed November 10, 2019].

2 Zeke Ashton, "Cree's Conference Call Blues," The Motley Fool, updated November 18, 2016, https://www.fool.com/investing/general/2003/10/24/crees-conference-call-blues.aspx [accessed October 19, 2019].

3 This list is derived from an excellent survey article titled "Corporate Ethics and Sarbanes-Oxley," which was published in 2003 by *Wall Street Lawyer*: https://corporate.findlaw.com/law-library/corporate-ethics-and-sarbanes-oxley.html [accessed October 19, 2019].

4 Milton Friedman, "The Social Responsibility of Business Is to Increase Its Profits," *New York Times Magazine*, September 13, 1970, http://umich.edu/~thecore/doc/Friedman.pdf [accessed November 12, 2019].

5 Larry Fink, "Purpose & Profit," https://www.blackrock.com/corporate/investor-relations/larry-fink-ceo-letter [accessed November 12, 2019].

6 Doug McMillan, "A Message from Our Chief Executive Officer," Walmart, https://cert-me
.walmart.com/content/walmartethics/en_us.html [accessed July 15, 2019].

7 "Patagonia's Mission Statement," Patagonia, https://www.patagonia.com/company-info.html
[accessed October 19, 2019].

8 These terms are shorthand for values that are spelled out for employees when they join Airbnb.
They refer to a mission of belonging, a spirit of hospitality, a willingness to embrace the unpredictability of business and travel with enthusiasm, and an ability to dig down in difficult
situations to find creative answers, as our founders once did when they kept the company afloat
by selling clever custom cereal boxes at political conventions.

9 My mother loved Dear Abby and used to read her letters out loud at breakfast. One of my all-
time favorite responses was to a letter from a reader who purported to be up in arms because
"strange-looking" people of different races and sexual orientations were visiting a house across
the street. The writer asked, "Abby, these weirdos are wrecking our property values! How can
we improve the quality of this once-respectable neighborhood?" Abby wrote: "Dear UP: You
could move." For more of Abby's most memorable responses, see https://theweek.com/articles
/468550/13-dear-abbys-best-zingers [accessed November 22, 2019].

10 "Integrity: The Essential Ingredient," The Coca-Cola Company, https://www.coca-colacompany
.com/content/dam/journey/us/en/private/fileassets/pdf/2018/Coca-Cola-COC-External.pdf
[accessed October 19, 2019].

11 "Code of Business Conduct and Ethics," Amazon, https://ir.aboutamazon.com/corporate
-governance/documents-charters/code-business-conduct-and-ethics/ [accessed October 19,
2019].

12 "Corporate Ethics," Hewlett Packard Enterprise, https://www.hpe.com/us/en/about/governance
/ethics.html [accessed August 7, 2019].

13 Nick Bilton, "Inside Elizabeth Holmes's Chilling Final Months at Theranos," *Vanity Fair*, February 21, 2019, https://www.vanityfair.com/news/2019/02/inside-elizabeth-holmess-final-months
-at-theranos [accessed October 19, 2019].

14 Henry Blodget, "Mark Zuckerberg on Innovation," *Business Insider*, October 1, 2009, https://
www.businessinsider.com/mark-zuckerberg-innovation-2009-10 [accessed November 22,
2019]. Note, even Zuckerberg has changed his motto to "Move fast with stable infrastructure."
https://www.businessinsider.com/mark-zuckerberg-on-facebooks-new-motto-2014-5 [ac-
cessed November 22, 2019].

Chapter 5: What will derail your mission

1 Vault Careers, "Finding Love at Work Is More Acceptable Than Ever," Vault, February 11, 2015,
http://www.vault.com/blog/workplace-issues/2015-office-romance-survey-results/ [accessed
October 19, 2019].

2 Maureen Farrell, "Two Snap Executives Pushed Out After Probe into Inappropriate Relationship," updated January 18, 2019, https://www.wsj.com/articles/two-snap-executives-pushed-out
-after-probe-into-inappropriate-relationship-11547850401 [accessed October 19, 2019].

3 David Margolick, "Inside Stanford Business School's Spiraling Sex Scandal," *Vanity Fair*, October 17, 2015, https://www.vanityfair.com/news/2015/10/stanford-business-school-sex-scandal
[accessed October 19, 2019].

4 Alexandra Berzon, Chris Kirkham, Elizabeth Bernstein, and Kate O'Keeffe, "Casino Managers Enabled Steve Wynn's Alleged Misconduct for Decades, Workers Say," updated March 27,
2018, https://www.wsj.com/articles/casino-managers-enabled-wynns-alleged-misconduct-for
-decades-workers-say-1522172877 [accessed October 19, 2019].

5 Tiffany Hsu and Mohammed Hadi, "Wynn Leaders Helped Hide Sexual Misconduct Allegations Against Company's Founder, Report Says," *New York Times*, April 2, 2019, https://www
.nytimes.com/2019/04/02/business/wynn-resorts-sexual-misconduct-steve-wynn.html [ac-
cessed October 19, 2019].

6 U.S. Department of Justice press release: Theranos Founder and Former Chief Operating Officer
Charged in Alleged Wire Fraud Schemes, June 15, 2018, https://www.justice.gov/usao-ndca/pr
/theranos-founder-and-former-chief-operating-officer-charged-alleged-wire-fraud-schemes
[accessed November 12, 2019].

7 Jennifer Medina, Katie Benner, and Kate Taylor, "Actresses, Business Leaders and Other Wealthy Parents Charged in U.S. College Entry Fraud," *New York Times,* March 12, 2019, https://www .nytimes.com/2019/03/12/us/college-admissions-cheating-scandal.html?module=inline [accessed November 12, 2019].

8 Wired Staff, "A True EBay Crime Story," *Wired*, May 8, 2006, https://www.wired.com/2006/05/a -true-ebay-crime-story/ [accessed October 19, 2019].

9 Kevin Sack, "Patient Data Landed Online After a Series of Missteps," *New York Times*, October 6, 2011, https://www.nytimes.com/2011/10/06/us/stanford-hospital-patient-data-breach-is -detailed.html [accessed October 19, 2019].

10 Ibid.

11 Jack Morse, "'F*ck ethics. Money is everything': Facebook Employees React to Scandal on Gossip App," Mashable, January 30, 2019, https://mashable.com/article/facebook-employees-react-teen -spying-app-blind/ [accessed October 19, 2019]. Note: It is only fair to mention that it is impossible to confirm whether or not the person who posted this is a current Facebook employee.

Chapter 6: Mix it up, blast it out, repeat

1 https://www.thedishonestyproject.com/film/ [accessed November 12, 2019].

2 When Airbnb began to get reports from guests of color that they were being denied access to Airbnb listings, I reached out to Eric immediately for his counsel on how to navigate the situation, and his firm has provided legal advice to Airbnb on several occasions during my tenure.

3 Jacobellis v. Ohio, https://www.law.cornell.edu/supremecourt/text/378/184 [accessed November 12, 2019].

Chapter 7: The welcome mat for complaints

1 Ann Skeet, "A Conversation with Theranos Whistleblower Tyler Shultz," Markkula Center for Applied Ethics at Santa Clara University, May 22, 2019, https://www.scu.edu/ethics/focus-areas /leadership-ethics/resources/a-conversation-with-theranos-whistleblower-tyler-shultz/ [accessed October 19, 2019].

2 Reid Hoffman, "The Human Rights of Women Entrepreneurs," LinkedIn, June 23, 2017, https:// www.linkedin.com/pulse/human-rights-women-entrepreneurs-reid-hoffman/ [accessed October 19, 2019].

3 "Suboxone Maker Pays $1.4 Billion to Settle Fraud Investigation," *FDA News*, July 22, 2019, https://www.fdanews.com/articles/192064-suboxone-maker-pays-14-billion-to-settle-fraud -investigation [accessed October 19, 2019].

4 Sue Reisinger, "Justice Department, 6 Whistleblowers Win $1.4B Settlement with Opioid Maker," Law.com, July 11, 2019, https://www.law.com/corpcounsel/2019/07/11/justice-department-6 -whistleblowers-win-1-4b-settlement-with-opioid-maker/ [accessed October 19, 2019].

5 Matt Richtel and Alexei Barrionuevo, "Finger in Chili Is Called Hoax; Las Vegas Woman Is Charged," *New York Times*, April 23, 2005, https://www.nytimes.com/2005/04/23/us/finger-in -chili-is-called-hoax-las-vegas-woman-is-charged.html [accessed October 19, 2019].

Chapter 8: When the other shoe drops

1 Rebecca Grant, "McDonald's Workers Walk Out over Sexual Harassment," *The Nation*, September 18, 2018, https://www.thenation.com/article/mcdonalds-workers-walk-out-over-sexual -harassment/ [accessed October 19, 2019]; see also Sarah Jones, "McDonald's Workers Say Time's Up on Sexual Harassment," *New York Magazine*, May 21, 2019, http://nymag.com/intelligencer/2019 /05/mcdonalds-workers-say-times-up-on-sexual-harassment.html [accessed October 19, 2019].

2 Elahe Izadi and Travis M. Andrews, "Former CBS Chairman Les Moonves Fired for Cause, Will Not Receive Severance in Wake of Sexual Misconduct Allegations," *Washington Post*, December 17, 2018, https://www.washingtonpost.com/arts-entertainment/2018/12/17/former -cbs-chairman-les-moonves-fired-cause-will-not-receive-severance-wake-sexual-misconduct -allegations/?utm_term=.23e0896b50bb [accessed October 19, 2019].

3 Reid Hoffman, "The Human Rights of Women Entrepreneurs," LinkedIn, June 23, 2017, https:// www.linkedin.com/pulse/human-rights-women-entrepreneurs-reid-hoffman/ [accessed October 19, 2019].

Chapter 9: Check the canaries

1 Kat Eschner, "The Story of the Real Canary in the Coal Mine," *Smithsonian*, December 30, 2016, https://www.smithsonianmag.com/smart-news/story-real-canary-coal-mine-180961570/ [accessed October 19, 2019].

2 Susan Fowler, "Reflecting on One Very, Very Strange Year at Uber," Susan Fowler blog, February 19, 2017, https://www.susanjfowler.com/blog/2017/2/19/reflecting-on-one-very-strange-year-at-uber [accessed October 19, 2019].

3 Maya Kosoff, "Mass Firings at Uber as Sexual Harassment Scandal Grows," *Vanity Fair*, June 6, 2017, https://www.vanityfair.com/news/2017/06/uber-fires-20-employees-harassment-investigation [accessed October 19, 2019].

4 Eric Holder, "Uber Report: Eric Holder's Recommendations for Change," *New York Times*, June 13, 2017, https://www.nytimes.com/2017/06/13/technology/uber-report-eric-holders-recommendations-for-change.html [accessed October 19, 2019].

5 "FAQs," Blind, updated March 2019, https://www.teamblind.com/faqs [accessed October 19, 2019].

6 "Ethics Complaints," Blind, September 13, 2017, https://www.teamblind.com/article/Ethics-complaints-eQUWfpH4 [accessed October 19, 2019].

Chapter 10: Dude, you're not just "bad at dating"

1 Globe Newswire, "Research Finds Businesses May Soon Feel Financial Impacts of #MeToo in Staffing and Revenue," FTI Consulting, October 15, 2018, https://www.fticonsulting.com/about/newsroom/press-releases/research-finds-businesses-may-soon-feel-financial-impacts-of-metoo-in-staffing-and-revenue [accessed October 19, 2019].

2 Alexandra Berzon, Chris Kirkham, Elizabeth Bernstein, and Kate O'Keeffe, "Casino Managers Enabled Steve Wynn's Alleged Misconduct for Decades, Workers Say," *Wall Street Journal*, updated March 27, 2018, https://www.wsj.com/articles/casino-managers-enabled-wynns-alleged-misconduct-for-decades-workers-say-1522172877 [accessed October 19, 2019].

3 Deanna Paul, "Harvey Weinstein's Third Indictment Could Open the Door for Actress Annabella Sciorra to Take Stand," *Washington Post*, August 26, 2019, https://www.washingtonpost.com/arts-entertainment/2019/08/26/harvey-weinsteins-third-indictment-could-open-door-another-accuser-take-stand/ [accessed October 19, 2019].

4 U.S. Equal Employment Opportunity Commission, "Enforcement Guidance," https://www.eeoc.gov/eeoc/publications/upload/currentissues.pdf [accessed November 12, 2019; emphasis added].

5 Rosenberg's original post on Facebook was taken down, but it has been reprinted widely, including on Deadline: Mike Fleming Jr., "'Beautiful Girls' Scribe Scott Rosenberg on a Complicated Legacy with Harvey Weinstein," Deadline, October 16, 2017, https://deadline.com/2017/10/scott-rosenberg-harvey-weinstein-miramax-beautiful-girls-guilt-over-sexual-assault-allegations-1202189525/ [accessed October 19, 2019].

Chapter 11: Who you do business with defines you

1 Mike Snider and Edward C. Baig, "Facebook Fined $5 Billion by FTC, Must Update and Adopt New Privacy, Security Measures," *USA Today*, July 24, 2019, https://www.usatoday.com/story/tech/news/2019/07/24/facebook-pay-record-5-billion-fine-u-s-privacy-violations/1812499001/ [accessed October 19, 2019].

2 I'm following the growing convention of not using the killer's name, since experts say mass murderers are motivated by the thought of becoming infamous, even after death.

3 Kevin Roose, "'Shut the Site Down,' Says the Creator of 8chan, a Megaphone for Gunmen," *New York Times*, August 4, 2019, https://www.nytimes.com/2019/08/04/technology/8chan-shooting-manifesto.html [accessed November 13, 2019].

4 Drew Harwell, "Three mass shootings this year began with a hateful screed on 8chan. Its founder calls it a terrorist refuge in plain sight," *Washington Post*, August 4, 2019, https://www.washingtonpost.com/technology/2019/08/04/three-mass-shootings-this-year-began-with

-hateful-screed-chan-its-founder-calls-it-terrorist-refuge-plain-sight/ [accessed October 19, 2019].

5 Kevin Roose, "Why Banning 8chan Was so Hard for Cloudflare: 'No One Should Have That Power,'" *New York Times*, August 5, 2019, https://www.nytimes.com/2019/08/05/technology/8chan-cloudflare-el-paso.html [accessed October 19, 2019].

6 Matthew Prince, "Terminating Service for 8Chan," The Cloudflare Blog, August 4, 2019, https://blog.cloudflare.com/terminating-service-for-8chan/ [accessed October 19, 2019].

7 Monica Nickelsburg, "Amazon Seeks to Root Out Any Ties to 8chan, as Tech Firms Grapple with Implications of Extremist Sites," *GeekWire*, August 8, 2019, https://www.geekwire.com/2019/amazon-seeks-root-ties-8chan-tech-firms-grapple-implications-extremist-sites/ [accessed November 12, 2019].

8 Mike Isaac, *Super Pumped: The Battle for Uber* (New York: W. W. Norton, 2019), 174.

9 Ibid.

10 Community Standards, Facebook, https://www.facebook.com/communitystandards/introduction [accessed November 12, 2019].

11 Simon van Zuylen-Wood, "'Men Are Scum': Inside Facebook's War on Hate Speech," *Vanity Fair*, February 26, 2019, https://www.vanityfair.com/news/2019/02/men-are-scum-inside-facebook-war-on-hate-speech [accessed October 19, 2019].

12 Elizabeth Dwoskin, "YouTube's Arbitrary Standards: Stars Keep Making Money Even After Breaking the Rules," *Washington Post*, August 9, 2019, https://www.washingtonpost.com/technology/2019/08/09/youtubes-arbitrary-standards-stars-keep-making-money-even-after-breaking-rules/?noredirect=on [accessed October 19, 2019].

13 14th Annual Board of Boards, CECP Executive Summary, https://cecp.co/wp-content/uploads/2019/03/2019_BoB_Exec_Summary-Final-WEB.pdf [accessed November 13, 2019].

14 Ibid.

15 Meg Whitman, with Joan O'C. Hamilton, *The Power of Many: Values for Success in Business and in Life* (New York: Crown Publishing, 2010).

Conclusion: A superpower for our times

1 Cindy Boren, "Clippers Owner Donald Sterling Allegedly Tells Girlfriend Not to Bring Black People to Games, Disses Magic Johnson, Report Says," April 26, 2014, https://www.washingtonpost.com/news/early-lead/wp/2014/04/26/clippers-owner-donald-sterling-tells-girlfriend-not-to-bring-black-people-to-games-disses-magic-johnson/ [accessed November 22, 2019].

2 Yahoo Sports Staff, "The NBA World Reacts to Donald Sterling's Lifetime NBA Banishment," Yahoo! Sports, April 29, 2014, https://sports.yahoo.com/-the-nba-world-reacts-to-donald-sterling-s-lifetime-nba-banishment-191344427.html?y20=1 [accessed October 19, 2019].

3 Jonah Goldberg, "Op-Ed: America Is Sick, and Both Liberals and Conservatives Are Wrong About the Remedy," *Los Angeles Times*, August 6, 2019, https://www.latimes.com/opinion/story/2019-08-06/liberal-conservative-nationalism-socialism-communities [accessed October 19, 2019].

4 David Brooks, "The Remoralization of the Market," *New York Times*, January 10, 2019, https://www.nytimes.com/2019/01/10/opinion/market-morality.html [accessed October 19, 2019].

5 Jamie Dimon and Warren E. Buffett, "Short-Termism Is Harming the Economy," *Wall Street Journal*, June 6, 2018, https://www.wsj.com/articles/short-termism-is-harming-the-economy-1528336801 [accessed October 19, 2019].

6 Martin Lipton, "Wachtell Lipton Shines a Spotlight on Boards," July 9, 2019, reprinted in "The CLS Blue SkyBlog," http://clsbluesky.law.columbia.edu/2019/07/09/wachtell-lipton-shines-a-spotlight-on-boards/[accessed November 16, 2019].

7 Mark Weinberger, "How the Role of Global CEO Is Changing," EY.com, January 18, 2019, https://www.ey.com/en_gl/wef/how-the-role-of-global-ceo-is-changing [accessed October 19, 2019].

8 Tim Cook, 2019 Commencement Address, https://news.stanford.edu/2019/06/16/remarks-tim-cook-2019-stanford-commencement/ [accessed November 16, 2019].

9 AP, "LUNA Bar Pledges to Make Up Roster Pay Gap for US Women," *USA Today*, April 2, 2019, https://www.usatoday.com/story/sports/soccer/2019/04/02/luna-bar-pledges-to-make-up-roster-pay-gap-for-us-women/39289701/ [accessed October 19, 2019].

Appendix

1 Rajeev Syal and Sybilla Brodzinsky, "Body Shop Ethics Under Fire After Colombian Peasant Evictions," *The Guardian*, September 12, 2009, https://www.theguardian.com/world/2009/sep/13/body-shop-colombia-evictions [accessed November 16, 2019].

Postscript: Integrity in a crisis

1 Lindsay Weinberg and Falen Hardge, "More Fashion Retailers Make Medical Masks and Scrubs for Coronavirus Doctors," *Hollywood Reporter*, March 25, 2020, https://www.hollywoodreporter.com/news/coronavirus-fashion-brands-make-medical-masks-scrubs-hospitals-1286609.

2 "Jennifer Garner & Amy Adams Launch #SAVEWITHSTORIES to Help Kids Learn, Get Nutritious Meals During Coronavirus School Closures," press release, Scholastic, March 16, 2020, http://mediaroom.scholastic.com/press-release/jennifer-garner-amy-adams-launch-savewithstories-help-kids-learn-get-nutritious-meals-.

3 Russ Mitchell, "How to Protect Workers from the Coronavirus: This CEO Has Good Advice," *Los Angeles Times*, March 26, 2020, https://www.latimes.com/business/story/2020-03-26/coronavirus-manufacturer-safety.

4 Dalvin Brown, "COVID-19 Claims Lives of 30 Grocery Store Workers, Thousands More May Have It, Union Says," *USA Today*, April 14, 2020, https://www.usatoday.com/story/money/2020/04/14/coronavirus-claims-lives-30-grocery-store-workers-union-says/2987754001/.

5 Annie Palmer, "Amazon Lawyer Calls Fired Strike Organizer 'Not Smart or Articulate' in Meeting with Top Execs," CNBC, April 2, 2020, https://www.cnbc.com/2020/04/02/amazon-lawyer-calls-fired-warehouse-worker-not-smart-or-articulate.html.

6 Nick Ellis, "How Marriott Plans to Manage a 45% Drop in Hotel Occupancy Rates," The Points Guy, March 20, 2020, https://thepointsguy.com/news/how-marriott-will-manage-huge-drop-in-occupancy/.

Index